# 20 Years of G20

Rajat Kathuria · Prateek Kukreja
Editors

# 20 Years of G20

## From Global Cooperation to Building Consensus

Springer

*Editors*
Rajat Kathuria
Indian Council for Research on International Economic Relations (ICRIER)
New Delhi, India

Prateek Kukreja
Indian Council for Research on International Economic Relations (ICRIER)
New Delhi, India

ISBN 978-981-13-8105-8 ISBN 978-981-13-8106-5 (eBook)
https://doi.org/10.1007/978-981-13-8106-5



This Springer imprint is published by the registered company Springer Nature Singapore Pte Ltd.
The registered company address is: 152 Beach Road, #21-01/04 Gateway East, Singapore 189721, Singapore

# Foreword

As India prepares to assume the G20 presidency in 3 years from now, this volume comes just at the right time. In 2022, India will host the G20, or Group of 20 nations, the world's most influential economic multilateral forum. It is worth reflecting on the 20 years of its existence, since it was formed as a replacement to the G-7 to include a larger set of countries that together constituted an overwhelming share of global GDP and global population. G20, over time, has emerged as a premier leaders-led-platform to address the challenges confronting the global economy, by promoting short-term as well as long-term solutions to support human prosperity and well-being. For emerging economies, such as India, G20 has served as a unique global institution championing a global economic architecture that seeks to achieve even-handed outcomes. The representation of both developed and emerging countries ensures that the G-20 provides a just platform for the latter to manifest their economic, political and global leadership on par with the former.

India is engaging with the global economy more strongly than ever and is increasingly voicing its opinion on several important global issues in multilateral forum. It also often builds coalitions with other like-minded countries and takes up causes on behalf of weaker countries. There are several challenges, however, which emerging markets confront. There is a continued threat from the monetary policies of select advanced economies and coupled with oil price volatility, it creates financial vulnerabilities among emerging markets. In the past, some of these countries including India have been characterized as the 'fragile five'. There is no doubt there is a need for domestic reform, but a strong case can be made for responsible policies from advanced nations, thus enabling financial vulnerabilities to be managed better and with equity. Other sources of worry confronting the global economy are the escalating trade tensions, youth unemployment and the uncertainty around AI. Employment in many G20 nations is shifting towards the kind of jobs that require high-level cognitive skills, whereas most of the routine jobs are increasingly being automated or offshored to varying degrees. History reveals that the world has an extraordinary ability of adapting to shocks, technology and economic. These lessons are etched in our minds and together with new global platforms like the G20, I am convinced we will be able to harness the benefits of technology and AI while minimizing the hazards. The global approach must be heterodox, without falling prey to ultra-nationalist sentiments.

The issues investigated in this book are highly contemporary and extremely relevant to G20. I am sure that this volume will appeal to a wide range of stakeholders including academicians, policymakers, governments and experts in these areas.

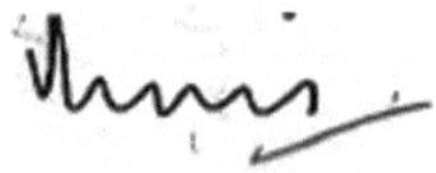

New Delhi, India
April 2019

Amitabh Kant
CEO, NITI Aayog (National Institution for Transforming India)

# Contents

# About the Editors

**Rajat Kathuria** is the Director and Chief Executive of the Indian Council for Research on International Economic Relations (ICRIER), New Delhi. He has over 20 years' teaching experience and 15 years' experience in economic policy. His research interests include a range of issues relating to regulation and competition policy. He has worked as a consultant for the World Bank, Washington DC, and carried out project assignments for a number of international organizations, including ILO, UNCTAD, LirneAsia, World Bank and ADB. He has published in international and national journals, as well as in popular magazines and newspapers. He has served on the Board of Delhi Management Association and is currently an independent director on the Microfinance Institutions Network (MFIN) and on several government committees. He has an undergraduate degree in Economics from St. Stephens College, a Masters from Delhi School of Economics and a Ph.D. degree from the University of Maryland, College Park.

**Prateek Kukreja** is a Research Associate at the Indian Council for Research on International Economic Relations (ICRIER), New Delhi. He has over 5 years of research experience and has previously been associated with various government and non-government organizations in India. His broad areas of research interest include labour economics, trade and development economics. He has authored papers and articles in respected journals, newspapers and magazines and has also presented papers at various national and international conferences. He holds an M.Phil. degree in Economics from the Jawaharlal Nehru University and a Masters degree from the South Asian University, New Delhi. He is currently pursuing his Ph.D. at Jawaharlal Nehru University.

# Chapter 1
# Introduction

**Rajat Kathuria and Prateek Kukreja**

The Group of Twenty (or G20 in common parlance) was formed in 1999 in the aftermath of the Asian financial crisis as a forum for dialogue between the finance ministers and the central bank governors of 19 countries and the European Union in order to respond to the crisis. Such meetings at the leader level go back to the 1970s. In the beginning, the discussions were limited to a small group of 5 industrialized economies—France, Germany, Japan, the United Kingdom, and the United States- and on topics that were of immediate relevance to them. Thus, the oil price shocks of 1973 and 1979 and the collapse of the Bretton Woods system of fixed exchange rates were the early items on the agenda. This group, called the Group of Five, or G-5 morphed into the G7 to include Canada and Italy in the mid-1980s. In 1998, Russia also joined, creating the G8. Macroeconomic policies reviewed in the G7 context included exchange rates, balance of payments, globalization, trade, and economic relations with developing countries. Over time, the focus of G7 and subsequently the G8 on macroeconomic policy coordination expanded to include a variety of other global and transnational issues, such as the environment, crime, drugs, AIDS, and terrorism (Nelson 2018).

As growth momentum shifted towards Asia and emerging markets, it became necessary to design a more inclusive platform to reflect global shifts in economic and political power. G20 naturally includes a much larger set of countries that together constitute an overwhelming share of global GDP and global population compared to either the G7 or G8. With time, G20, has emerged as a premier leaders-led stage to address the challenges confronting the global economy, by promoting short-term as well as long-term solutions to support human prosperity and well-being. For emerging economies, such as India, G20 has served as a unique global institution championing a global economic architecture that seeks to achieve evenhanded out-

R. Kathuria · P. Kukreja (✉)
Indian Council for Research on International Economic Relations, New Delhi, India
e-mail: prateekukreja89@gmail.com

R. Kathuria
e-mail: rkathuria@icrier.res.in



R. Kathuria and P. Kukreja (eds.), *20 Years of G20*,
https://doi.org/10.1007/978-981-13-8106-5_1

comes. The representation of both developed and emerging countries ensures that the G20 provides a just platform for the latter to manifest their economic, political and global leadership on par with the former.

The intellectual persuasion of the forum was never in doubt. The members represent around two-thirds of the world population, generate 85% of the global GDP, and account for 75 percent of international trade. G20 faced its first true test during the global financial crisis, which was triggered by the collapse of Lehman Brothers in September 2008 in the United States, and which eventually almost pushed the world economy into deep recession. During the global financial crisis, the then US President George W. Bush invited leaders of the G20 members to coordinate actions in order to respond to the crisis. The G20 Leader's Summit been held annually since its first meeting in 2008 by the different member countries holding presidencies on a rotational basis. The Leader's Summit was conceived to manage or handle the crisis in 2009 and its success in doing so led it to become institutionalized as a permanent feature. Comparisons with the Great Depression were ubiquitous at that time and the heads of government took decisions which the finance ministers by themselves would not have been able to take.

As a crisis response body, the G20 therefore played a central role in providing the political momentum for greater policy coherence and helped avoid a situation that could have been decidedly worse in its absence. This has kept alive the essence of G20 as a deliberative international forum, when several other multilateral bodies have gone into hibernation. At the same time many new regional and multilateral bodies and forums have emerged which are further binding countries and enabling North-South cooperation. As economic integration increases, international economic policy coordination is even more significant. In this background, the need for deliberative forums that involve Leader Summits such as the G20 is more pronounced.

While the G20 has achieved widely acclaimed progress in containing the crises through short term policy responses, it faces multifaceted challenges, and doubts over its effectiveness for long-term economic governance. Short-term stabilization only buys time and does not produce robust growth unless accompanied by structural reforms and investments that boost productivity and open new sources of growth (Qureshi 2015). So, the perennial question is whether the G20 will remain an effective crisis response body, with a limited role in longer-term goals such as strong, sustainable and balanced growth? In other words, is there a peace-time role for G20? The best way to answer this is to look at some of the salient achievements of the group since the 2008 crisis.[1]

## 1 Salient Achievements Since the Global Financial Crisis

By virtue of being a non-treaty based institution, the G20 is often described as an informal forum. This weakness is in fact its strength. It is more flexible and less bound

[1] Sharma (2017) provides a detailed account on the achievements of the G20.

compared to formal treaty based institutions and therefore, has the potential to act more swiftly to global economic matters. It provides an accommodating, problem-solving framework where established and emerging powers can forge consensus and negotiate breakthroughs on pressing global issues. While the group during the early years attempted to build consensus on issues related to international financial stability, with time, it has expanded to encompass a wide array of economic issues, such as discussion on trade and investment, energy and climate change, empowering women, global health, agriculture, development policy, digitization, employment policy and terrorism. Because of the involvement of Leaders, it is possible to achieve commitments in major policy areas where there are trade-offs such as in climate change and trade. This may not always be possible in issue specific forums and institutions.

Concerted efforts in the direction of coordination began in earnest in the aftermath of the global financial crisis of 2008. In the **first-ever G20 summit** in Washington, the Leaders agreed to strengthen financial regulation, with agreement on a 47-point action plan to improve financial regulation over the medium term. In the area of trade and investment, the first-ever commitment to resist protectionism took place during the summit. But a major breakthrough came in the year 2009, at the **second G20 summit** in London, when the then prime minister of UK, Gordon Brown successfully coordinated a deal in which world leaders agreed on a $1.1 trillion injection of financial aid into the global economy. This was expected to reinvigorate the International Monetary Fund (IMF) by greatly increasing the capital available to it. In order to bring further reform into the global financial architecture, a Financial Stability Board (FSB) was set up through mutual consensus among the member nations to include major emerging market economies with a stronger financial regulation mandate. Reform of the global financial system, including the banks, quasi banks and shadow banks were at heart of the proposals. Reform of the international financial system pointed towards the IMF, the World Bank and the regional development banks. Commitment of members to impose tight financial regulations continued during the **third G20 summit** in Pittsburgh, with a view to reform the international financial system into the one that has a higher capacity to absorb losses and novel incentives to avoid a return to past excesses. The group agreed on tougher regulations on hedge funds and rating agencies, as well as a crackdown on tax havens. A fresh emphasis was placed on the commitment to create employment opportunities through income, social protection, and training support for the unemployed. Further, in an attempt to shift to a low-carbon global economy, the leaders committed on phasing out and rationalizing fossil fuel subsidies over the medium-term, while providing targeted support to the poorest. The **fourth summit** took place in Toronto, with global economic recovery as the prime focus area. A general consensus among the members was achieved towards initiating measures to sustain private demand. It was committed by the members to cut deficits by at least 50% by the end of 2013 and stabilize or reduce government debt-to-GDP ratios by 2016. An important accomplishment during the Toronto summit was the agreement to reform the IMF for better representation of emerging economies and developing economies. An intense debate during Toronto was the move away from fiscal stimulus. While there was an acknowledgement of short term problems, many felt it was time to focus on long term private demand. But was it really feasible or desirable to reduce public sector demand? Would that not lead to too much of slowing down? Structural reforms were expected to revive investment spirits and lead to a great revival of demand. Even though it was right to focus on structural reform, would it really enthuse the private sector. The **fifth summit** in Seoul was the first G20 summit in Asia and came at a critical phase of fragile, uneven global recovery with possibility of another financial crisis looming over Europe, the potential threat of "currency war" and debates about containing current account imbalances hogging the discourse space. Nonetheless, the summit concluded with some key achievements. It managed to develop a Framework for Strong, Sustainable and Balanced Growth, and intensify international effort to contain current account imbalances and any prospective currency wars. The launch of Global Partnership for Financial Inclusion (GPFI) was a major breakthrough. It is an inclusive platform for all G20 countries, interested non-G20 countries and relevant stakeholders to carry forward work on financial inclusion. Coordinated actions and policies continued into the **sixth G20 summit** in Cannes, where general consensus was developed to remove impediments to global economic recovery and to give special attention to the social dimension of globalization. Further, the group committed on managing capital flows to reap the benefits from financial globalization and ensure resilience against volatile capital flows. The members also agreed to sign a multilateral convention to regulate tax information exchange. With growing emphasis on jobs and employment, the group agreed to put in place an Action Plan for Growth and Jobs to foster employment and social protection. The Cannes summit also saw one, the launch of the Agriculture Market Information System to ensure transparency of agricultural product markets and two, promotion of an Action Plan on Food Price Volatility and Agriculture. The **seventh summit** took place in Los Cabos, Mexico in 2012, which led to an agreement between the members on an Accountability Framework to enhance implementation of the G20 policy commitments on growth. The members also committed to raise IMF resources through bilateral loans. Russia hosted the **eighth summit** at Saint Petersburg in the year 2013, wherein the members committed on country specific medium-term fiscal strategies to support economic growth and job creation, while putting debt as a share of GDP on a sustainable path. The summit also saw the launch of the St. Petersburg Action Plan which set forth reforms for achieving strong, sustainable and balanced growth. On the trade front, a greater emphasis was placed on coherence between regional trade agreements and the multilateral trading system. The **ninth summit** in Brisbane saw the leaders agreeing on boosting their collective GDP growth by 2.1% over the next five years. This was known as the Brisbane Action Plan and was drawn up by the finance ministers from G20 countries. Infrastructure investment was underscored to boost growth and the creation of a Global Infrastructure Hub was seen as the way to provide a link between governments, the private sector, development banks, and other international organizations to improve the functioning and financing of infrastructure markets. The summit also addressed climate change, trade, female participation in the workforce, anticorruption efforts, and IMF reforms. They agreed on Principles for Energy Collaboration and Action Plan for Voluntary Collaboration on Energy Efficiency for strong, resilient energy markets critical to economic growth. Additionally, members collectively set a target to reduce the gender gap in women's labour market participation in G20 countries by 25% by 2025. Recognizing the significant negative impact of corruption on economic growth, trade and development, the leaders agreed on what came to be known as the 2015-16 Anti-Corruption Action Plan. While the focus of the summit was on economic issues, conflict in Ukraine also attracted significant attention, raising disquiet around Russia's involvement in the Summit. The G20, in its **tenth summit** in Antalya, reaffirmed the goal of strong, sustainable and balanced economic growth. Further, it was agreed to tax multinational companies and prevent them from exploiting loopholes in the global system through endorsing and adopting measures on G20/OECD Base Erosion and Profit Shifting. On the employment front, members targeted to reduce the number of youth who are at risk of being permanently left behind in the labour market by 15% by 2025 in G20 countries. Also, a specific engagement group was established which aimed at promoting gender equality in the G20 called the Women 20. Migration, was recognized for the first time as a global challenge that needs to be addressed. A commitment was made to strengthen support for efforts to protect the unprecedented global refugees and internally displaced persons. Further, on agriculture, an increased focus was placed on the need of smallholder farms, rural women and youth. The **eleventh summit** in Hangzhou focused on inclusive and innovative growth, building on the efforts of previous Presidencies. The members endorsed a G20 Innovative Action Plan to pursue pro-innovation growth strategies. There was an agreement among the leaders on some new financial inclusion indicators to measure the use, availability and quality of digital financial services in more than 200 economies worldwide. The members also endorsed the G20 Action Plan on the 2030 Agenda for Sustainable Development. With a view to foster favorable conditions for the digital economy and to address the digital divide, G20 Digital Economy Development and Cooperation Initiative was launched. Also, in order to strengthen their inclusive growth and development potential, the members collectively launched a G20 initiative on Supporting Industrialization in Africa and LDCs. Progress on these was then reviewed in the **twelfth summit** hosted by Hamburg, Germany, which focused primarily on global co-operation. Consensus was built on issues such as fight against terrorism, global warming and protectionism. The members also pledged to strengthen health systems and to combat the menace of antimicrobial resistance (AMR), which was recognized as a "growing threat" to public health and economic growth. Further, the leaders adopted a World Bank funding plan of up to USD 1 billion for women entrepreneurs in developing nations. India presented a 10-point action plan for G20 nations to counter terrorism. Further, steps taken by India for sustainable and inclusive growth as well as support to global economy were greatly acknowledged by the G20 members. The commitments made in the Hamburg summit were evaluated during the **thirteenth summit** in Buenos Aires, where a declaration focusing on the future of work, infrastructure for development, a sustainable food future and on gender equality was adopted. The signatories to the Paris Agreement on Climate, which included all members, but the US, pledged the "full implementation" of the pact, which they called "irreversible". A note was also taken of the UN scientists' call for a more ambitious target of reducing warming to 1.5 degrees Celsius above pre-industrial levels. On the trade front, the members called for a reform in the WTO and decided to review its progress in the **fourteenth summit** in Osaka. Further, recognizing the significance of the IMF, the leaders committed to provide adequate funding and to meet a goal of finalising new national quotas in time for the global lender's spring 2019 meetings. With a view to reduce gender inequality, the group recommitted to a four year old goal of closing the gender gap in the labour force by 2025.

The G20 has undoubtedly made significant progress in reshaping the governance of global finance and reforming the global financial system in the last 20 years. More however needs to be done in regard to International Financial Institution (IFI) reform, especially quota enhancements in the IMF. There is an entrenched view that the global financial architecture is loaded against emerging markets. Moreover, many economists argue that monetary policy is a blunt instrument and can at best stabilise the business cycle rather than address structural weaknesses such as those relating to jobs, growth (or lack thereof) and inequality. More emphasis thus has to be placed on making growth inclusive. The world is experiencing severe socio-economic problems such as increasing income inequality, youth unemployment, the threat from technology, growing protectionism and gender inequality. These problems increase social tensions and undermine democracy and therefore require coordinated efforts of the nations. The ability of G20 to deal with such issues has been questioned since it has no enforcement mechanism beyond "naming and shaming" and with little follow-up will not be able to enforce its commitments. Besides, G20's effectiveness since the crisis has diminished because the issues covered by the G20 have broadened (agenda creep), and there is now little follow-through from one summit to the next. As a crisis management body, it has been effective, but its contribution in "normal" periods has been doubted. Admittedly, its major strength is to facilitate coordinated action, and at the same time one must recognise that getting there in normal periods may be difficult due to diverse interest group pressures within and across countries. Sovereign governments often have intense differences and each of those democratic governments take a position in the context of considerable domestic controversy. The silver lining in these other areas such as inequality, protectionism, technology, jobs etc. is that after the talks at G20, the discussions could filter back to their relevant ministers for action later. Be that as it may, there is surely value in informal discussions at a high level even if no resolution is forthcoming in the short term (Kathuria and Nagpal 2016).

In this backdrop, India is preparing to assume the G20 presidency in three years from now in 2022. India is engaging with the global economy more strongly than ever and is increasingly voicing its opinion on several important global issues in multilateral forum. It also often builds coalitions with other likeminded countries and takes up causes on behalf of weaker countries. There are several challenges however which India and other emerging markets confront. There is a continued threat from the monetary policies of select advanced economies and coupled with oil price volatility, it creates financial vulnerabilities among emerging markets. In the past some of these countries including India have been characterized as the 'fragile five'. There is no doubt of the need for domestic reform, but a strong case can be made for responsible policies from advanced nations, thus enabling financial vulnerabilities to be managed better and with equity. Other sources of worry confronting the global economy are the escalating trade tensions, youth unemployment and the uncertainty around artificial intelligence (AI). Employment in many G20 nations is shifting towards the kind of jobs that require high-level cognitive skills, whereas most of routine jobs are increasingly being automated or offshored to varying degrees. History reveals that the world has an extraordinary ability of adapting to shocks, technology and economic. Together with new global platforms like the G20 and the abundant knowledge that already exists, it is possible to adopt coordinated strategies to harness the benefits of technology and AI while minimizing the hazards for the global economy.

Since 2009, Indian Council for Research on International Economic Relations (ICRIER) has been organizing annual G20 conferences prior to the G20 summits, providing a platform for engaging eminent researchers, academicians and policy-makers in rich debate on topics of relevance to the Summit.

ICRIER's 10th G20 conference was held on October 11–12, 2018 in New Delhi in partnership with the Ford Foundation and the International Monetary Fund (IMF). The conference was centered on the key issue of moving beyond global cooperation to building consensus and the participants deliberated on various thematic areas that were relevant for the 2018 Argentinean presidency. Argentina focused on "building consensus for fair and sustainable development."

This book explores the past 20 years of the G20 through subjects of contemporary relevance to the G20 countries and therefore to the global economy, including those discussed during the Argentinean Presidency. The issue of Global Financial Architecture and Regulatory Practices is a permanent theme in the G20 and is always relevant. Indeed it was the coordinated policy response to the global financial crisis that resulted in G20 being designated as the premier forum for international economic cooperation. Following its initial success in overcoming the financial and economic crisis through prompt action, the G20 faces an existential challenge. Questions are being asked if it can graduate from crisis-management to crisis-prevention by establishing international standards for global governance. The heterogeneity in the group is a weakness, but also a strength. Strength because it gives it legitimacy to be a standing world economic governing board and weakness because coordination may be hard due to diverse interest group pressures. In general, the overarching idea of the conference was to examine the G20 objectives of reducing risk and volatility in the global financial markets, prepare for impending disruptions in the job market, build viable structures for open trade and investment regime, and promote sustainable and inclusive development. The invited contributions from the participants in the conference are organised under five thematic areas. The volume begins with an introductory chapter by the editors outlining the scope of the content presented in the volume as well as summarizing the achievements of the G20 in the last two decades. The following sections contain a brief on the content of papers under each thematic area. For G20 that excelled in international coordination following the financial crisis, issues like trade, climate change and future of work are begging for similar coordinated global attention. Greater emphasis in these areas will provide a raison d'etre for the continued legitimacy of G20 as an institution. This book, is a compilation of invited contributions from experts in the following five broad themes, namely:

(a) Global Financial Architecture and Regulatory Practices;
(b) Future of Work;
(c) Role of Technology for Adaptation and Mitigation of Climate Change;
(d) Trade Investment and the Multilateral Process; and
(e) Financing Infrastructure for Sustainable Development.

I. ***Global Financial Architecture and Regulatory Practices***

Following the global financial crisis in 2008, the need for a better regulatory structure took centre stage as consensus emerged among the members to deal with risks stemming from financial fragility. Regulatory institutions in general play catch-up with financial markets, creating underlying risk. The Financial Stability Board, which works under the auspices of G20 has issued several recommendations to the G20 members to combat systemic risk and to strengthen the international financial system. A number of regulatory reforms like Basel III, over-the-counter (OTC) derivatives market, changes affecting the regulatory and accounting framework for institutional investors, policy measures for globally systemically important financial institutions (G-SIFIs) are being implemented. G20 has played an important role in pushing improvement in financial regulatory structure not only in the case of member countries but also for multilateral institutions.

In the lead chapter in this section, "Emerging markets perspectives on G20 led financial reforms", Ashima Goyal and Akhilesh Verma examine progress as well as continuing concerns in G20 led financial reforms, with particular emphasis on emerging markets. The Financial stability board (FSB) set up in 2009 was tasked with coordinating reforms with 24 countries including G20 countries under FSB jurisdiction and monitored for timely and consistent implementation to reduce regulatory arbitrage across countries. The reforms have been designed to (1) Strengthen the financial system and make it more resilient through lower leverage, higher buffers, better risk management and governance and a sound compensation structure. (2) End too big to fail (TBTF) institutions through requirements for higher loss absorbency for global systemically important financial institutions (G-SIFIs) subjecting such institutions to intensive supervision and establishing a legal and regulatory framework to allow resolution without government support. (3) Make derivative markets safer through the requirement to report all over-the-counter (OTC) derivatives to trade repositories, clearance of all standardized contracts through central counter-parties with trading on electronic platforms or exchanges and subjecting non-centrally cleared contract to minimum margin and higher capital requirements, (4) Transform shadow banking into market-based finance through oversight and strong regulation (5) Develop a macro prudential policy framework, improve accounting, auditing and disclosure, promote adherence to international standards and increase international policy coordination.

They find that while risks remain, they are of a lower order of magnitude compared to those in the pre global crisis period. For Emerging Markets especially they worry about leverage and spillovers, creating difficulties in maintaining an open and integrated global financial system. As quantitative easing is withdrawn emerging markets face risk-off outflows and volatile exchange rates during this period. Moreover leverage is high in some emerging markets after a period of low global interest rates and risk-on inflows in search of yields. Therefore arguments for and against financial tightening as the best response to ensure financial stability are examined in the context of experiences in some specific emerging markets. Implications are drawn for G20 policies and for advice to emerging markets. They find policy advice and action to be highly asymmetric. For example, emerging markets are advised to reduce fiscal spending to reduce reliance on and risks of foreign borrowing, while advanced economy governments are advised to borrow more at the low interest rates prevailing. The macro prudential regulations are not applied in advanced economies since they may increase the cost of financing, especially for the small borrower, but the effect of volatility in raising risk and rates throughout the world is ignored.

The third chapter, by *Alok Sheel* titled "Global Finance Ten Years after the Global Financial Crisis" provides a comprehensive overview of the evolution of macroeconomic policies from the time of the Great Depression as well as of the policy response to the recent Global Financial Crisis. The chapter explores how the global economy and the financial markets have adjusted in the wake of the crisis. It analyzes near term risks, provides an overview of longer term prospects of the global economy in the backdrop of the Global Financial crisis emanating from the US. While it was a problem of other countries, the authors point out that not only did the dollar strengthen as a result of a flight to safety, but the US Federal Reserve bailed out other countries, rather than the IMF, the traditional lender of last resort. This strength ultimately derives from the special role of the US dollar as the defacto global reserve currency. The seemingly bottomless global appetite for the dollar allows it to fund levels of domestic and external deficits that would normally be penalized by markets elsewhere. It also gives it the economic clout to discipline other countries—through sanctions without calling upon its deep military strengths. In a recent article in Financial Times, Rachman (2019), chief Foreign Affairs commentator, sees the globalized world yielding to a two bloc world dominated by the US and China. While the contours of a new global economic order in the wake of the global financial crisis are still unclear, it has nevertheless begun to take shape. The policy mix of how this new order will grapple with the continuing pre-crisis trends of stagnant wages, falling labour participation rates, growing inequality and stalling growth that is creating geopolitical instability and a backlash against globalization in advanced economies, is less clear.

II. ***Trade, Investment and the Multilateral Process***

Most G20 summits have recognized international trade and investment as the engine for growth, productivity, innovation, job creation, and development. Interestingly, the world merchandise trade growth posted its largest increase in six years in 2017 (WTO estimates). Continued expansion, as per the WTO, however depends on robust global economic growth and governments pursuing appropriate monetary, fiscal and trade policies. The G20 secretariat has always encouraged adoption of free market principles. Unfortunately, the long-held consensus over trade has recently come under threat from protectionist stance by some developed countries, which includes plans to impose tariffs on steel and aluminium. In this regard, the chapters in this section discuss the implications of the policies pursued by a few advanced economies on the global trade and investments and measures to avoid further decline in the global trade volumes. They also deliberate on the future of the multilateral trading system.

Anwarul Hoda, in his chapter titled, "Where is the US trade policy headed under the Trump Administration?", provides an excellent overview of the recent trade policy developments in the United States. The anti-globalisation rhetoric of candidate Donald Trump's election campaign has shaped the trade policy of the new Administration. Bilateralism is the favoured approach but unilateral measures have also been taken to pursue the protectionist agenda. A number of trade policy actions have focused on China, inducing a trade war. Donald Trump lamented the loss of manufacturing jobs in the US and put the blame on his predecessor administrations for two trade agreements responsible for the loss, namely the North American Free Trade Agreement (NAFTA) and the World Trade Organization (WTO). He has charged that 'China's entry into the WTO has enabled the greatest jobs theft in history. Increased protection of domestic manufacturing by raising tariffs has become the dominant objective of US trade policy. Anwarul Hoda critically analyses the protectionist stance taken by the US,and the disruptive effects of some of the particular trade policy actions, including opposition to appointments to vacancies in the Appellate Body and how this poses serious questions over the future of the multilateral trading system. The unrelenting opposition by the US to appointments to vacancies in the Appellate Body has caused a crisis in the WTO and given rise to doubts on its commitment to the rules based multilateral trading system.

Sugandha Huria and Manoj Pant take this discussion forward in their chapter titled, "Trade, Investment, and the Multilateral Trading System", by reiterating that the recent attempts by some of the world's largest trading countries towards protectionism seem to have furthered the extent of uncertainty involved in establishing a multilateral trading/investment system. They emphasize on the role of bilateral/plurilateral or regional trade agreements, which have the WTO rules as their foundations, in paving a way towards multilateralism. This is contrary to what Jagdish Bhagwati has stated in 1992 when describing them as stumbling blocs (Bhagwati 1991). Another aspect explored is the increasing inseparability between trade in goods, services, and investment or the so-called trade-services-investment nexus. While recent events towards protectionism involve only a handful of economies, yet their effects are far reaching. Fragmentation of production activities, rising trends of offshoring and outsourcing and rapid expansion in the activities of lead multinational firms have made economies interdependent so that a disturbance in one spills over very quickly on others. Measures and countermeasures resulting from steel and aluminium tariffs imposed by the US are therefore not limited to the seller only. In essence, this means that even though adopting a beggar-thy-neighbour policy may lead to some short-term gains it would ultimately generate longer-term world-wide inefficiencies, an effect of which may fall on to those who initiated the crises as well. Other impacts may be felt on jobs/employment, GDP, purchasing power, productive-efficiency, -all benefits that were created as a by-product of higher trade. The concern goes even deeper, in that many now fear that the existing multilateral system (or the WTO) may become abraded by exceptions, discriminatory trading arrangements, and by exploitation of various trade measures and distortions that are not yet covered by its rules. Accordingly a common set of norms that guide trade and investment volumes at the multilateral level are essential.

III. ***Future of Work***

Jobs have been central to the G20 agenda. The G20 Employment Working Group, constituted by transforming the Task Force on Employment (TFE) in 2014, recognizes the need for developing policies that are adaptable to the needs of the future job market. The broad objectives have been to help improve functioning of labour markets, enhancing social protection, equity and cohesion, improving measures related to labour mobility, skills portability, demographic and other related challenges, achieving healthier and safer workplaces through enforcement of regulations, implementation and investments and address inequality and promote sustainable growth. Under the Argentinian presidency in 2018, some additional aspects related to the future of work were discussed, such as technological change and its impact on employment and productivity, the informal economy, job security, and social protection initiatives. Given this, the discussions in this section focus on the structural transformation in the job market looking at the impact of technological change on job creation and displacement, social protection and gender inequality as well as the changing nature of informality in the labour market.

The section begins with the chapter by Kim Jurgensen and Imraan Valodia, titled, "Technological Change and the Future of Work—Some Issues from a Developing Country Perspective", where they examine the challenges and opportunities for developing countries that may emanate from the so-called fourth industrial revolution (4IR). Earlier the third industrial revolution saw information technology and electronics being used to automate production, while the 4th IR builds on it, the speed of development and scope of its impact are quite different. Developments in artificial intelligence, the Internet Of Things, robotics, automated vehicles, 3-D printing, nanotechnology, biotechnology, quantum computing, materials science and energy storage, coupled with how many people have access to some form of technology, means there are few aspects of our lives which will not be touched by the 4IR. In developing countries, and countries with high levels of inequality, planning for the likely impacts of the 4IR is crucial. The authors argue that technological change is a process that can be shaped and influenced. As more jobs in manufacturing become automated, countries will look to other industries to absorb the workforce. But this approach should be cognisant of how jobs are broken into components, and where to build on the human capital and where to invest in technology. Furthermore, a careful examination of the likely churning effects of the 4IR is necessary rather than on making policy on the hype about job losses. Helpfully, they find no concrete evidence to suggest that the new artificial intelligence and machine learning based technologies will necessarily destroy large number of jobs, especially in developing economies, where a large proportion of workers are employed in the informal sector. They go on to discuss the potential of new technology to improve working conditions in the care economy.

The next chapter by Radhicka Kapoor, "The Changing World of Work in Developing and Emerging Economies", attempts to widen the ambit of the discussion on the future of work by examining the issue from the lens of developing and emerging economies. The existing discourse on the future of work largely focuses on the advanced world. Out of the 3.4 billion global labour force that we have in the world today just about 20% is accounted for in the developed world. A large part of it is in developing and emerging economies where informality and precariousness is the norm and not the exception.

Accordingly, Radhicka Kapoor stresses the importance of inter-country heterogeneity in determining the impact of technological progress on the world of work. She looks at the future world of work, in a comprehensive way by analyzing the implications of the ongoing technological revolution on different actors in the world of work. The fact that it is changing is obvious. The workplace has been transformed by globalization, changing power dynamics, and new and emerging technologies—including artificial intelligence, robotics, and big data. These changes are playing an increasingly important role in shaping the jobs of the future, by shifting jobs between sectors, transforming the kinds of tasks that are done in existing jobs, and changing how people connect to work. However, these changes are not impacting people equally, with some workers bearing the brunt of these challenges disproportionately, thereby exacerbating overall inequality. Not only are the implications different across individuals but also across countries. The way the future of work is going to pan out across countries depends on their history, culture, demography, politics and social and economic development.

IV. ***Role of Technology for Adaptation and Mitigation of Climate Change***

Energy is an indispensable building block for economic growth. The energy appetite of the world is growing exponentially with economic advancement. As most of the world's energy is produced from fossil fuels, the role of technology is going to be crucial in replacing the current sources and processes with cleaner alternatives that create an avenue for climate change mitigation. We are already witnessing a technology revolution with the advancement of solar and wind technologies and their footprint globally. However, more technological innovation and development is necessary to effectively replace the existing greenhouse gas emitting sources and provide stable, reliable, and affordable energy as an alternative. The international climate change negotiations have witnessed deliberations on matters of technologies and technology cooperation. The United Nations Framework Convention on Climate Change (UNFCCC) also mentions technology issues related to addressing climate change. As it has been already recognized under the G20 framework, the countries need to come together and form a collaborative approach towards the development, adoption and implementation of environmentally-sound technologies and move towards a low-carbon sustainable future. The G20, which accounts for 85% of global GDP and 75% of global GHG emissions can play a leadership role in the transition to a decarbonized world by mid-century to stay within 1.5 °C warming. This section, therefore includes discussions on several existing energy alternatives, the importance of technologies, transfer of technology and technological cooperation towards mitigation of climate change, the various barriers associated with the adoption of innovative technology, and other related issues.

In this regard, Ulka Kelkar and Apurba Mitra, in their paper titled, "Rethinking technology for a 1.5 °C world" skillfully examine the role of technology and supporting policies in the transition to a decarbonized world by mid-century. They discuss the types of technologies and policies that are needed for India, to stay on track for 1.5 degree Celsius global warming. This requires the adoption of a range of low carbon technologies as well as enabling policies. Some technologies may not be major contributors to mitigation at present but may have high scalability potential. For instance, the costs of solar panels have fallen sharply over time due to economies of scale in their production. As another example, purchases of electric vehicles today can create a network externality, whereby the charging stations that are set up today will lower the effective cost for future purchasers of electric vehicles. Furthermore, some technologies and policies may have significant interaction effects such that the combined effect is more than the sum of its parts. For example, in India, higher grid penetration of renewables brought about by the National Solar Mission presents a less GHG intensive baseline for the Perform-Achieve-Trade (PAT) scheme for energy savings.

The discussion is taken forward in the next chapter titled, "Climate Ambition Needs Targeted Technology Collaboration", by Arunabha Ghosh, Vaibhav Chaturvedi and Shikha Bhasin, where they shed light on the elements that hold key to actualising technologies through frameworks that allow for cooperative and collaborative arrangements of burden-sharing, rather than maintaining strategic competitive advantages. Apart from highlighting the kind of technologies that are crucial for meeting climate goals, they also look at the uncertainties associated with them. Importantly, they provide templates of three alternative modalities for technological development, ranging from those that are ready to scale but need commercial pilots to horizon technologies that have significant risks. India has been right to argue that low-carbon growth would need much greater focus on shifting technologies "from lab to field". The shift to a 1.5 °C target from the 2 °C target agreed in Paris, requires a step change in technological collaboration, development, testing, deployment, manufacture and commercialization at scale. Action, thus far, has not been in line with ambition according to the authors. To be effective the transformations must occur with speed, and at scale. Given the range of uncertainties that exist in deploying and diffusing low-carbon technologies, from costs to governance to impacts, technology partnerships will have to strategically surge ahead as platforms to tackle these uncertainties through targeted research, development and deployment.

V. ***Financing Infrastructure for Sustainable Development***

All nations, including the G20 have recognised the role of investment in infrastructure in boosting growth and productivity, especially the role of private sector in improving infrastructure. However, despite continued efforts, infrastructure investment gap remains significant in both developed and emerging economies. Just as in tackling climate change, what is needed here too is a collaborative approach for development of infrastructure that involves both domestic and international institutions as well as both public and private sector funding. This will entail setting global standards, addressing data gaps, standardization of contracts, processes, financial instruments and financial engineering, among other things. The chapters in this section, therefore, look at these issues, and attempt to identify the instruments and mechanisms, which can be scaled in G20 countries, particularly India, given the current infrastructure financing scenario and the financial standards that need to be put in place to ensure overall stability of the system.

The section begins with a chapter by Kumar V Pratap and Mira Sethi, "Infrastructure Financing in India—Trends, Challenges and Way Forward", where they highlight the infrastructure financing history of India, how this has changed over the years, and the factors responsible for it. They provide a rich discussion on the need for deepening and diversifying sources of infrastructure financing and the challenges and issues that need to be addressed. Drawing lessons from other countries, they attempt to identify the instruments and mechanisms which can be adopted to mobilize increased infrastructure finance and also highlight the lessons that India holds for other countries on infrastructure financing.

Historically, the government and banks have been the most important sources of funding infrastructure projects in India. Both these traditional sources of funding infrastructure are constrained at present; government because of fiscal constraints and the banking system because of inter alia the Non-Performing Assets (NPAs) problem. On the other hand, the need for infrastructure investment is massive, given the infrastructure deficit in the country and the imperative of providing infrastructure to a fast growing economy. Given these factors, there is a strong recognition of the need for diversification of infrastructure funding sources, including introduction of new and innovative instruments of financing and enabling regulatory and institutional reforms. In this context, the untapped potential of long-term institutional investors such as insurance and pension funds and debt capital market offer both a challenge and an opportunity to meet the future financing needs. India has launched several new and innovative initiatives to channelize long-term funding to infrastructure sector such as Infrastructure Debt Funds, monetization of brownfield infrastructure assets (asset recycling strategy) through models such as Toll-Operate-Transfer and Infrastructure Investment Trusts, mainstreaming of Public Private Partnerships, developing a new credit rating scale for infrastructure projects and a proposed dedicated credit enhancement NBFC to raise credit rating of bonds floated by infrastructure companies. These new alternative financing instruments and avenues hold immense potential to provide fillip to infrastructure investment in India and may find traction with countries across the world who are looking to diversify their infrastructure financing options.

Sebastian Morris, in his chapter titled, "The Problem of Financing Private Infrastructure in India Today" highlights the importance of private sector involvement in financing infrastructure. Looking at the challenges involved, he emphasizes the importance of a commercially oriented banking sector that can facilitate flow of funds to the infrastructure sector and can help in exercising due diligence in funding projects, highlights the role of DFIs for overcoming the large interest rate risks, calls for an improvement in contracts and PPPs and also suggests a reform in the Indian public sector banks as well as civil service and administrative reforms in order to effectively respond and deal with the problem of financing private infrastructure in India. According to the author, contracts and PPPs have to improve much before there are a larger number of "good" infrastructure projects into which private capital can flow. "Good" projects are not those through which rents can be sought, but those where profits are adequate and private capital does not bear risks that it is ill equipped to bear. Moreover, Indian public sector banks need to be reformed, and the mess has gone far enough that nothing short of disinvestment would now work. While politically hard, this is also a suggestion in the previous chapter. The government cannot be relied to be at arm's length. Ultimately it is the weakness within the government (non-learning organisations, and lack of a systems approach, little ability to coordinate across many government departments, mind space of decision makers being too busy with fire fighting procedures, that results in enhancing risks and in failure. Correction of the same would require civil service and administrative reform.

And finally, an issue that always comes up with respect to the G20 is whether it is effective. Or will it degenerate and go back to the G7 or become just G2 (US and China) and overlook the others. A superficial response to this criticism is that once established, international institutions have an amazing capacity to perpetuate themselves. Therefore the G20 is there to stay. More seriously however, there is an opportunity for the G20 to try and resolve deep tensions in the global economy that are already there and threaten the future—trade wars, climate change and technological disruptions to name a few. For the G20 a relevant question is whether international cooperation in these areas can help. Trade and Climate Change are both extremely important, but these are also areas where negotiations are legally and formally taking place in different forums. The expectation from the G20 is that it can somehow give a lead on issues being negotiated elsewhere since negotiations between 190 odd countries are not only gruelling but more often than not, are inconclusive. Therefore the intent could be to use the G20 to build consensus and then wait for it to drive the rest of the system. The demand for legitimacy has pushed the G20 to sometimes stretch itself and do a little bit more (Kathuria and Nagpal 2016). And that can still be the touchstone. Only that it should do more in a narrow set of issues especially where international cooperation can be effective and of value—such as trade and climate change. From India's point of view international cooperation can be brought to bear through multilateral development banks (MDB) to leverage private money into infrastructure. There is a yawning gap in India and indeed in other emerging and even in developed markets between what is available and what is necessary to bridge the quality infrastructure gap. This is another area where international cooperation can be of immense value in the G20 and beyond.

## References

Bhagwati, J. (1991). *The World Trading System at Risk*. Princeton, NJ: Princeton University Press.
Kathuria, R., & Nagpal, N. K. (2016). Introduction. In R. Kathuria & N. Nagpal (Eds.), *Global Economic Cooperation*. New Delhi: Springer.
Nelson, R. M. (2018). The G-20 and International Economic Cooperation: Background and Implications for Congress. Library of Congress Washington DC Congressional Research Service.
Qureshi, Z. (2015). G20: From Crisis Management to Policies for Growth. In M., Larionova, & J. J. Kirton (Eds.), *The G8-G20 Relationship in Global Governance*. Ashgate Publishing.
Sharma, A. (2017). The road to hamburg: A reflection on the achievements of G20. *Issue Brief*, Indian Council of World Affairs (ICWA).

# Part I
# Global Financial Architecture and Regulatory Practices

# Chapter 2
# Emerging Markets Perspectives on G-20 Led Financial Reforms

**Ashima Goyal and Akhilesh Verma**

**Abstract** The chapter examines progress as well as continuing concerns in G-20 led financial reforms, with particular emphasis on emerging markets (EMs). Although risks remain they are of a lower order of magnitude compared to those in the pre global crisis period. But progress is slowest in areas of concern to EMs. Question marks over liquidity in markets as quantitative easing is withdrawn are echoed in EMs, which also face risk-off outflows and volatile exchange rates in this period. Leverage is high in some EMs after a period of low global interest rates and risk-on inflows in search of yields. But EMs are largely left to handle volatility themselves. Even the advice given to them or its understanding in policy circles or markets is not sufficiently nuanced. There are arguments for and against financial tightening as the best response to achieve financial stability. These are examined in the context of experiences in some specific EMs. Implications are drawn for G-20 policies and for its advice to EMs.

**Keywords** G-20 · Financial reforms · Emerging markets

**JEL Codes** F42 · F53 · G15

## 1 Introduction

G-20 countries aim to maintain the open and integrated structure of the international financial system while initiating a comprehensive program of global financial reforms[1] to:

(1) **Strengthen the financial system and make it more resilient** through lower leverage, higher dbuffers, better risk management and governance and a sound compensation structure.

[1] FSB (2015, 2016 and 2017) annual reports.

A. Goyal (✉) · A. Verma
Indira Gandhi Institute of Development Research, Mumbai 400 065, India
e-mail: ashima@igidr.ac.in



R. Kathuria and P. Kukreja (eds.), *20 Years of G20*,
https://doi.org/10.1007/978-981-13-8106-5_2

(2) **End too big to fail (TBTF) institutions** through requirements for higher loss absorbency for global systemically important financial institutions (G-SIFIs), subjecting such institutions to intensive supervision and establishing a legal and regulatory framework to allow resolution without government support.
(3) **Make derivative markets safer** through the requirement to report all over-the-counter (OTC) derivatives to trade repositories, clearance of all standardized contracts through central counter-parties with trading on electronic platforms or exchanges and subjecting non-centrally cleared contract to minimum margin and higher capital requirements,
(4) **Transform shadow banking** into market-based finance through oversight and strong regulation.
(5) **Develop a macroprudential policy framework**, improve accounting, auditing and disclosure, promote adherence to international standards and increase international policy coordination.

Financial stability board (FSB) set up in 2009 was tasked with coordinating reforms, with 24 countries including G-20 countries under FSB jurisdiction and monitored for timely and consistent implementation to reduce regulatory arbitrage across countries.[2]

Global banks capital and liquidity buffers have improved. The financial system has become more diversified through enhancement of market-based finance. Growth in total and bank credit has improved in most countries and the cost of financing remains low mainly due to advanced economies' (AEs) accommodative monetary policy. While there is steady progress in objectives (1) to (3), progress is slow for (4) and (5).

Over the past few years, FSB has completed an assessment of two core reforms: OTC derivatives and shadow banking. Central clearing has simplified the earlier complex process of derivative exposure and central counterparties have strengthened. Higher collateral in the financial system, improved transparency through trade repositories, better data quality are some outcomes of reforms in OTC derivatives, while those in the shadow banking system have reduced vulnerabilities in money market funds and repo markets.

There are still areas of weakness, however, such as concerns about market liquidity, leverage and spillovers on emerging markets (EMs). These create difficulties in maintaining an open and integrated global financial system.

International bank lending through European banks has declined since the global financial crisis (GFC). The move towards regionally funded lending increases the risk of geographic market segmentation. Financing through international debt markets has substantially increased, which further requires the development of global infrastructure for trading, clearing, settlement and measures to reduce volatility. On the EM side, there are challenges in implementing FSB reforms and concerns expressed over the excessive focus on banks, leading to slowdown in domestic bank credit,

[2]These countries are Argentina, Australia, Brazil, Canada, China, France, Germany, Hong Kong, India, Indonesia, Italy, Japan, Mexico, Netherlands, Republic of Korea, Russia, Saudi Arabia, Singapore, South Africa, Spain, Switzerland, Turkey, United Kingdom and the United States.

reduction of global bank exposure in their domestic markets and rising volatility of non-bank capital flows. Overall credit growth has been robust, however, in most countries.

The remainder of the paper is structured as follows: Sect. 2 discusses reform successes; Sect. 3 brings out the key challenges remaining and assesses global risks; in this context Sect. 4 further develops the risks and challenges from an EM perspective before Sect. 5 concludes the paper with some suggestions for G-20.

## 2 Reform Successes

### *2.1 Stronger and More Robust Banks*

Much of the reforms have focused on banks, which are now stronger and more resilient with higher capital buffers. Leverage is lower although it can still go as high as 20–33 times loss-absorbing equity.

Funding profiles have improved for banks due to less dependence on short-term wholesale funding and larger holding of more liquid assets such as government bond and deposits at the central banks, indicating that the core of banking has become more resilient than it was before GFC. Credit default swaps (CDS) premium and other indicators suggest that bank risk has declined. The credit rating of several international banks shows reduced expectations of too-big-to-fail stress.

The share of domestic systemically important banks (SIBs) in the global banking system has marginally decreased, but it remains large in absolute levels. Balance sheet size of SIBs in the US and Europe has remained stable in last few years (although post crisis it did rise with mergers), but it has increased in Asia (mostly in China).

All countries within FSB jurisdiction have put in place risk-based capital and liquidity rules from the Basel III regulatory framework. Rules on leverage ratio and net stable funding ratio (NFSR) came into force in most of the G-20 countries in January 2018. 20 countries published final rules for leverage ratio and 15 countries have published the final draft on NFSR.

Higher loss absorbency requirements for G-SIFIs are in place in all G-SIFIs headquarters; 23 jurisdictions have loss absorbency requirements for SIBs. Crisis management groups (CMG) have been formed in all SIBs and there are significant advances in resolution planning, however, cross-border resolution remains incomplete. The absence of insurance resolution regime with broader tools in G-SIFI home countries still impedes resolvability.

### *2.2 Safer Derivative Markets*

Implementation of OTC derivative market reform is underway. Reforms related to trade reporting and interim capital requirement for non-centrally cleared derivatives are in advanced stages. Progress in final capital requirement, however, is relatively slow. Comprehensive central clearing framework is implemented in three-fourth while comprehensive margin requirement and trading framework are implemented in half of the countries under FSB jurisdiction.

Till end-2017 comprehensive trade reporting requirements were in place in all but one jurisdiction; 12 countries had adopted a framework for mandatory platform trading of standard OTC derivative covering 90% of the market. EU rules have increased margin and decreased leverage. Migration to electronic platforms has reduced counterparty risk

Aspects such as availability of client clearing service are constantly monitored. Additional work is underway to increase central counterparties (CCP) resilience, resolvability and recovery planning. Although home authorities have started to establish CMGs for systemically important CCPs, cross-border resolution mechanism is not in place. A joint group of regulators investigated interconnectedness of CCPs and SIBs, possible systemic risk and macroprudential (MaP) regulations required.

## 2.3 *Transformation of Shadow Banking into Market-Based Finance*

FSB, in collaboration with standard-setting bodies, has created a system-wide monitoring framework to analyze risk and global trends and strengthen oversight in the shadow banking system. Several issues are identified for further work such as data gaps in assessing financial stability risk, information sharing between authorities and bringing non-bank entities that could pose stability risk under regulation. Three countries, including the US, that account for a substantial part of the global market, have completed implementation of shadow banking reforms.

Liquid money market funds (MMFs) invest in risky corporate paper but offer fixed returns, which they were unable to sustain during the GFC, so that they 'broke the buck'; 21 FSB jurisdiction countries have now implemented the fair value approach for the evaluation of MMFs portfolios.

Improvements in auditing, disclosure, the spread of legal entity identifiers (LEI) and more uniform standards all aim to push shadow banking towards market-based finance. Haircuts are proposed for bonds and equities as well so as to extend countercyclical regulation beyond banks and cover markets more uniformly and broadly. Basel III wants banks to hold capital against client positions as well. Progress on liquidity management in the shadow banking system is not significant as yet, however.

### 2.4 *Adherence to International Financial Standards and Other Reforms*

FSB jurisdiction countries undergo a financial sector assessment program every five years. Most of them publish their compliance assessment report in line with the "Report on Standard and Codes" published by World Bank and IMF. FSB completes the country peer review and publishes its recommendations. A global code of conduct was issued in May 2017 to promote integrity and effective functioning of the wholesale foreign exchange market.

G-20 countries have established a MaP authority and inter-agency bodies to implement MaP regulations, strengthen system-wide monitoring and to manage financial stability risks. An oversight framework for hedge funds or their managers is also established, and there are requirements for oversight and registration of credit rating agencies.

To address data gaps and to assess international risks, FSB started a "G20 data gaps initiative", which was in its second phase in 2018. Under this initiative, G20 members enhance sharing granular data at national and international level. 500000 LEIs issued over 195 countries would help to collect information on parent entities, and aid FSB in regulatory activities especially with financial transaction reporting and correspondent banking.

BCBS is also working on measures to enhance timeliness and quality of information sharing among regulatory supervisors and promote cooperation between host and home countries of SIBs.

To address concerns about manipulation at the global level the robustness of interest rate benchmarks is being improved. Market participants are also working with authorities to identify risk-free benchmarks and increase their market use. Although migration away from the existing benchmark, LIBOR, in 2021 risks instability as contracts have to be re-priced, scope for market manipulation would reduce. Also inter-bank borrowing rates have become less important since many other money market instruments are now developed. Banks borrowing from each other will have less effect on their cost of funds.

## 3 Key Challenges and Impact Assessment

BCBS evaluation of G-20 and other countries under FSB jurisdiction found 18 countries (containing 68% of the total market) to be largely compliant with risk-based capital rules while six European Union members (containing the remaining 32% of the total market) were non-compliant. G-20 countries were fully compliant with the liquidity coverage ratio. Further, all 10 countries with G-SIFIs were compliant.

Despite progress, some key regulations under Basel III standards due to be implemented during early 2017 were still delayed in most G-20 countries. These include capital requirements for equity investment, standardized approach for counter-party credit risk, the capital requirement for exposure to central counterparties, and margin requirement for non-centrally cleared derivatives. So country progress is not uniform. Delays prevent a level playing field and put extra pressure on compliant countries.

Reforms in financial market infrastructure have led to an increase in the number of CCPs for clearance of OTC derivatives, including those operating at cross-border levels. In post-trade services that include expanded portfolio reconciliation, there are better documentation practices and support for risk mitigation.

While reforms have increased rates of central clearing, liquidity and reduced spread in product markets, there are, however, views expressed that interaction of reforms may have reduced the depth of liquidity. Compliance cost has increased but has to be weighed against possible long-term benefits from increased financial stability. Banks have more capital but they also have more concentration and lower profitability.

BCBS analysis found strategic variation in bank's risk-weighted assets and recommended further revision of Basel III standards to reduce risk arbitrage. Shadow banking and liquidity management remains an issue. There are data and information sharing gaps.

There is pushback from markets (FSB 2018), which expect more volatility due to tough global standards and therefore want them to be made more risk sensitive. For example, they want cross border flows to be forced to have similar standards only if they are systemic.

QE has led to a rise in debt as a percentage of GDP from 145 in 2007 to 256 in 2017. At $182 tn it is 60% higher than in 2007. In China alone it doubled to 300%. For governments leverage increased 31 percentage points; non-financial corporates 29, and households 11 points. Corporate bonds increased 2.7 times to $11.7 tn, while credit quality fell. In China the CAGR was 39.9, other developing economies 14, AEs 7.8–10.5. Non-financial corporate debt ratio to GDP reached 73% in the US (Lund et al. 2018). Leveraged loans alternatives to bonds like mortgage-backed securities doubled since 2010 to more than $1 tn, at the expense of credit standards. A majority of these loans had weak protection against default. A string of defaults could freeze lending to firms.

Strong BASEL III regulation targeting them led to arbitrage away from banks. Mutual Funds global assets under management increased from $50 tn in 2004 to $ 79.3 tn in 2016 and exchange-traded funds from $400 bn in 2005 to $4.7 tn in March 2018. Shadow banking has grown to $45.2 tn. Growth was 7.6% in 2016 amounting to 13% of global financial assets (in 29 jurisdictions). It reached 2.5 times GDP in the US (FSB 2017). High asset prices make non-bank investors vulnerable to a rise in interest rates and possible crash in prices.

## *3.1 Assessment of Risks*

Even so, a distinction needs to be made between asset prices and excess leverage. If interest rates go up due to higher growth, asset prices may not crash. There is some diversification and discrimination among countries based on longer term fundamentals, and a long term movement away from the US towards diversified EMs.

The current leverage itself is different. While leverage of governments, firms and households has increased, financial sector leverage now comes from hedge funds not from banks. Equity funds lending arms are substituting for banks. Private equity is even buying banks and multiplying leverage. Even so, leverage in loan funds is 2:1,[3] much less than the 30:1 banks had reached before the GFC. Private equity funds assets under management rose from nothing in 2006 to $200 bn.[4] This is still less than 1% of banking assets but is a large share in smaller and more leveraged businesses. There are long-term investors who would lose but this would not be systemic unless growth collapses. But private equity does not have high quality assets or access to a lender of last resort facility as banks do.

However, annual gross cross border capital inflows, including foreign direct investment (FDI), debt securities, equity, and lending and other investment fell 53% from a peak of 12.7 $ tn in 2007 to 5.9 in 2017 (Lund et al. 2018). There are no large swaps as in 2008 when derivatives outstanding increased from $100 tn in 2002 to $516 tn in April 2007. The unsecured inter-bank market has shrunk and there is reform to make manipulation in benchmark rates difficult.

Larger buffers and stronger capital rules, however, imply banks are retreating from traditional market maker roles of providing two-way quotes. There is therefore a question mark over liquidity supply. Can exits for trades become crowded especially as interest rates rise? Technology has enhanced market liquidity. For example, the adoption of MIFID II rules in Europe encouraged electronic trade. Volumes rose as the compliance burden fell. But algorithmic trade tends to be pro-cyclical.

Will this lead to more reliance on CBs? AE CBs are providing wider support, but should it continue? After the large expansion in balance sheets and extended period of low rates they now have little space for further stimulus. Moreover, after the experience of the GFC, lender of last resort power has been reduced for many CBs.

Cooperation among national authorities is required for regional and global financial stability because of large cross-border financial activity. It would create a level playing field and reduce regulatory arbitrage. Uneven pace of reform implementation leads to time-consuming bilateral recognition processes in the derivative regulatory framework. But the current political climate of populist nationalist rhetoric makes coordination difficult. Adherence to international standards, transparency in reporting, sharing resolution related information, maybe critical but is voluntary.

---

[3]Equity Funds as the new banks. https://www.ft.com/content/ec43db70-ba8e-11e8-94b2-17176fbf93f5.

[4]Prequin research reported in the Economist September 8, 2018.

## 4 The Emerging Market Perspective

From the EM perspective excessive focus of reforms on banks has been costly because their financial systems tend to be more bank focused. In addition, bank regulation together with QE encouraged arbitrage towards portfolio flows, increasing capital flow volatility for EMs. Since objectives (4) and (5) are aimed to address this volatility relatively slower progress in these items is a negative for EMs. In the post GFC period, and even before, EMs suffered from capital flow volatility, which was largely due to global risk-on risk-off, not the domestic cycle. Rey (2015) argues global risk off, when funds choose to return to the US, is largely due to US financial tightening. Periods of risk-off in 2011, 2013 and 2018 that followed the GFC have hurt EMs more than the GFC itself. And risk-on contributes to subsequent risk-off.

The 19 largest EMs saw outflows of $0.5 tn in 2008/09 and $1 tn in 2014/15, recent risk-off periods. The IMF (2018) forecasts $40–$60 bn outflows per annum during the period of QE exit; Lagarde sees this going up to $100 bn in 2019. Over risk on periods such as July 2009–June 2014, when US interest rates were almost at the zero bound, EM inflows amounted to $2 tn. In 2017 they were $160 bn.

Although domestic macroeconomic vulnerabilities affected individual countries, the reasons for these surges were largely global. Low interest rates in AEs led to outflows in search of yield. Large liquidity made available through QE was multiplied through pro-cyclical balance sheets in financial institutions. In 2018, another risk-off year, US political actions such as sanctions against Iran led to an oil price rise, while its pro-cyclical fiscal stimulus strengthened the dollar.

EMs concerns remain peripheral. The 10th anniversary, in 2018, of the Lehman crash stimulated a large amount of discussion, but hardly any from EMs point of view. 2011, 2013 and 2018 were actually larger shocks for EMs than 2008. Despite the G-20, not enough was done to moderate spillovers on EMs. This was short-sighted because EMs now account for a large and growing share of global GDP. AEs share, which was 54% in 2004 fell to 41.31% in 2017. So an EM slowdown can now create negative spillovers for AEs, reducing world growth.

### *4.1 Sources of Negative Spillovers to EMs*

#### 4.1.1 Bank Dependence

Compared to AEs, EMs remain much more bank dependent. Therefore decreasing cross border and trade finance, as regulations were tightened for banks, was a concern for them. EMs raised several issues during FSB's third annual EM forum (February 2017). Global regulatory reforms could conflict with the financing needs of these economies. Major implementation challenges of FSB regulatory reforms are related to domestic factors (narrow fixed-income markets, capacity constraints etc.) as well as cross-border spillovers. Bank lending grew slowly in some EMs whereas the non-bank sources of financing increased. As home jurisdictions of international banks implemented reforms (delays in bilateral recognition assessment of OTC derivatives, risk weighting of host countries' debt), adopted national policies to improve financial stability that went beyond internationally agreed standards, along with other macroeconomic developments such as slower growth, low commodity prices etc. the presence and activities of global banks reduced in some EMs.

#### 4.1.2 Cross-Border Banking Flows

Cross-border banking flows to EMs reduced and remained volatile in the post-GFC period. BIS consolidated banking data suggest that reduction in banking flows were mainly from US and UK whereas Japanese banks continued to increase their presence in EMs. Domestic and international banks were adversely affected due to emphasis on capital adequacy ratios in the Basel III framework. This reflected in the rising cost of funding, its availability, loan pricing and in a selection of countries. Rising interest rates in AEs could further reduce investors' appetite towards EM assets and add pressure on EM financial and non-financial corporates (Tiftik et al. 2017).

#### 4.1.3 Trade Finance

European and U.S. banks reduced their trade credit flows to EMs due to modest recovery since 2010. Some EM banks attempted to fill in the gap in financing needs, but tighter global funding conditions pose a risk for trade credit and these banks have lower capacity to fund cross-border trade. Since the Basel III framework does not fully identify risk profile of large corporations and banks and penalizes all off balance exposure, low-risk characteristics of trade finance would not be considered making it a less attractive portfolio for banks. Therefore, the higher capital requirement leads to a reduction in trade credit.

#### 4.1.4 Bank Lending and Debt Capital Markets

The financial system in EMs is mostly bank dominated and financial markets are in a nascent stage of development. However, EM non-financial corporate bonds have grown substantially in the previous decade, reaching $4 trillion in 2016 (Tiftik et al. 2017). Despite such a trend in the debt market, the domestic banking sector remains the primary source of funding in many EMs and accounts for more than half of non-financial corporate debt. Lack of external credit ratings of EMs corporates forces banks to increase their lending standards, in form of higher capital requirement, to lend to such firms. It negatively affects domestic and cross-border lending in EMs, and raises cost of capital.

### 4.1.5 Corporate Hedging

EM non-financial corporate debt has increased from $5 trillion in 2005 to $26 trillion in 2016 (Tiftik et al. 2017). Given such exposure in corporate firms in international markets, it becomes important for EM corporate to hedge interest rate risk, exchange rate risk, inflation risk etc.

The published Basel proposals sharply penalize trading activity that includes all financial instruments used for hedging purpose by SME and corporates. Proposed regulatory amendments create potential headwinds for corporates with foreign currency denominated debt through their negative impact on international funding available for hedging. During stressed periods, it might become difficult for EM corporates to pay foreign currency debt due to lack of foreign currency funding sources. Core sectors in EMs could be at larger risk due to lack of natural hedges and access to derivative markets. Corporate in the real estate and consumer sectors with local currency revenue and foreign expenses are more exposed to currency risk.

### 4.1.6 Infrastructure Investment

Since infrastructure investment needs are higher compared to national saving especially in EMs, cross-border finance continues to an important source of funding for infrastructure investment. The post-crisis regulatory environment has made international banks reluctant to take a risk in this sector. Long-term infrastructure investment in EMs seems vulnerable to further de-risking by foreign banks. For regulatory purposes infrastructure project finance falls under Specialized Lending Exposure category of financing. According to the current Basel framework, these types of investment would not be assessed through the internal model and would require high collateral and guarantee from the government or credit agencies. This makes banks reluctant to fund such investment due to the risk of mispricing the cost of the investment.

*Financial inclusion* is another neglected area of particular importance to EMs. BCBS did issue guidance in 2016 on the application of Basel in the context of financial inclusion.

### 4.1.7 Synchronization of Macroprudential Regulations

Given the need to regulate cross-border capital to maintain financial stability in EMs, IMF (2011, 2012) recognized that countries may have to 'synchronize' or co-ordinate macroprudential (MaP) regulations at international as well as domestic levels, although there has been least progress in this area. MaP regulations mainly address systemic-wide financial risk within an economy. Countercyclical rules help to reduce market volatility, provide stability to the financial system, and obtain growth and investment objectives ( Akdogan 2018; IMF 2012). They mitigate balance sheet exposure from short-term debt flows, and reduce incentives to take risks, unlike capital controls that directly act on capital flows. But poorly designed and un-coordinated MaP regulations and capital flow measures such as aggressive capital controls might result in 'regulatory or capital war' and impose excess burden on a few countries, reducing global welfare (Jeanne 2014; da Silva and Chui 2017).

At the international level, EMs and AEs need to coordinate their policies to maintain global financial stability and mitigate negative spillovers which may constrain the supply of global capital. Coordination of MaP regulations with domestic monetary policy could control possible policy spillover. It is more important for EMs since they are exposed to cross-border flows and its mismanagement can have repercussion for their domestic financial stability.

International policy coordination has become more relevant in the post-crisis era. After GFC, EMEs faced excess capital flow volatility and its policymakers used several MaP tools to reduce the intensity and negative spillover of such inflows (da Silva and Chui 2017). Some MaP tools, such as countercyclical capital buffers, are relatively new and their possible spillovers are yet to be known. Given the size and outreach of several global banks, some form of international co-operation in MaP regulations could be helpful to not only restrain local credit booms but also affect the credit conditions in those economies where these banks have a larger presence. Global finance is highly mobile, adaptive and innovative which can generate negative externalities. Policy coordination would help to moderate excessive co-movements of asset prices globally and reduce the possibility of hasty capital controls or capital flow measures by any individual country (Cecchetti and Tucker 2016). Exposure to risk across sectors, borders and institutions requires transparent exchange among authorities. It is beyond the ability of one supervisor to accurately aggregate information and to assess vulnerabilities. A common standard in MaP regulation would avoid regulatory arbitrage, fragmentation, and balkanization of the system. A key role of FSB is to promote such coordination among countries, identify vulnerabilities and address them in time.

On the domestic level of policy synchronization, monetary policy focusses on the inter-temporal allocation of spending whereas MaP regulations restrain borrowing. Monetary policy mainly controls risk-free interest rates and MaP regulation focuses on risk premium or the spread between risk-free rate and lending rates (IMF 2012). Achieving financial and price stability may not be possible with one instrument (via monetary policy) in case of capital account openness (IMF 2012). For example, domestic currency appreciation due to capital inflows can lead to economic imbalances. Increase in policy rates alone may not be enough to dampen credit incentives. MaP policy alone is also inefficient to manage output and price stability because it highly restrains the financial sector. MaP regulations are more successful when it is complemented with the monetary policy (Bruno et al. 2017). A case study of five inflation targeting European countries (IMF 2012) shows policy interest rates can stay relatively low, reducing incentives for unhedged FX borrowing when complemented with MaP regulations. These also enhance monetary policy effectiveness and its transmission in small open economies.

Well designed and coordinated MaP regulations reduce the costs and tradeoffs. Claessens (2014) shows before the GFC MaP regulations were used 4 times more by EMs compared to AEs; after the GFC the gap reduced to 3.3. AEs use though increasing is still limited. This reduces coordination possibilities that can improve the effectiveness and reduce the costs of MaP regulations. In the section below we see the unilateral use of regulations in EMs faced with foreign portfolio flows.

## *4.2 Regulation of Foreign Portfolio Flows in EMs*

QE has led to an especially large rise in EM corporate debt and in fixed income flows to EMs.

Even so regulatory measures for cross border FPI flows to EMs are largely implemented in destination countries (EMs) with hardly anything for source countries (AEs).

Financial regulation of cross-border finance evolved over three generations of regulation. The first phase of regulation immediately after the Bretton Woods agreement was in the form of quantity-based controls such as restrictions on currency mismatches, minimum end-use restrictions, and minimum stay requirements. The second phase was price based such as unremunerated reserve requirement and minimum stay requirement in Chile, tax on inflows in Brazil and outflows in Malaysia (1998). Finally, in the third phase of financial regulation after the GFC, a few economies experimented with first and second-generation capital controls while others imposed regulations on foreign exchange derivatives to contain risk in currency and credit markets (Gallagher 2015). Some of the third-generation regulation EMs implemented were:

1. **China**: Outright ban or limit on entry of certain investments.
2. **India**: Directed limits on dollar-rupee trade, margin requirement on dollar-rupee trade increased to 100%.
3. **Brazil**: Tax on portfolio investment (2% tax on bond and equities purchased by foreigners). Non-interest reserve requirement on short dollar position in FX spot market. These measures did not reduce the volume of capital inflows but switched foreign investment towards long-term investment.
4. **South Korea**: Withholding tax on non-resident holdings of treasury and monetary bonds; restrictions on bank FX derivatives. Liberalized capital outflows reduced net inflows and exchange rate pressures.
5. **Peru**: Tax on portfolio investment, position limits on FX short dollar trades and reserve requirement for all FX deposits. These did not, however, make a significant impact on the total inflows of capital or the composition of inflows.
6. **Indonesia**: One month holding period on central bank bills.
7. **Thailand**: Tax on nonresident purchase of public bonds.

Post GFC period also witnessed a more favourable view from the IMF on capital flow measures (CFMs) for EMs (IMF 2011, 2012). While capital account liberalization was to continue as the goal, it was recognized, the appropriate level of liberalization depends on institutional thresholds and country-specific circumstances.

Nations should be cautious and sequenced when liberalizing the capital account. They should first liberalize FDI, then longer-term portfolio flows, and lastly short-term flows. Capital controls (now referred to as CFMs) may be used under certain circumstances.

Nations should, however, respond to inflow surges first with appropriate macroeconomic policies such as: allowing the exchange rate to appreciate; accumulating reserves; tightening fiscal policy or managing interest rates.

CFMs could be used if the exchange rate was not undervalued, reserves were at optimal levels or were too costly to accumulate further, the economy was overheating and there was little scope for fiscal tightening. CFMs can buy time for the first three, since inflow surges raise systemic risk. After a country has substantially liberalized its capital account, CFMs on capital outflows can be considered in crisis or near-crisis conditions, to provide breathing space while more fundamental policy adjustments are implemented. Even so, nations should give precedence to CFMs that do not discriminate on the basis of residency. They should be temporary and should be lifted when the conditions for their removal have been met.

Source countries (where capital flows originate) and nations deploying CFMs should be conscious of the multilateral aspects of their policies. Nations should strive for reciprocity when MaP policies are being deployed. The design of policies should "minimize the scope for regulatory arbitrage." The IMF recognizes that its advice on CFMs may be at odds with international trade and investment commitments of IMF members. De facto the onus remains on EMs, and there is little coordination. More market-based MaP regulations, such as those that reduce lowering of credit standards in source countries would allow EMs also to graduate to less distorting market-based regulations.

## *4.3 Risks and EM's Resilience: Global Liquidity Tightening*

Post GFC, several EMs took advantage of easy external financial conditions to build buffers and correct economic imbalances but this also built financial vulnerabilities. Central banks in AEs normalized monetary policy in tandem with their gradual economic recovery, especially in the US leading to higher rollover risk, capital outflows and negative implications for productive investment for EMs. Depending on their domestic fundamentals, EMs experienced currency volatility and deterioration in debt sustainability with rising debt service due to increase in global interest rates.

IMF (2017) suggests that expected federal funds rate increase to 3.6% by early 2020 may lead to reducing portfolio flows in EMs, especially countries with weaker fundamentals, by $40 billion a year in 2018–19. If policy normalization is accompanied by investors' risk aversion, capital portfolio flows could reduce by $60 billion a year. EMs would be disproportionately affected due to in face of a rise in global interest rates (Sahay et al. 2014).

Shim and Shin (2018) show financial stress measured through CDS spread in AEs where international banks headquartered is a big driver of banking outflows from EMs. International banks decrease their exposure to EMs in face of financial instability in lender countries. Cross-border lending is more vulnerable to financial stress in lending countries compared to local lending by foreign banks. Diversification among financial lenders could be a way to reduce risk emanating through financial stress in lender countries.

However, except for a few, EMs are in a better position to withstand global volatility, with stronger macro-fundamentals, better reserve holdings and availability of cross-country swaps. After the East Asian crisis EMs increased the share of risk-sharing foreign equity investment compared to debt, which helped them survive the GFC. But the subsequent QE has led to a rise in corporate dollar debt in some EMs. They have also gained experience in macro and micro prudential regulations.

## *4.4 Country Experiences*

EMs are largely left to face global volatility on their own, but even the advice on how they should do this is not very clear. As a result, they tend to swing between extremes. But in the latest bout of global risk-off neither worked in vulnerable countries. Neither orthodox currency defense implemented by Argentina (with interest rates rising by 15–60%) nor Turkey's heterodox polices (where despite Erdogan's resistance interest rates rose 24%) were effective. Both their currencies depreciated by 40–50%. Neither conservative pro-market nor idiosyncratic policies that ignore markets do well.

Context sensitive pragmatic counter-cyclical policies perform better. For example, China seems to be navigating trade shocks with counter-cyclical macroeconomic policies. After the post GFC credit boom there was contraction in attempts to contain shadow banking. But capital controls were increased after 2015–16 so that domestic interest rates can decrease even if US rates are rising. Cuts were implemented in CRR to increase liquidity.

In the post GFC period India saw large growth volatility, although its growth rate remained the highest in the world as growth slowed elsewhere. Its macroeconomic policies swung from too much stimulus to too much tightening. The post GFC G-20 coordinated macro stimulus was too large and aggravated already high commodity-led inflation. There was over-reaction after that as fiscal consolidation took place together with strictly implemented inflation targeting. There was some useful structural reform but in Larry Summers words 'stone-age monetary ideas' ruled in India. The micro and market fundamentalist view that only the supply-side determined output neglected the countercyclical actions that were feasible even with the flexible inflation targeting legally adopted. Systemic risk and possible financial instability from spillovers were also neglected. As a result industry and investment continued in a slowdown over 2011–2018, banks NPAs festered and grew, credit growth slowed and inadequacies in infrastructure financing manifested as concerns in non-bank financial companies also. Inflation did fall, but with major contribution from falling commodity prices.

The asset quality review undertaken by the RBI increased NPAs and provisioning, but the government was reluctant to recapitalize banks until the Indian Bankruptcy Code, 2017, was functional and there was some governance improvement. As a result bank credit fell steeply. As in AEs, there was a greater role for NBFCs and markets as banks retreated. This can be a healthy diversification that builds on local customer knowledge and fin tech to improve market stability. But for NBFCs in infrastructure, such as IL&FS, that were financing long term assets with short-term debt, and funding more and more in short term money markets, under rising interest rates, the default was waiting to happen.

After the oil price crash of 2014, since the country was on an inflation targeting path, policy rates were not adequately adjusted downwards. Real interest rates were too high and investment and manufacturing collapsed, after a brief revival in 2014. The fall in oil prices turned India's net exports removing oil negative, implying a negative demand shock, which policy needed to alleviate. A rise in taxes on oil reduced a possible consumption boost from a fall in oil prices.

After 2011 Indian credit growth was the slowest among EMs; it actually turned negative for industry. Indian corporate dollar debt also did not rise as it did in most EMs in this period. Even borrowing limits available were not utilized, suggesting the credit slowdown was due to low demand. Industrial growth became negative in the April 2015 quarter after oil prices crashed, exports slowed, and the real interest rate reached a peak of 4%.

A sharp fall in growth of gross fixed capital formation followed in the July 2016 quarter. As a result of the slowdown in industry, India was not able to take advantage of the boom in world exports.

As caps on debt inflows were lifted 2017 saw a surge of inflows, and real appreciation further hurt export growth. Debt inflows gained from appreciation, leading to more inflows. Intervention added \$53 bn to reserves in 2017–18, but it was not enough to prevent appreciation over-fundamentals. Even so, the US treasury called it manipulation, and put India on their watch-list since one of their criteria is persistent one-sided FX intervention of at least 2% of GDP over 12 months. They recognized that India does not have a current account surplus but felt it does not need \$400 bn of reserves since it has capital controls. But excess inflows had come in, appreciating the rupee, precisely because controls had been relaxed. And reserves seemed inadequate in 2018 as oil prices touched \$85 and inflows were inadequate to finance the current account deficit. The rupee plunged despite interventions that only aimed to reduce excess rupee volatility.

The debt inflows did not help finance government borrowing either since the sterilizing swap of foreign for domestic securities only increased G-Sec yields.

Despite the perverse effects of high real interest rates, markets wanted a rise in policy repo rates in the October 2018 meeting to decrease domestic demand and increase inflows, suggesting the dominance of orthodox thinking opposing views on whether financial tightening or growth is necessary to review inflows. An interest rate defense of the rupee was attempted but did not work during the taper tantrum of 2013.

Majority of inflows are growth sensitive. Even debt inflows get capital gains from softening interest rates. If over depreciation indicates future appreciation and interest rates have peaked indicating future softening they are likely to return. This happened in India as oil prices crashed in November and the rupee appreciated.[5]

Impact of equity flows on Indian stock market indices has reduced since large domestic retail flows are coming in through mutual funds. Similar deepening of domestic debt markets is required before allowing more debt inflows. Retail fixed income flows are the most volatile and can create considerable interest rate volatility in thin markets that disrupts the domestic cycle.

India had a 0.5% policy rate rise in 2018 with debt inflows capped at 5% of the domestic market. Indonesia, where the share is 40% the rise was 1.75%. Therefore the caps on debt flows need to be lifted more gradually, keeping in mind, not just the share of domestic debt market, but also international debt and impact on capital flows and intervention. This is an example of better domestic policy coordination.

Apart from direct intervention, there are many ways of financing an oil shock driven widening of the current account deficit and reducing rupee volatility in the short-term. For example, reducing oil companies' dollar demand by making dollar swaps available to them was the most effective measure in 2013. In the long-term, of course, the CAD has to be reduced through easier industrial conditions to stimulate exports, and substitution away from oil.

As strictly implemented inflation targeting led to a narrow focus there was poor coordination of monetary policy with capital flow management tools. The MPC acted as if the exchange rate was a float, although there was active intervention in the managed float. Coordinating MaP regulations, capital flow management and monetary policy could have given better results.

## 5 Conclusion

The G-20 financial reforms have seen many successes, and on the whole financial sector risks are lower than they were pre GFC. Although financial sector leverage is less, that of households, firms and governments is higher. EM corporate cross border leverage is regarded as a large potential risk as global interest rates rise towards normal. QE and the regulatory focus on banks have increased the volatility of portfolio flows to and from EMs, creating large fluctuations in interest and exchange rates, and therefore growth rates. EMs should not have to handle capital flow volatility alone.

EMs size has grown. They now account for more than 50% of global growth. Therefore preserving EM growth and reducing risks facing them aids global growth. AEs stand to lose as growth reduces in EMs. For example, global growth forecasts have been reduced after the volatility affecting EMs in 2018. Better coordinated

---

[5]Inflows of Rs. 1.9 tn in liquid funds in October and November 2018, without any rise in policy rates in these months, largely reversed the Rs. 2.1 tn outflow during September.

prudential policies that are applied in source as well as destination countries can therefore benefit both. Better design can reduce tradeoffs, spillovers and costs.

At present policy advice and action are highly asymmetric. For example, EMs are advised to reduce fiscal spending to reduce reliance on and risks of foreign borrowing, while AE governments are advised to borrow more at the low interest rates prevailing. MaP regulations are not applied in AEs since they may increase the cost of financing, especially for the small borrower, but the effect of volatility in raising risk and rates throughout the world is ignored.

Since both conservative and heterodox policies have not been successful in dealing with capital flow volatility it would be helpful to build up a body of case studies for balanced context-based advice that co-ordinates monetary policy and MaP regulations with capital flow management, and creates better understanding of the nuances of and interactions among policies. The G-20 can help in this. Without better policies, there is a risk of democratic backlash in both EMs and AEs, against the open international financial system G-20 want to preserve.

Finally, there are many specific actions and institution building that can help EMs ride out global volatility. Calvo (2005) argues during risk-off episodes, spreads on debts rise even for EMs not undergoing a crisis. Indices such as the Morgan Stanley emerging market bond index (EMBI) show a sharp widening, implying the problem originates with creditors and their perceptions, not with the EMs. As EM firms' productivity or its perception becomes more volatile the returns to acquiring information rise. This increases price volatility, which causes further problems if firms are highly leveraged. Markets tend to underprovide information since it has a cost and benefits others (it creates an externality)—some EMs and firms are sound but the spread widens for all. Therefore institutions need to be created to provide credible information on EM firms. For example, a global emerging market fund (EMF) or a global information agency; or warranty or credit rating from international institutions. An EMF can help stabilize EM bond prices or spread index. The information provided by EMF support would be credible since it would be backed with money.

Liquidity facilities need to be further improved for EMs. More regional cooperation is improving the availability of bilateral CB swaps; an IMF backstop for these may decrease the moral hazard involved. Countercyclical infrastructure investment credit from international institutions can help smooth cycles. As international development banks are set up in EMs, competition among these banks may improve fund availability without compromising on credit standards.

**Acknowledgments** Some of these ideas were presented at the 10th Annual International G20 Conference at ICRIER. We thank the participants for useful feedback and Reshma Aguiar for secretarial assistance.

## References

Akdogan, I. U. (2018). The effects of macroprudential policies on managing capital flows. *Empirical Economics*, 1–21.

Bruno, V., Shim, I., & Shin, H. S. (2017). Comparative assessment of macroprudential policies. *Journal of Financial Stability, 28,* 183–202. https://doi.org/10.1016/j.jfs.2016.04.001.

Calvo, G. (2005) Crises in emerging market economies: A global perspective. http://www.nber.org/papers/w11305.pdf.

Cecchetti, S. G., & Tucker, P. (2016). *Is there macroprudential policy without international cooperation?* CEPR Discussion Paper No. DP11042. https://ssrn.com/abstract=2717591.

Claessens, S. (2014). *An overview of macroprudential policy tools*. IMF Working Paper No. WP/14/214. https://www.imf.org/external/pubs/ft/wp/2014/wp14214.pdf.

da Silva, L. A. P., & Chui, M. (2017). Avoiding 'regulatory wars' using international coordination of macroprudential policies. In *Financial Volatility and Foreign Exchange Intervention: Challenges for Central Banks*, p. 24.

Financial Stability Board. (2015). *Implementation and effects of the G20 financial regulatory reforms: 1st annual report*. Report of the Financial Stability Board to G20 Leaders. Financial Stability board.

Financial Stability Board. (2016). *Implementation and effects of the G20 financial regulatory reforms: 2nd annual report*. Financial Stability board.

Financial Stability Board. (2017). *Implementation and effects of the G20 financial regulatory reforms: 3rd annual report*. Financial Stability board.

Gallagher, K. (2015). *Ruling capital: emerging markets and the reregulation of cross-border finance*. Cornell studies in money. Ithaca, NY: Cornell University Press.

IMF. (2011). *Macroprudential policy: An organizing framework*. IMF.

IMF. (2012). *The interaction of monetary and macroprudential policies—Background paper*. IMF.

IMF. (2017). Is growth at risk? *Global financial stability report*. Washington, DC: IMF.

IMF. (2018). *Regulatory reform 10 years after the global financial crisis: Looking back, looking forward*. Global Financial Stability Report. Washington, DC: IMF.

Jeanne, O. (2014). *Macroprudential policies in a global perspective*. CEPR Discussion Papers 9875. C.E.P.R. Discussion Papers.

Lund, S., Mehta, A., Manyika, J., & Goldshtein, D. (2018, August). *A decade after the global financial crisis: What has (and hasn't) changed?* Executive Briefing McKinsey Global Institute.

Rey, H. (2015). *Dilemma not trilemma: The global financial cycle and monetary policy independence*. NBER Working Paper No. 21162. https://www.nber.org/papers/w21162.

Sahay, R., Arora, V., Arvanitis, A., Faruqee, H., N'Diaye, P., & Griffoli, T. M. (2014). Emerging market volatility: Lessons from the taper tantrum. *Staff Discussion Notes, 14*(9), 1. https://doi.org/10.5089/9781498318204.006.

Shim, I., & Shin, K. (2018, September). *Financial stress in lender countries and capital outflows from emerging market economies*. BIS Working Papers 745 (p. 45).

Tiftik, E., Vazquez, J., Stallings, J., Bailey, N., Nguyen, F. (2017). *Basel capital reforms: Impact on emerging markets*. International Institute of Finance. Published on January 3, 2017. https://www.iif.com/Publications/currentpage/87.

# Chapter 3
# The Global Economy and Financial Markets 10 Years After the Global Financial Crisis

**Alok Sheel**

**Abstract** The paper gives a synoptic view of the evolution of macroeconomic policies from the time of the Great Depression and the current thinking in stabilizing business cycles and financial markets, and makes an overview of the policy response to the recent Global Financial Crisis. It analyses the adjustments made in the global economy in the wake of the Global Financial Crisis, as also the adjustments in financial markets. The concluding section discusses the current prospects of the global economy, and the risks that possibly lie ahead.

## 1 The Evolution of Macroeconomic Policies

It has been over ten years since the global economy was buffeted by what is by general consensus the most severe financial crisis since the Great Depression. At first blush, when the crisis broke, it appeared that the global economy was headed for a crisis as, if not more, severe than the Great Depression (Eichengreen and O'Rourke 2012). These fears proved unfounded. Both financial markets, and the global economy, rebounded more strongly and quickly than what was expected in the circumstances. The macroeconomic policy response, coordinated globally under the stewardship of a revamped G 20 upgraded to summit level, is usually credited for this swift turnaround and stabilization (see Blanchard and Summers 2017).[1]

[1] Olivier Blanchard, chief economist of the IMF, and Lawrence Summers, president of Barrack Obama's National Economic Council, when the financial crisis broke, are in "no doubt that, absent the strong monetary and fiscal policy responses we have observed, the financial crisis would have led to an outcome as bad or worse than the Great Depression". See Blanchard and Summers (2017).

The original version of this book was revised: Missing abstracts of chapters 3, 6, 8, 9 and 11 have now been included. The correction to this book can be found at https://doi.org/10.1007/978-981-13-8106-5_12

A. Sheel (✉)
Indian Council for Research on International Economic Relations, New Delhi, India
e-mail: asheel@icrier.res.in; aloksheel@aloksheel.com



R. Kathuria and P. Kukreja (eds.), *20 Years of G20*,
https://doi.org/10.1007/978-981-13-8106-5_3

Macroeconomic policy was spawned during the Great Depression in the 1930s. Economists and historians alike have over the years faulted those at the helm of policy making at the time in the use of fiscal, monetary and trade policies in managing the firestorm, missteps that transformed the financial crash of 1929 into what we now call the Great Depression. The imperatives of the Gold Standard, to which most major economies adhered to at the time, also acted as a constraint on fiscal and monetary discretion (Bernanke 2002; Christiano et al. 2004; Fishback 2010; Romer 1991; Eichengreen 1986; Irwin 1996). Arguably, it was the war economy that provided the aggressive stimulus that finally pulled the western world out of the long Great Depression.

The Great Depression is largely credited for the Keynesian Revolution that followed in its wake. Fortified by the Keynesian halo, expansionary fiscal policy (fuelled by President Lyndon Johnson's 'Great Society' initiative and the Vietnam War) from the mid sixties, assisted by accommodative monetary policy however drove up consumer price inflation in the United States. This expansion ultimately led to the collapse of the gold standard and morphed into stagflation following a steep hike in international oil prices in the seventies.

Even as the debate whether inflation is mostly a monetary phenomenon,[2] or at root a fiscal phenomenon on account of the unpleasant monetarist arithmetic associated with it, continues to rage to this day (Sargent and Wallace 1981; Dotsey 1995; Uribe 2016; Bhattacharya and Haslag 1999), the big macroeconomic policy take away from the stagflationary seventies was that fiscal policy encountered far too powerful political tailwinds at entry, and headwinds at exit, to be entrusted with the pole position in the conduct of macroeconomic policy. Beginning with Federal Reserve governor Paul Volcker's success with taming inflation, monetary policy conducted by independent central banks came to occupy this position to underwrite macroeconomic stability. Over time monetary policy became less discretionary, and more rule bound, with most central banks adopting, at least informally, some variant of the Taylor Rule,[3] targeting a mix of inflation and growth. Until the Global Financial Crisis, fiscal policy was mostly relegated to providing automatic stabilizers that expanded and contracted in synch with the business cycle, as envisaged in Keynesian economics.

Under the policy stewardship of central banks western economies now enjoyed remarkable macroeconomic stability, characterized by stable inflation and growth, in what came to be described as the 'Great Moderation' (see Hakkio 2013). Inflation indeed became puzzlingly[4] stable, not only in advanced economies, but also in EMDEs that were long plagued by supply constraints, as asset prices scaled new highs amidst high levels of liquidity (Chart 1).

---

[2]The most articulate proponent of this view was of course Friedman (1963) according to whom "Inflation is always and everywhere a monetary phenomenon."

[3]The Taylor Rule formula interest rate = 0.5 (current GDP − potential GDP) + 0.5 (Actual consumer price inflation − target core consumer price inflation) + 2. The constant, 2, in the equation is the neutral policy rate, i.e., the policy rate when both inflation and growth are on target.

[4]This decline has been attributed to technological change, productivity improvements, globalization and ageing. See Sanchez and Kim (2018).

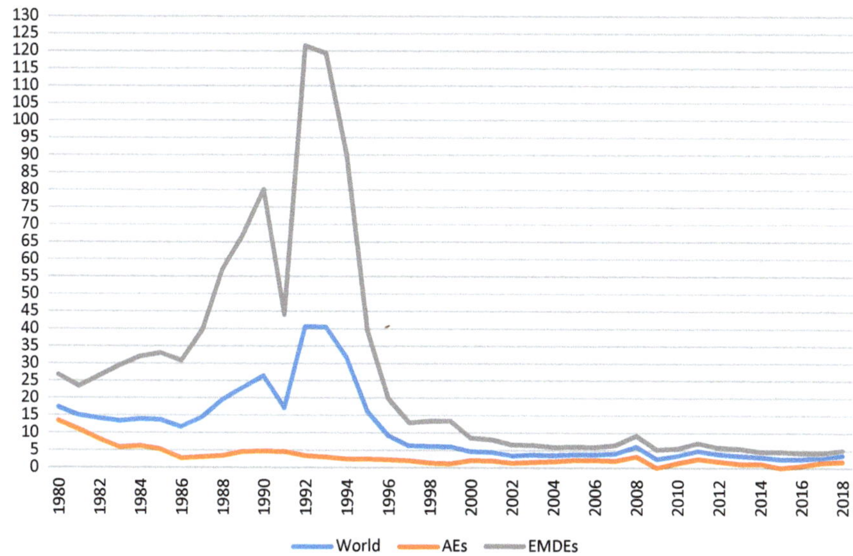


**Chart 1** Global consumer price inflation. *Source* IMF WEO Database

Consumer price Inflation was a critical signaling device for central banks in the conduct of monetary policy, with a number of central banks explicitly setting their sights on inflation as their primary target. As inflation became increasingly unresponsive to the business cycle, monetary policy tended to become accommodative and started deviating from the Taylor Rule, possibly because advanced country central banks, looking at the Japanese experience, now became more concerned about the dangers of deflation than of inflation (Bernanke 2010; Taylor 2010a, b). Asset price inflation on the other hand not only continued unchanged, but might indeed have been fueled by low real rates set by central banks in their pursuit of growth with macroeconomic stability. In the process central banks in advanced economies lost sight of their original mandate, and for which they were created in the first place, namely financial stability. Alan Greenspan, the long-serving Chairman of the Federal Reserve from the time the hawkish Paul Volcker demitted office in 1987 and until Ben Bernanke took office was of the view that the job of the central bank was not to lean against asset bubbles, but to clean up after they burst (see Greenspan 2002).

The Great Moderation lasted up to the Great Financial Crisis of 2007, but the collapse of the Japanese asset bubble in the early nineties had bared the limits of monetary policy as a stabilizing tool in addressing economic instability deriving from financial crises, and to stimulate demand in the face of structural headwinds. As the Bank of Japan's benchmark interest rate hit the zero bound from the second half of the nineties, and where it has been stuck even since, monetary policy appeared to fall into a liquidity trap. To head off deflation the Bank of Japan switched from using the benchmark interest rate to using its balance sheet as the primary tool of monetary policy tool, a monetary policy innovation that has come to be more popularly known as Quantitative Easing (QE). The Bank of Japan however had limited success with combating deflation and raising Japanese growth through QE.[5] Japanese growth that averaged 4.3% between 1980 and 1991, averaged under 1% in the 27 years since (until 2018), with six years of negative growth (*IMF WEO database*).

Under the IS-LM Keynesian framework, when monetary policy falls into a liquidity trap, where money and bonds become perfect substitutes, the burden of fiscal policy falls squarely on fiscal policy. Discretionary fiscal policy now gained a new lease of life as a macroeconomic policy tool (see Krugman 1998; Correia et al. 2012). Japan's fiscal balance declined from an average of 1.2% between 1998 and 1992 to a deficit of 5.6% between 1993 and 2007. Such stimulative fiscal policy, largely in the form of tax cuts, however could do little to take Japan out of the economic crisis to anywhere near its former trend growth.[6]

Meanwhile, risks were mounting in the financial system on account of incremental deregulation and increasing sophistication and innovation in the financial system as banks increasing supplemented deposits with wholesale funding from money markets as their source of funds. The policy response to the Great Depression had led to the passage of the Glass Steagall Act in 1933 that created a firewall between commercial 'deposit' banks, and their affiliates that traded in securities to reduce depositors' exposure to stock market losses such as those that occurred on Black Tuesday and Black Thursday in 1929. Although there were occasional bank failures, this firewall between commercial and investment banking, also prevented largescale commercial bank runs. The Glass Steagall Act was effectively repealed in 1999 through the Gramm-Leach-Bliley Act which did away with this firewall. This led to the emergence of giant 'universal banking' full-service conglomerates, such as through the $33 billion merger of J.P. Morgan and Chase Manhattan in September of 2000.

Since no major financial crisis occurred in the US since the passage of the Glass Steagall Act, and the global financial crisis occurred within less than a decade of its appeal, it is often held as a villain of the piece for the latter crisis, especially as this facilitated greater concentration in the banking industry. Others have however pointed to the fact that most of the dodgy, poorly underwritten products that later spread financial panic were put together and traded by the big stand-alone investment banks that never felt the need to become bank holding companies following the Gramm-Leach-Bliley Act. It was these investment banks, almost entirely dependent on wholesale funding from money markets, and not the universal banks, that were the worst affected by the crisis. All the five major investment banks (Goldman, Merrill, Morgan Stanley, Lehman, and Bear Stearns) ran up huge losses and were acquired by other banks and incorporated as part of universal banks during the crisis. The Act's culpability is most likely indirect, as it changed the conservative culture of

[5]Bernanke (2003) was critical of Japanese QE because according to him it was not aggressive enough.

[6]Kuttner and Posen (2002) have argued that despite the sharp increase in nominal deficits, when the revenue shock is factored in, Japanese fiscal policy was actually contractionary in the nineties.

commercial banks and made them more prone to speculation and risk taking (Stiglitz 2009).

This speculation and risk-taking was facilitated by incremental deregulation of various financial sector markets. The Commodities Futures Modernization Act of 2000 lowered the regulatory threshold for the derivatives market and allowed self-regulation of over-the-counter derivatives. In 2004 the US Securities Exchange Commission relaxed capital rules, enabling investment banks to substantially increase debt, fueling the boom in mortgage-based securities, including sub-prime mortgages, that lay at the heart of the asset bubble to follow. Regulators and accounting standard setters also permitted banks to move assets and liabilities off balance sheet through complex structured investment vehicles (SIVs) that masked the weakness of their capital base relative to their actual leverage.

In retrospect it became clear that there were several weaknesses in the pre crisis regulatory stricture. Multiplicity of domestic regulators and an uncoordinated cross border regulatory structure allowed regulatory arbitrage. Regulation was too procyclical and micro-prudential. Banks were required to hold more capital during downturns when default risks were higher, and lower capital during upturns when these risks decreased. This amplified rather than mitigated credit cycles and biased the system in favour of excessive leverage, and ultimately financial instability. Regulators focused too narrowly on assessing the robustness of individual institutions, and with and central banks preoccupied with inflation and growth concerns, there was no agency watching financial stability in markets as a whole.

## 2 The Global Financial Crisis and the Policy Response[7]

As global financial markets crashed in 2008 policy makers were acutely conscious of the need to not repeat the policy failures of the 1930s. Somewhat fortuitously, Governor Ben Bernanke, at the time at the helm of the US Federal Reserve, was also an economist of the Great Depression. He had long ruminated on the monetary policy failure of the 1930s (Bernanke 1994) in not injecting adequate, indeed large amounts of, liquidity to avoid deflation and stabilize financial markets in times of financial panic as had been advocated by Walter Bagehot in his iconic ***Lombard Street*** published about half a century before the Great Depression.

Strains in US financial markets initially surfaced with defaults in the relatively small subprime segment of the US housing mortgage market in March 2007, with LIBOR (the rates at which banks lend to each other) rising and TED (Treasury-EuroDollar) spreads beginning to widen, crossing the 'risk aversion' threshold of 50 basis points by May 2007. Markets however still expected the problem in financial markets to be contained (Bernanke 2007), as the Dow Jones Industrial Average continued to ascend to new highs, peaking at over 16700 by end September 2008.

[7]A more detailed account of the onset of the Global Financial Crisis and the macroeconomic policy response can be seen in Sheel (2014).

The stresses kept growing however, as the underlying problem lay way beyond US housing markets. The government sponsored enterprises Freddie Mae and Freddie Mac, the investment bank Bear Stearns, and the global insurance firm AIG, had to be bailed out. Uncertainty regarding the financial institutions on whose books "toxic assets" lay led to liquidity drying up by August, with the market for Asset Backed Commercial Paper (ABCP) through which mortgage securitizers funded their operations, collapsing. Following the collapse of the investment bank Lehman Brothers these growing strains snowballed into a full-blown Global Financial Crisis by October 2008, with TED spreads exceeding 450 basis, and the Dow Jones going into a tailspin, bottoming out in February 2008 to halve at around 8300. As asset prices plunged, and financial institutions recalibrated their balance sheets to current market prices, the market fell into a vicious spiral of falling prices and increasing firesales in a scramble for liquidity to meet liabilities and square account books. Financial market participants' response to this liquidity squeeze was to reduce their exposure to all complex derivative investments—not just related to the housing sector—on the assumption that they could not properly assess associated counterparty risks. The market for these derivatives, mostly traded 'over the counter' (OTC) with no central clearing system, disappeared almost overnight as their market prices went into free fall. Data from Markit.com showed triple AAA rated ABX (asset backed) paper trading at about a third of the issue price, with AA ABX securities trading below 5 cents to a dollar. The major investment banks that were almost entirely dependent on wholesale market funding teetered on the brink of collapse and had to absorbed by other banks to avoid collapse.

Going on the assumption that this was the usual crisis of liquidity rather than insolvency, characteristic of financial crises, the Fed moved swiftly into crisis fighting mode to inject large amounts of liquidity into the financial system. It lowered the Fed Funds Rate to zero. It supplemented its traditional discount window lending to depository institutions with new instruments like TAF (Term Auction Facility), PDCF (Primary Dealer Credit Facility), TSLF (Term Securities Lending Facility), providing liquidity directly to major crisis affected institutions through other instruments like CPFF (Commercial Paper Funding Facility), AMLF (Asset-Backed Commercial Paper Money Market Mutual Fund Liquidity Facility), MMIFF (Money Market Investor Funding Facility) and TALF (Term Asset-Backed Securities Loan Facility). It entered into bilateral swaps with major central banks around the world, including the ECB, Bank of England and the Bank of Japan. The US Treasury also chipped in to buy troubled assets, and help distressed homeowners, under the Troubled Assets Relief Programme under the new Emergency Economic Stabilization Act enacted by the US Congress on October 3, 2008.

As the US sub-prime housing crisis unraveled, and growth concerns surfaced, the long cycle of monetary tightening ended and the Fed began easing monetary policy from 2007 with periodic lowering of rates. The cycle accelerated following the collapse of Lehman brothers, and by December 2008 US monetary policy was at the zero lower bound. This pattern was repeated across advanced economies with both the bank of England and the European Central Bank following suit.

Although monetary policy's primary objective in financial markets is to influence medium to long term interest rates that have a bearing on investment and consumption, and thereby on the business cycle, the primary monetary policy instrument of central banks is setting the overnight rate, and defending it through open market operations. The overnight rate then works its way through various transmission channels to influence the entire yield curve. These transmission mechanisms break down at the zero bound since no further rate reductions are possible. In such circumstances monetary policy could be said to fall into a liquidity trap. Even prior to the crisis however, economists, including Ben Bernanke himself, had argued that it was possible for the central bank to influence the yield curve even at the zero bound by (a) expanding its balance sheet, (b) changing the composition of the existing balance sheet through purchases of longer dated securities, (c) better coordination with fiscal authorities for a more aggressive bond purchase programme, should this be required, and (d) an appropriate communication strategy.[8]

As things turned out, the Federal Reserve used all these mechanisms once the zero bound was reached. The first instrument was three rounds of quantitative easing that dramatically expanded the central bank balance sheet from 6% of US GDP to over 25% by August 2014 (Chart 9a); the second was credit easing that altered the existing composition of the balance sheet through 'operation twist'; the third led to the virtual conflation of monetary policy with fiscal policy on account of the aggressive treasury purchase programme; and the fourth was forward guidance that influenced market participant behavior. As monetary policy became increasingly unconventional, and depository institutions were inclined to park their funds with the Federal Reserves at levels far exceeding levels mandated under fractional banking, the interest paid on these reserves soon became the primary monetary policy instrument, eclipsing the Feds Fund and discount rates.[9]

Aggressive and innovative monetary policy was matched by aggressive fiscal policy, as the US cyclical (budget deficit controlled for the decline in revenue on account of below trend growth) fiscal balance declined to −7.3% in 2009, −9.3% in 2010, −7.9% in 2011 and −6.1% in 2012. Once again, other advanced economy central banks followed the US lead, with policy coordination through the G 20 that was upgraded to summit level. The ECB's balance sheet exceeded 40% of the Euro area's GDP by 2017. The cyclical fiscal balance in the Euro Area declined to −4.8% in 2009, −5.1% in 2010, −3.9% in 2011 and −2.7% in 2012. The Bank of Japan's

---

[8]The fourth instrument was the 'forward guidance' on Fed policy that affected market participants' behavior. See Bernanke et al. (2004).

[9]The *Feds Fund Rate (FFR)* is the rate at which depositary institutions *trade balances they hold at the Federal Reserve*, and is set by the Federal Reserve. (LIBOR type benchmarks, on the other hand, are rates at which banks borrow from each other in the interbank market, and are market determined). The *discount rate* is the *liquidity window at which depositary institutions can borrow from the Federal Reserve* as a 'last resort', and is therefore usually set at a small spread above the FFR. The reserves held by depositary institutions with the Federal Reserve were interest free till the global financial crisis. It was constrained to pay interest on them in view of their growing size, as risk averse banks preferred to park their funds with the Federal Reserve as a result of risk aversion (Chart 9a). Large, sudden withdrawals can put downward pressure on the benchmark FFR.

balance sheet is now equivalent to the size of the country's GDP. Its cyclical fiscal balance declined to −5.8% in 2009, −6.9% in 2010, −6.8% in 2011 and to −6.3% in 2012.[10] Most of the stimulus in advanced countries was through tax cuts and income support for low income or distressed households, unlike in the bigger EMDEs, such as China and India where it was more focused on boosting infrastructure spending (see IILS 2011).

Such aggressive injections, and monetary and fiscal policy actions, were effective in keeping deflation at bay—US consumer price inflation had entered negative territory for a few months—and in stabilizing financial markets within a few months, with TED spreads back under 50 basis points by mid 2009. Consumer Price inflation was back in positive territory by January 2009. Asset prices recovered smartly, with the DJIA bottoming out in February 2008 and crossing its 2007 pre-crisis peak of 13000 by 2012, even as the economic recovery was punctuated by a 'double dip'. The VIX, a common measure of stock market instability in the US, that had crossed the fear threshold of 25 by mid September 2008, was back below the 25 by July 2009. The DJIA soon turned ballistic and is currently at around twice the pre-crisis peak.

The economic recovery, however, was comparably far slower (Table 1). Although the Advanced Economies had negative growth for just one year, the recovery gained momentum only from 2014, and growth is still hardly robust by pre-crisis standards, despite both monetary and fiscal policies remaining stimulative. The strong recovery came a few years down the line, at a time fiscal policy was being tightened. The economic recovery of 2010 was short lived as it soon morphed into a debt crisis in the Eurozone in 2011. Public debt exploded in advanced economies within a very short period, as OECD (December 2018) indicates. This was the lagged effect of a number of years of two simultaneous fiscal shocks—a negative shock to revenues, and a positive shock to expenditures on account of the need to provide fiscal stimulus—both occasioned by growth significantly below trend over a number of years. The market impact of these shocks was asymmetric because the capacity to absorb these shocks varied from country to country. Eurozone governments were particularly vulnerable to market revolt because of a basic design flaw in the monetary union project that provided neither for a fiscal (bailout) backstop nor a monetary one (printing your way out of a nominal default). Moreover, unlike the US, the assets of some of the bigger banks dwarfed the size of sovereign balance sheets and were therefore too small to bail out the too big to fail financial institutions (Sheel 2011).

Fiscal deficits have to be financed. The conventional wisdom is that this is done through a combination of market borrowing, that can raises interest rates to crowd out private investment, and can expose sovereigns to market revolt if sovereign balance sheets are seen to be unsustainable, and through monetization of the deficit which can destabilize the macroeconomy through inflation. It is for these reasons that fiscal deficits are kept within reasonable limits, with the dissaving during economic down-

[10]Data on cyclical fiscal balances is from IMF's Fiscal Monitor database. https://www.imf.org/external/datamapper/datasets/FM.

**Table 1** Global growth

| | World | Adv Econs | EMDEs | US | Euro area |
|---|---|---|---|---|---|
| **1980–01** | **3.2** | **2.9** | **3.7** | | |
| **2002–07** | **4.5** | **2.5** | **7.1** | **2.8** | **2.0** |
| 2002 | 2.9 | 1.6 | 4.7 | 1.7 | 1.0 |
| 2003 | 3.7 | 1.9 | 6.3 | 2.9 | 0.7 |
| 2004 | 4.9 | 3.1 | 7.5 | 3.8 | 2.3 |
| 2005 | 4.6 | 2.6 | 7.3 | 3.5 | 1.7 |
| 2006 | 5.3 | 3 | 8.2 | 2.9 | 3.2 |
| 2007 | 5.4 | 2.8 | 8.7 | 1.9 | 3.1 |
| 2008 | 2.8 | 0.1 | 6.1 | −0.1 | 0.5 |
| 2009 | −0.6 | −3.5 | 2.7 | −2.5 | −4.5 |
| 2010 | 5.4 | 3.1 | 7.4 | 2.6 | 2.1 |
| 2011 | 4.3 | 1.7 | 6.4 | 1.6 | 1.6 |
| 2012 | 3.5 | 1.2 | 5.3 | 2.2 | −0.9 |
| 2013 | 3.5 | 1.4 | 5.1 | 1.8 | −0.2 |
| 2014 | 3.6 | 2.1 | 4.7 | 2.5 | 1.4 |
| 2015 | 3.5 | 2.3 | 4.3 | 2.9 | 2.1 |
| 2016 | 3.3 | 1.7 | 4.4 | 1.6 | 1.9 |
| 2017 | 3.8 | 2.4 | 4.7 | 2.2 | 2.4 |
| 2018 | 3.7 | 2.3 | 4.6 | 2.9 | 2.0 |
| **2011–13** | **3.8** | **1.4** | **5.6** | **1.9** | **0.2** |
| **2014–18** | **3.6** | **2.2** | **4.5** | **2.4** | **2** |

***IMF WEO database***

turns reversed through increased saving following the recovery so as to keep public debt GDP ratios stable and within prudent limits.

Policy makers in advanced economies were able to get around this unpleasant fiscal arithmetic during the Global Financial Crisis through the conflation of fiscal and monetary policy. Quantitative easing was no doubt an appropriate monetary policy tool at the zero lower bound. But by purchasing treasury bonds—what Ben Bernanke called coordinating with fiscal policy—on an epic scale it also served as a fiscal tool by keeping sovereign borrowing costs low. The consequential largescale monetization was deferred/moderated by incentivizing depository institutions to keep their balances through sale of bonds with the Federal Reserve by paying interest on bank reserves. It was this dual role of quantitative easing that led to a legal challenge in the European Court of Justice, which ultimately ruled that the European Central Bank's OMT (Outright Monetary Transactions) targeting the bonds of distressed countries facing market revolt was an instrument of monetary policy authorized under European treaties, and not fiscal policy. It was the ECB's declared commitment to open-ended purchase of sovereign bonds of distressed countries that finally quelled the market revolt and stabilized the Eurozone.

With the exception of the US and Japan, all major advanced economies have brought their (nominal) fiscal deficits to under 3% of GDP, the maximum under the Maastricht Treaty, with burden of stimulus now resting entirely on monetary policy. However, except for Germany public debt to GDP ratios have not been rolled back, and these now far exceed the Maastricht maximum of 60% (Chart 17).

How have the global economy and financial markets adjusted in the wake of the GFC? Have the two underlying forces behind the GFC, namely growing global imbalances and their spillovers into financial markets facilitated by financial deregulation been addressed? Looking ahead, what are the risks to the global economy?

# 3 Adjustment in Economic Growth

## *3.1 The Recovery in Advanced Economies*

The consensus view amongst economists is that despite the current near term weakness going forward, advanced economies have by and large recovered as much as they possibly could from the Global Financial Crisis of 2008, with both inflation and unemployment rates at levels that indicate that the economy is firing at full potential. According to the IMF's October 2018 *World Economic Outlook* "the steady expansion (is) under way since mid-2016 continues....(this is) a time of above-potential growth in many economies....the economy is above full employment" (see IMF 2018). As a result central banks across major advanced economies—with the exception of the Euro Area and Japan, where these are still stuck at the zero lower bound—have been raising policy rates.

## *3.2 Hysteresis and Secular Stagnation*

The recovery was not the usual V shaped that usually follows recessions—through which the economy grows above trend to quickly recover the loss in potential output loss (Table 1). According to IMF's *World Economic Outlook database* the output loss in advanced economies was recovered only over 10 years, by 2018, and in the process there may have been some permanent loss of growth potential through hysteresis and a secular decline in private demand (Eggertsson et al. 2016; Summers 2018). The IMF also appears to be of this view: "Beyond the next couple of years, as output gaps close and monetary policy settings continue to normalize, growth in most advanced economies is expected to decline to potential rates—(which is now) well below the averages reached before the global financial crisis of a decade ago. Slower expansion in working-age populations, and projected lackluster productivity gains, are the prime drivers of lower medium-term growth rates" (IMF 2018). To this one can perhaps add increasing income inequality deriving from stagnant median wage growth that constrains demand.

## 3.3 *Macroeconomic Stimulus Still Not Withdrawn*

The return to potential growth nothwithstanding, the macroeconomic stimulus put in place during the crisis is still mostly in place in major advanced economies, and they remain on life support. In the US, policy rates have more or less normalized, but the oversized Federal reserve balance sheet has still to be mostly rolled bank, cyclically adjusted fiscal deficits remain high, and are not projected to decline in the foreseeable future. The dramatic expansion in public debt as a proportion of GDP continues. In the Euro Area, while there has been fiscal tightening, policy rates are still at the zero lower bound, and the ECB's balance sheet is still expanding. In Japan, too policy rates are still stuck at the zero bound, with accommodative monetary policy and expansionary fiscal policy comprising two of the three arrows of 'Abenomics'. The Bank of Japan's balance sheet now equals the GDP, and public debt is very near twice the GDP. The Bank of England's bank rate remains below single digit, and while fiscal deficits have declined, public debt as a proportion of GDP remains at the crisis peak levels. The real test of the recovery in advanced economies would be removal of macroeconomic life support.

## 3.4 *Long Term Income Convergence*

The global economy grew at an average of 3.2% in the roughly two decades preceding the boom of 2002–2007, when it grew at 4.5%, with Emerging Markets and Developing Economies (EMDEs) growing slightly faster than Advanced Economies (Table 1). Long-term averages may hide structural changes afoot. A trailing 10 year moving average reveals that over this earlier period AEs slowed down by about 30 basis points while EMDEs accelerated at an equivalent rate, with global growth remaining more or less constant at 3.2%. This declining growth trend is attributed to adverse demographics, a declining labour participation rate, and growing income inequality with the twin forces of globalization and automation keeping real wages stagnant in Advanced Economies. After having peaked at the turn of the century, US Labour participation rates started declining, including during the economic boom that followed, and the decline continued in the wake of the GFC (Chart 2). Despite increasing ten times in nominal terms since the sixties, when corrected for consumer price inflation US real wages have barely budged in real terms. With greater automation and use of new technologies in the economy, and global integration of labour markets through international trade, a big gap opened up between wage growth at the high end of the labour market and at the bottom, leading to growing inequality.

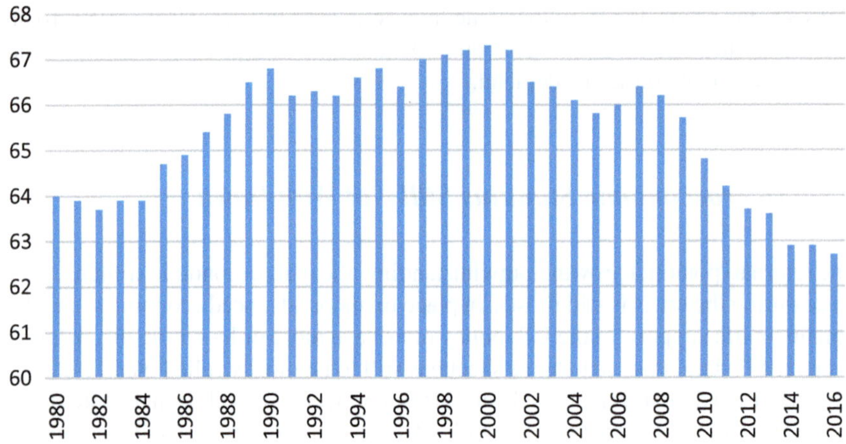


**Chart 2** US labour participation rate. US Dept of Labour (BLS). *Source* US Bureau of labor statistics

Thus while real wages of low wage workers declined by 5%, and those of middle wage workers increased by just 6%, those of high wage workers have increased by over 40%. The wage pyramid has become steeper, with the wages of the top 1% rising 138%, even as those of the bottom 90% rose by just 15%. The disparity in the ratio of incomes of the typical wage worker and CEOs, which was just 30 in 1980 increased steeply to over 300 (Pew Research Centre 2018; Mishel et al. 2015).

### 3.5 *Accelerated Convergence During the Boom*

This structural shift towards income convergence was sharply accentuated during the boom, during which EMDEs grew at rates that were on average almost twice as high as the preceding two decades. Indeed, the boom was largely an EMDE phenomenon (Table 1). This pushed up global growth by about 40%, despite AE growth rates continuing to decline on average.

### 3.6 *The Post Crisis Divergence*

In the post crisis period although Advanced Economies recovered more slowly, the divergence in growth between AEs and EMDEs has reduced. Within advanced countries, the Euro area, recovered more slowly than the US, on account of the Euro zone crisis that followed the GFC. Growth in EMDEs held up well in the immediate aftermath of the GFC, fuelling speculation that these economies had now 'decoupled'

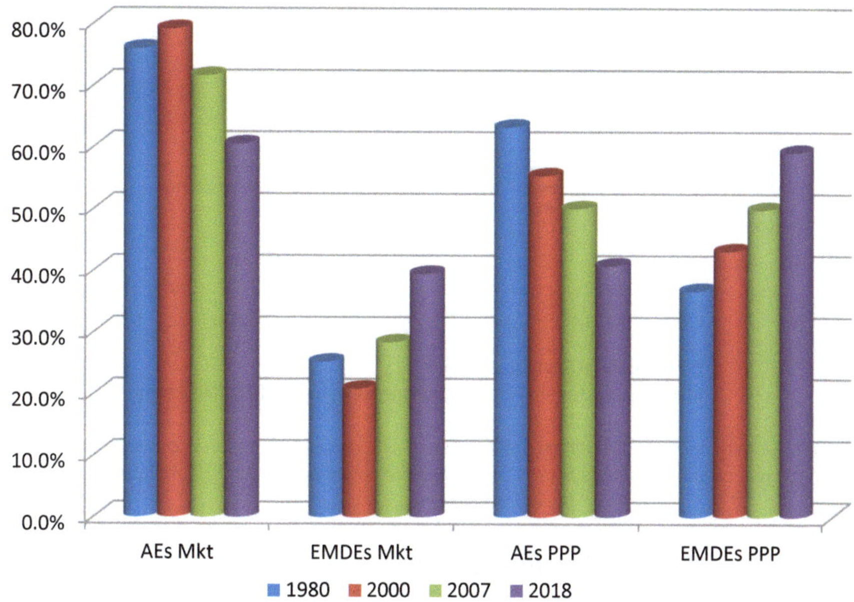


**Chart 3** Shift in global economic weights. *Source* IMF WEO database

from AEs,[11] on whose demand they had long been dependent for their own growth.[12] However, growth in EMDEs continued to decline steadily in EMDEs, puncturing the decoupling hypothesis, even as it accelerated in AEs. The latter turned the corner around 2014, growing on average at a rate 60% higher than in 2011–13. EMDEs, on the other hand, decelerated on average by 20% during the same period. While EMDEs are currently still growing at a pace that is about 20% higher than in the last two decades of the last century, it is still unclear whether the post crisis decline in growth in EMDEs has bottomed out or not. With the exception of India, near term central bank policy rates in the BRICS have either declined (Brazil and Russia) or remained stable (China and South Africa). Even so, the shift in global economic activity towards EMDEs over the last four decades has been remarkable. Their economic weight in world economic output rose from 25 to 40% measured at market exchange rates, and from about a third to 60% measured in Purchasing Power Parity. While the convergence in the period 1980–2000 was only when their incomes were measured at PPP, the convergence since is palpable at both market exchange rates and at PPP (Chart 3).

[11] Even the IMF lent its weight to the decoupling hypothesis (Akin and Kose 2007; The Economist 2008).

[12] In his Nobel Prize lecture delivered over three decades ago the economist Lewis (1979) observed that economic growth in developing countries was dependent on economic prospects in OECD countries that accounted for the major share of global demand.

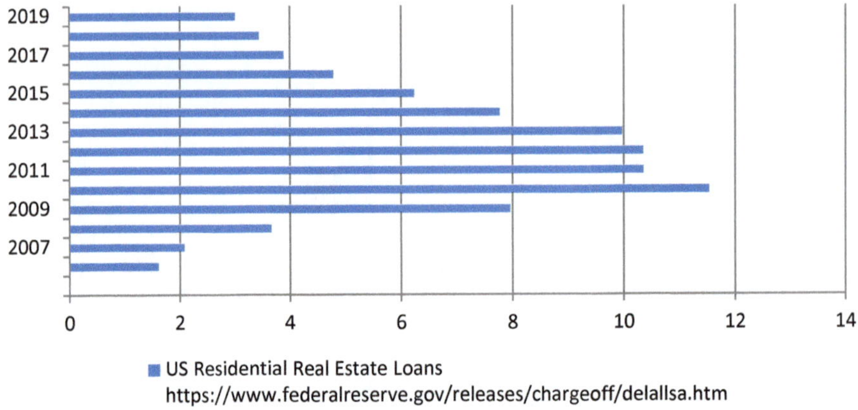


**Chart 4** Delinquency rates (Due past 30 days) of US residential real estate loans. *Source* US residential real estate loans https://www.federalreserve.gov/releases/chargeoff/delallsa.htm

## 3.7 *Factors Underlying the Slow Recovery*

A protracted recovery should have been expected, notwithstanding the aggressive monetary and fiscal stimulus, since the source of the crisis lay in the financial sector (Reinhart and Rogoff 2014). Macroeconomic policies can stabilize growth fluctuations arising out of cyclical shocks, but are unable to do so where the decline is on account of structural shocks. A financial crisis impairs the balance sheets of both creditors and borrowers, and repair takes time, as the flip side of increasing savings to deleverage is reduction in consumption.

Monetary policy is transmitted to the real economy through two separate channels, namely credit and wealth. Deleveraging households saw their incomes shrink further through low interest rates on deposits, protracting the time required to repair their balance sheets. Richer households with lower marginal propensities to consume and greater financial assets saw their wealth increase through rising asset prices. QE may therefore have exacerbated inequality that was undermining demand in the pre-crisis world, through the wealth effect, with transfer of income from those with a greater propensity to consume to those with higher propensity to save. This kept consumer demand, consumer price inflation and economic growth low even as asset prices boomed.

A good proxy to assess the timeline of the repair of household balance sheets is from the delinquency rates of US Residential Real Estate Loans, that lay at the heart of the financial crisis. These delinquencies were under 2% in 2006–2007, following which they rose sharply as the financial crisis escalated, peaking at over 10% between 2010 and 2013 (Chart 4). The rapid decline in delinquencies began in 2014, which coincided with the economic recovery gaining momentum.

With monetary policy arguably in a liquidity trap, the onus of stimulus increasingly fell on fiscal policy. Fiscal stimulus had expectedly high multipliers during the initial strong recovery. These multipliers however weakened considerably and the recovery petered out, most likely because the underlying problems were structural rather than cyclical.[13]

The recovery in the Eurozone was slower because of the market revolt that forced austerity in the midst of a continuing crisis, as sovereign debt in the European periphery saw prices plummet and yields rocket. The yield on Portuguese sovereign debt rose from 7 to 20% in 2011, while those on Greek bonds climbed as high as 200% in 2012.

Another possible reason why the US recovery was stronger than the Euro area was because authorities in the US took strong action to take toxic assets off and recapitalize bank balance sheets, while European governments have dithered in doing so not so much on account of moral hazard, but the recognition that sovereign balance sheets are not big enough to bail out their large banks (Sheel 2013). TARP, which authorized bailouts of $ 700 billion of the US financial system through Treasury funds, of which less than $ 500 was actually used, was just the tip of the iceberg. A Congressional audit of the Federal Reserve system in 2011 revealed that the bail outs through its targeted emergency lending windows such as TAF, PDCF, TSLF, CPFF, AMLF and TALF was over $ 16 trillion (US Government Accountability Office 2011). While there are moral hazards inherent in such bailouts, it nevertheless allowed the US banking system to bounce back faster and more strongly than that in Europe. Banking stocks in the US (proxied by the S&P 500 banks index) and Europe (proxied by the STOXX Europe 600 banks), fell by over 80% between 2007 and 2009. While European bank stocks have recovered only marginally from the crisis low, American banks have recovered almost 80% of value. Likewise, while both US and European banks gave equity returns of around 15% prior to the crisis, Banks, returns in the US fell far more sharply in the US in the wake of the crisis, to −10% between 2007 and 2009, while they fell to 5% in Europe. While returns in Europe have remained more or less at the post crisis levels, US banks caught up with European banks by 2009, and their returns are now significantly higher, although still under 10% (The Economist 2017).

[13]The experience with fiscal policy during both the Japanese financial crisis of the nineties, and the more recent Global Financial Crisis has reopened the debate on the effectiveness of fiscal policy, and fiscal multipliers, in a liquidity trap. The role of fiscal policy in the recovery from the Great Depression before the "second dip" remains contentious. Till recently, following Milton Friedman, the focus was more on monetary policy driving the recovery. See Brown (1956). Romer (1993) concluded that it was mainly monetary policy that drove the recovery. Eggertson (2005, 2010) and have underscored the role played by fiscal policy in the recovery. See also De Long and Summers (2012). More recently Romer (2011) has argued that but for the fiscal stimulus the fall in consumption during the Global Financial Crisis would have been higher.

## 3.8 The Decline in Trade

Much of the spurt in growth in EMDEs during the boom is attributed ultimately to supplementing domestic demand with external. Chart 5 (drawn from data in the IMF database) where annual perturbations have been smoothened out through five yearly moving averages, shows that the sharp increase in trend growth in EMDEs from the 1990s coincided with an even sharper increase in the growth of the volume of global trade in goods and services as a share of GDP. During the boom prior to the Global Financial Crisis trade grew at about twice the rate of GDP. The global financial crisis was also a trade shock, with this growth declining to 3.8% in 2008, and turning negative in 2009 (−10.3%). It however rebounded back by 12% during the brief global recovery of 2011, but fell back thereafter to levels of the early eighties despite the valiant attempts by the G 20 to keep markets open,[14] which is where it remains presently. Trade is now growing only about as fast as GDP. The Current Account measure actually underestimates the degree of de-globalization as the increase in domestic value addition of exports indicates that Global Value Chain (GVC) integration has also declined since 2011–12, especially in major EMDEs like China and India OECD (December 2018). It is therefore unsurprising that while EMDEs weathered the early shock of the GFC reasonably well, which spawned the decoupling hypothesis, their prospects have dimmed considerably since, even as growth has resumed its northward trajectory in AEs. Whatever may have been the experience of the colonies of free trade during the colonial era, EMDEs have certainly gained by the freeing up of global trade in the postwar era. It is in their interests to keep markets open.

On the strength of this data it is easy to come to the conclusion that trade has worked against AEs, and this is certainly the narrative that is leading to the resurgence of nationalist parties in some of these countries. However, as pointed out above, there are also long-term structural reasons that are leading to the lowering of demand and trend growth in AEs. Indeed, cross border trade enabled consumers with stagnant real incomes in advanced economies to benefit from wherever rapid productivity gains were taking place to maintain living standards through cheaper wage goods. Protectionism would lead to the loss of this welfare benefit in the absence of matching productivity shifts that can make manufacturing in Advanced Economies competitive.[15]

[14]The G20 resolve was mindful of the disastrous snowballing impact of the Smoot-Hawley Tariffs that aggravated the Great Depression in the 1930s (Sheel 2014, pp. 270–71).

[15]Although Chinese TFP has also fallen in tandem with that of the US (Chart 5), Conference Board (2018) data shows that there are other developing Asian economies, particularly India, which are becoming more competitive through robust productivity growth.

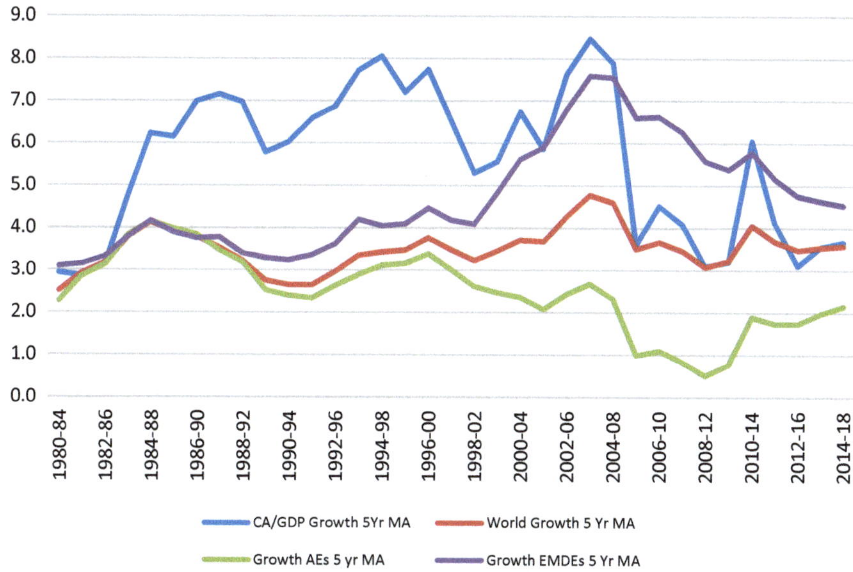


**Chart 5** World trade and growth. *Source* WEO, October 2015

## *3.9 The Unwinding of Global Imbalances?*

The decline in world trade mirrors the decline in external—global—imbalances. The flipside of the sharp rise in cross border trade in goods and services was growing current account imbalances that sent increasingly large amounts of capital uphill, as it were, from emerging markets (notably China, and oil surplus countries) to advanced economies (notably the USA). This was because despite the sharp increase in growth, aggregate savings exceeded aggregate investment in EMDEs on account of consumer demand limited by low median incomes. Corporates in AEs, meanwhile, were redirecting their own surpluses away from investment, possibly because productivity growth, and therefore returns, were higher in EMDEs (Chart 6). The US-China story is by and large applicable to AEs and EMDEs as a whole. The resultant global savings glut spilled over into financial markets, lowering interest rates, underpricing risk, which in turn fuelled innovation in, and deregulation of, financial markets in the recipient countries, to which the GFC is usually traced. This savings glut ultimately found its way into leveraged consumption in AEs, with the froth in financial markets boosting consumption even as labour wages remained stagnant, and was one of the ultimate drivers of the Global Financial Crises (Bernanke 2005, 2015).

External (Current Account) imbalances are merely external spillovers of domestic imbalances. Global rebalancing of demand entailed that economies with large external surpluses needed to save less and consume more, and those with large deficits needed to save and invest more. Knee jerk reactions to reduce current account deficits simply by targeting bilateral imbalances, as the United States is attempting to do

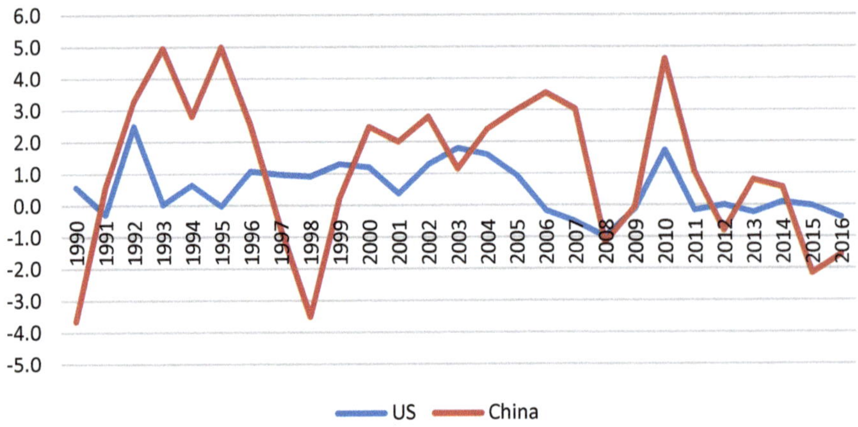


**Chart 6** Total factor productivity growth. *Source* Total Economy Database, The Conference Board

through trade negotiations with China, cannot work unless the underlying structural imbalances are addressed. In the absence of this, imports would simply shift to other countries supplying goods and services at higher prices.

In the post crisis period, China has partly rebalanced its economy away from excessive reliance on exports and towards a greater reliance on consumption. It is saving much less than what it did prior to the crisis. However the excessive reliance on investment has been exacerbated, even as total factor productivity growth has fallen sharply. This has inter alia lowered growth in China. The other big emerging market economy, India, which had a largely balanced economy on the eve of the global financial crisis, and was firing on all three growth cylinders, has seen its trend growth decrease through a decline in savings, and a loss of two growth engines, namely investment and exports. While India's current account deficit has remained the same, this is because of sharp declines in both exports and imports, that has seen its current account as a share of GDP fall from 55.6% of GDP in 2011–12 to 40.5% in 2017–18. With the two biggest emerging market economies losing engines of growth, growth in EMDEs as a group has drifted lower (Table 2).

While growth has revived in major Advanced Economies, the counterpart rebalancing has been modest. The US has increased savings marginally through a reduction in consumption, but there has been a further reduction instead of increase in investment. The increase in private savings through deleveraging has been mostly offset by the increase in public leverage. Germany has increased its savings further, and reduced instead of increased consumption. While hitherto this surplus spilled over only into the Euro area, which had a balanced current account with the rest of the world, the Euro area has now redirected its economy away from both consumption and investment to run a significant current account surplus.

**Table 2** Global imbalances

| Country/Group | Consumption/GDP | | | Investment/GDP | | | CAB/GDP | | | Savings/GDP | | |
|---|---|---|---|---|---|---|---|---|---|---|---|---|
| | 1997 | 2007 | 2017 | 1997 | 2007 | 2017 | 1997 | 2007 | 2017 | 1997 | 2007 | 2017 |
| China | 60.0 | 48.9 | 54.2 | 36.2 | 41.2 | 44.4 | 3.8 | 9.9 | 1.4 | ***40.0*** | ***51.1*** | ***45.8*** |
| India | 73.1 | 60.6 | 67.5 | 25.6 | 38.1 | 30.6 | −1.3 | −1.3 | −1.9 | ***24.3*** | ***36.9*** | ***28.8*** |
| Germany | 77.7 | 72.5 | 72.0 | 22.8 | 20.7 | 20.1 | −0.5 | 6.8 | 7.9 | ***22.3*** | ***27.5*** | ***28.0*** |
| Japan | 67.9 | 70.8 | 72.0 | 30.0 | 24.5 | 24.0 | 2.2 | 4.7 | 4.0 | ***32.1*** | ***29.2*** | ***28.0*** |
| United Kingdom | 82.1 | 85.2 | 86.4 | 18.0 | 18.4 | 17.4 | 0.0 | −3.6 | −3.8 | ***17.9*** | ***14.8*** | ***13.6*** |
| United States | 79.2 | 82.3 | 81.7 | 22.4 | 22.6 | 20.6 | −1.6 | −4.9 | −2.3 | ***20.8*** | ***17.7*** | ***18.3*** |
| Euro Area | 77.6 | 76.0 | 75.8 | 21.6 | 24.0 | 20.8 | 0.8 | 0.0 | 3.5 | ***22.4*** | ***24.0*** | ***24.3*** |
| EMDEs | 76.3 | 66.7 | 67.7 | 24.8 | 29.6 | 32.3 | −1.1 | 3.7 | 0.0 | ***23.7*** | ***33.3*** | ***32.3*** |

*Source* IMF WEO Database

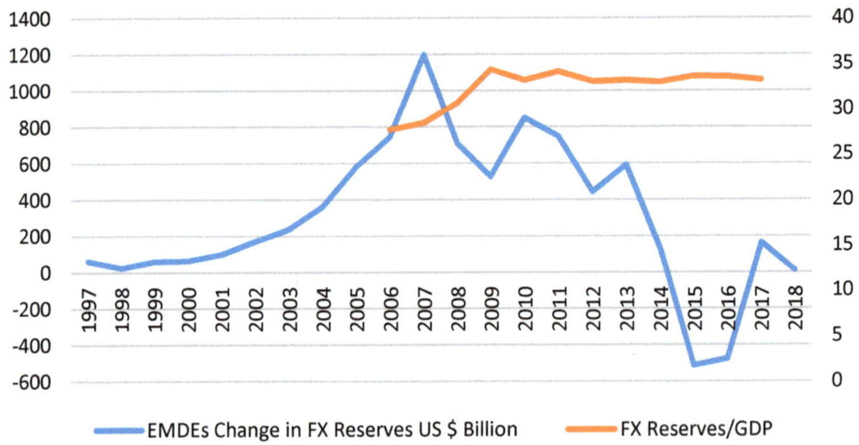


**Chart 7** FX reserves of EMDEs. *Source IMF*, International Financial Statistics; *CEIC*, Datastream; national data; BIS policy rate statistics; BIS calculations

The global economy is more balanced relative to 2007, the height of the economic boom, but it is much less balanced relative to 1997, the period preceding the boom. Both trade and growth have declined alongside global imbalances. With so little structural adjustment one could argue that the reduction in global imbalances is mostly the byproduct of lower growth rather than structural adjustments, and that if growth were to rise to former levels these imbalances might increase again.

## 3.10 *Flattening in FX Reserve Accumulation in EMDEs*

The flipside of the rise in global imbalances during the boom was the sharp increase in the foreign currency reserves of EMDEs, as these countries, particularly China, ran large current account surpluses during this period. Historically, US monetary policy is also a major determinant of global capital flows, with low rates sending a tsunami of capital flows into EMDEs in search of higher yields, mostly in the form of portfolio flows. With the decline in imbalances, combined with first the threat of rising US rates, and then the heir actual rise, the rate of increase in FX assets of EMDE central banks has declined, while the accumulated stocks of these reserves as a proportion of GDP has flattened out (Chart 7).

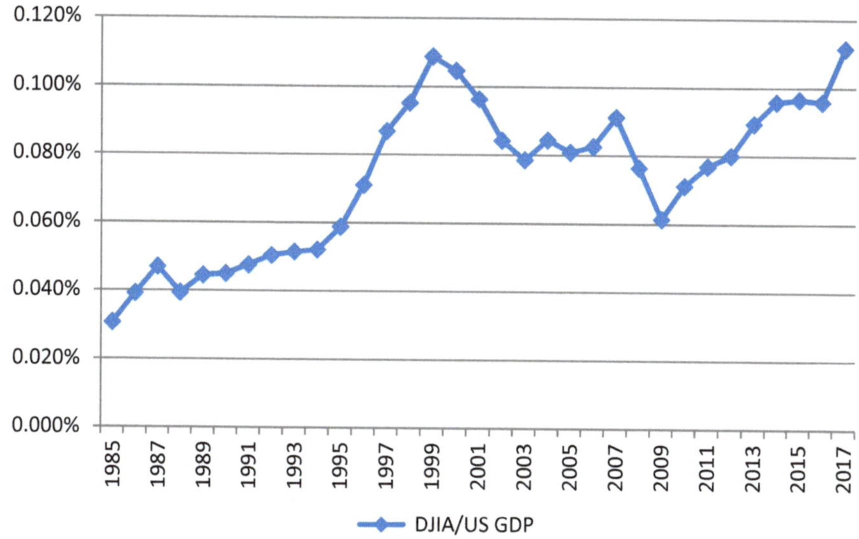


**Chart 8** Asset prices. *Source* Yahoo Finance and US Bureau of Economic Analysis (BEA)

## 4 Adjustment in Financial Markets

### *4.1 The Rapid Rebound in Financial Markets and Central Bank Balance Sheets*

The froth in financial markets is not only back with a bang, but the Dow Jones as a percentage of US GDP has crossed levels not seen during past thirty years, including during the dotcom bubble of the nineties, and the economic boom preceding the GFC when economic growth, and growth expectations going forward, were appreciably higher (Chart 8). The Federal Housing Finance Agency (FHFA) housing index crossed its nominal all time peak of March 2007 in 2016, and currently the real housing index is back at its peak housing boom level of November 2006 (Mislinki 2019). High yield corporate bond spreads are also close to historic lows. By these measures there now appears to be more liquidity in financial markets than there has ever been in over a third of a century.

Much of this liquidity overhang is arguably the result of large injections by central banks in advanced economies. The US Federal Reserve alone injected $ 4.5 trillion—equivalent to 5% of global GDP—through its three Quantitative Easing programmes. Its balance sheet increased dramatically from around 6% of US GDP in 2008 to over 20% by 2013, peaking at over 25% in 2014. Although the Fed has begun to shrink its balance sheet recently—Quantitative Tightening, or QT—it was still over 20% of GDP as late as August 2018. (Chart 9a) The European Central Bank has injected the equivalent of another $ 3.5 trillion, with its balance sheet still expanding and now standing at about 40% of the Euro Area GDP (Chart 9b). The Japanese and Chinese experinces are strikingly similar, with the Bank of Japan expanding its balance sheet by above $ 3 trillion, and the Bank of China by $ 2.5 trillion.[16] The Bank of Japan's balance sheet now exceeds the country's national income.

## 4.2 *Post Crisis Decline in the Growth of Financial Assets*

Global financial assets aggregated around $ 382 trillion at end-2017, or about five times global GDP. Data put out by the Financial Stability Board shows that the annual growth in aggregate financial assets of financial corporations—comprising banks, pension funds, insurance corporations, public financial corporations, central banks and other financial intermediaries—in the 29 systemically important areas monitored by the Financial Stability Board has slowed sharply in the post crisis period despite the sharp increase in asset prices This appears a little puzzling, and is possibly explained by the retreat in private leverage. Global financial assets increased annually on average by over 11% in nominal terms between 2002 and 2007, but by just over 6% the next ten years, between 2007 and 2017. Paradoxically, despite the slower growth in nominal terms, on account of slower economic growth in the post crisis period financial assets grew faster relative to GDP in the latter period. Financial assets grew from 3.7 times global GDP in 2002 to just 3.8 in 2007. By 2017 global financial assets were 4.8 times global GDP (Financial Stability Board 2019).

## 4.3 *The Shift Away from Riskier Assets*

The decline in financial assets is led by greater risk aversion, with a flight to quality away from riskier, higher yielding complex financial products, such as Collateralized Debt Obligations (CDOs), Credit Default Swaps (CDS) and other mortgage and asset backed[17] securities that took much of the blame for the global financial crisis,[18] towards less risky and particularly riskless sovereign paper (Chart 10), and those of government sponsored enterprises such as housing mortgage products.[19] This is

[16]The US and Euro area data is from the Federal Reserve and European Central Bank. The Japanese and Chinese data is from the FSB.

[17]Mortgage based securities are issued by pooling mortgage receivables, while asset backed securities are issued by pooling of receivables from non-mortgage assets, such as credit cards, student loans, auto loans and home equity loans.

[18]According to the Financial Stability Board (2017), those " aspects of shadow banking considered to have contributed to the global financial crisis have declined significantly and generally no longer pose financial stability risks".

[19]While US Mortgage Related Securities have not shrunk since the crisis, in 2006 and 2007, on the eve of the financial crisis, almost two thirds of mortgage related securities outstanding were

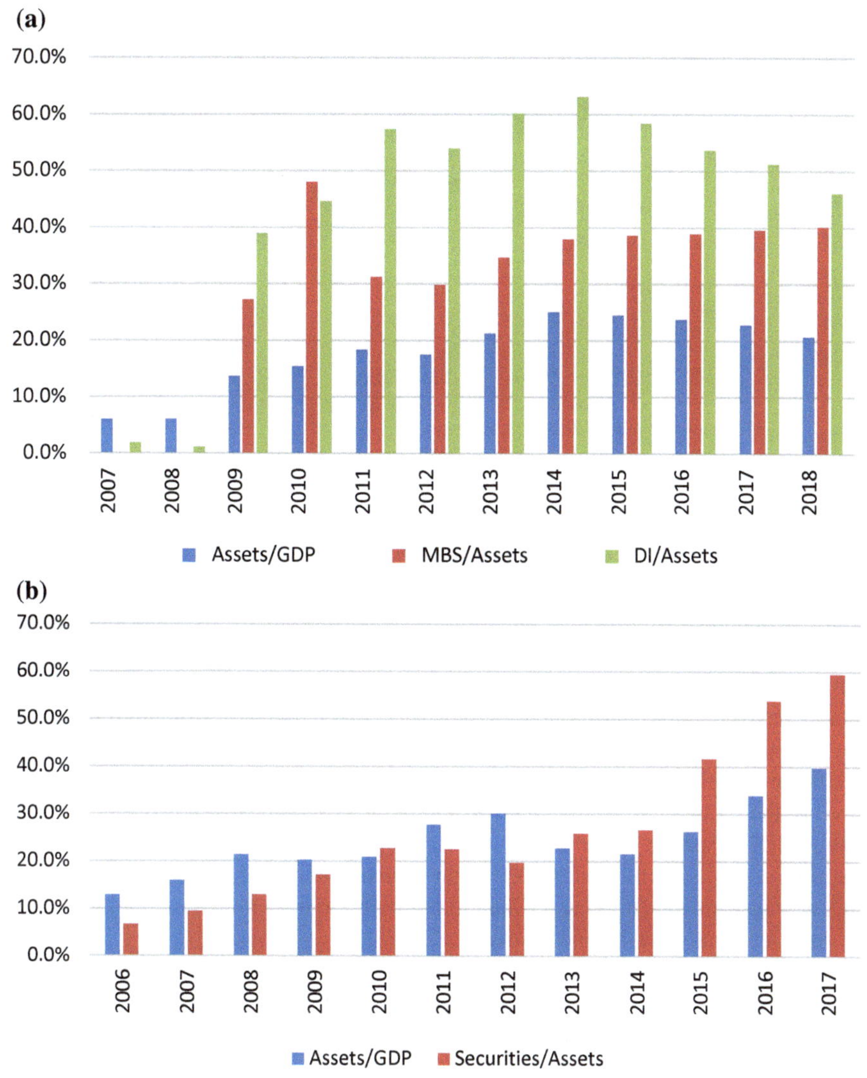


**Chart 9** **a** US Federal reserve Balancesheet. *Source* US Federal Reserve. **b** ECB balancesheet. *Source* European Central Bank. (MBS: Mortgage Based Securities; DI: Assets of Depositary Institutions)

not surprising as most of the increase in leverage was by governments in Advanced Economies. Non-financial corporates have also increased their share of financial assets by leveraging the low interest rate environment to borrow more.

---

issued by private companies. This declined sharply in the wake of the financial crisis, and in 2018 about 85% of all such instruments were guaranteed by Government Sponsored Enterprises, namely Freddie Mae, Freddie Mac and Ginnie Mae (*SIFMA* op. cit).

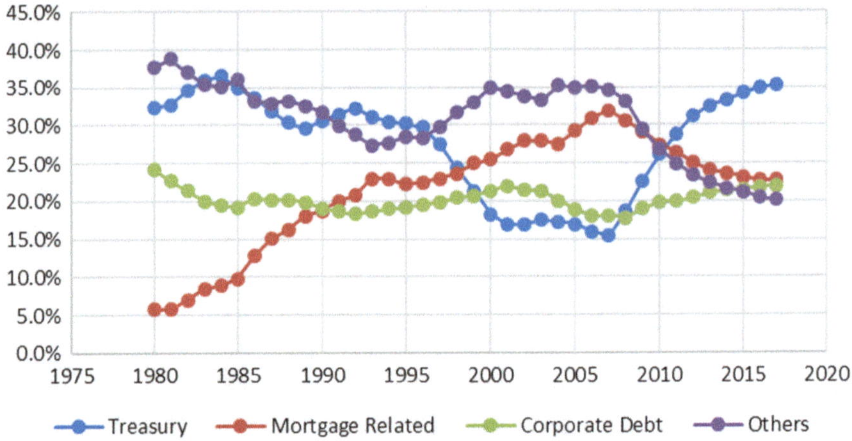


**Chart 10** Outstandings in US bond markets. *Source* SIFMA https://www.sifma.org/resources/archive/research/

Issuance of Collateralized Debt Obligations (CDOs), which restructured various kinds of incomes from assets, including housing mortgages, by securitizing them into new innovative financial instruments, such as CDOs, that lay at the heart of the panic in financial markets in the US (CDO issuance in Europe was on a much lower scale), have declined sharply in nominal terms. Taken together, structured finance in the US and Europe shrank from around $ 4.5 trillion in 2006 to just over 1 trillion in 2016 (Financial Stability Board 2017). In Europe the issuance has fallen back to the level of the second half of the nineties, and in the US to pre-boom levels (Chart 11). While CDO issuance has revived in the recent period, the issuance of the riskier and far more complex 'synthethic CDOs', that securitized income receivable from CDOs into new instruments, making it even more difficult to trace on whose books the risks of default actually lay, has not revived.

This shift away from riskier assets is also evident from the changing complexion of the balance sheets of global systemically important banks (G-SIBs) where the securities trading portfolio has shrunk, while loans and cash have increased (Chart 12).

## *4.4 The Rise and Rise of Shadow Banks*

Shadow banking is a feature of financial market sophistication, and is globally distributed across just 8 jurisdictions, US, UK, Canada, Netherlands, Japan, China, Cayman Islands and the Euro Area (Chart 16). The assets of shadow banking[20] have grown at a much faster clip than aggregate financial assets between 2002 and 2017 at 314% and 195% respectively (Financial Stability Board 2019). In 2008 the share

[20] Assets of 'other financial intermediaries', the FSB's broad measure of shadow banking.

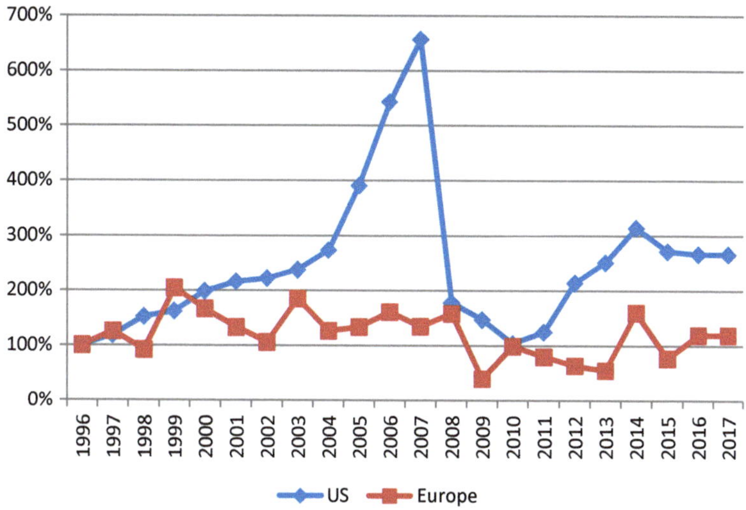


**Chart 11** CDO issuance (1996 = 100). *Source* SIFMA https://www.sifma.org/resources/archive/research/

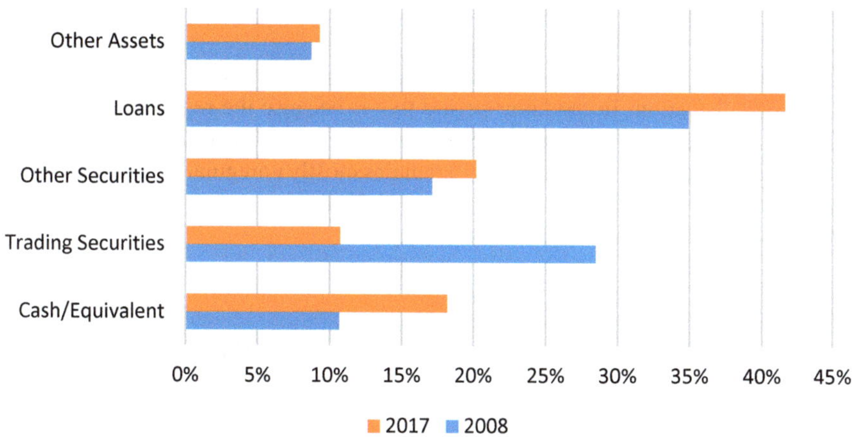


**Chart 12** G-SIB balance sheets. *Source* Bank of International Settlements (2018)

of Non-bank and Non-insurers among the top 20 financial institutions by size was 30%. By 2016 this had increased to 50%.[21]

At first glance it might seem surprising that this differential growth is true for both the period prior to the Global Financial Crisis, and in its wake, especially since the riskiest financial assets have declined sharply. The decline in these riskier assets have been more than countervailed by collective investment schemes/Money Market

[21]This corresponds to FSB's Monitoring Universe of Non-Financial Institutions, or MUNFI (Bank of International Settlements 2018).

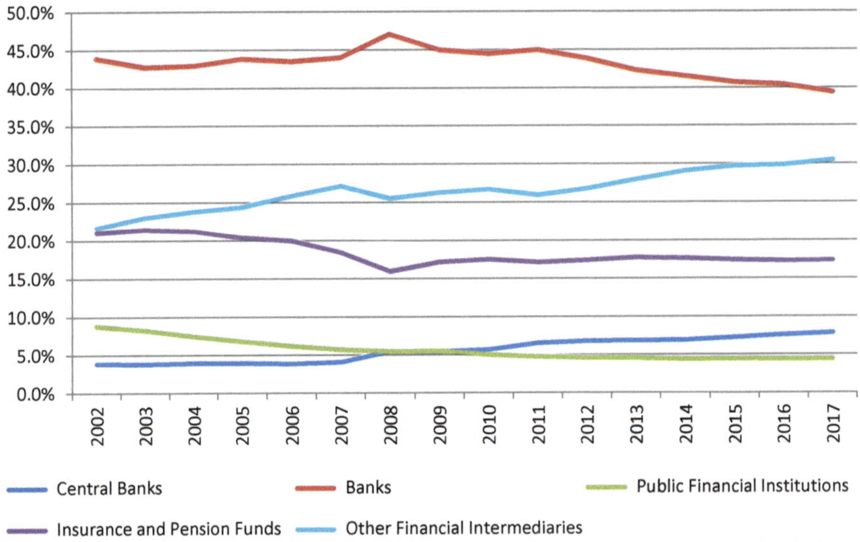


**Chart 13** Composition of global financial assets. *Source* Financial Stability Board (2019)

Funds that are subject to runs.[22] In the earlier period the growth was on account of financial deregulation. In the latter period this is because the regulatory noose has tightened around banks through the enactment of Basel III and national regulatory tightening, whereas shadow banking still remains mostly unregulated. Chart 13 shows that in the post crisis period the assets of shadow banks and central banks have grown at the expense of all other financial asset classes.

## 4.5 *Shifts in the Geographical Distribution and Composition of Financial Assets*

Financial asset aggregates hide some subtle, but significant, geographical shifts in global finance over the past decade. First, while just five jurisdictions (US, UK, Japan, China and the Euro Area) continue to account for about 85% of global financial assets the biggest shift in the distribution of global financial assets since 2005 is away from the US and Europe and towards China. In 2005 the US, UK, Japan and the Euro Area together accounted for 84.2% of financial assets, and China just 4.3%. By 2017, the

[22]Or Economic Function 1, one of the five narrow measures of shadow banking of the *Financial Stability Board*. This narrow measure aggregated 13% of global financial assets globally at the end of 2016. Of this over 70% constituted collective investment vehicles such as Money Mutual Funds, real estate funds, credit hedge funds, mixed funds etc. that are susceptible to runs. Financial Stability Board (2019).

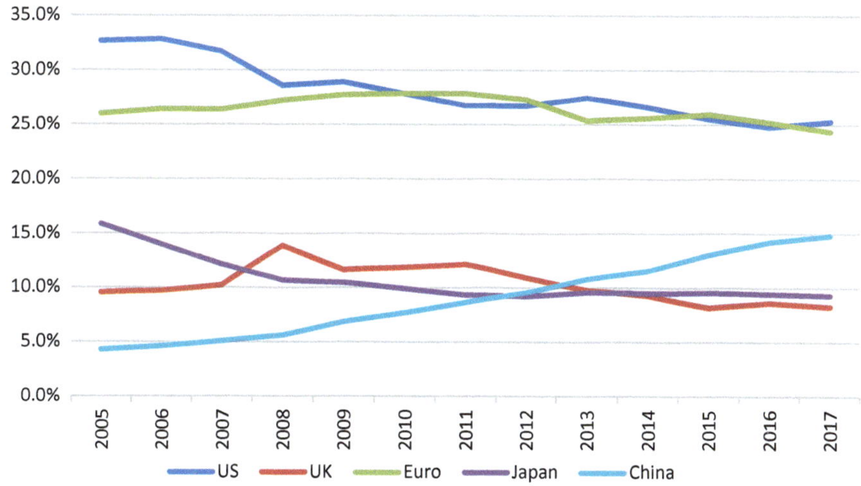


**Chart 14** Geographical distribution of financial assets. *Source* Financial Stability Board (2019)

former's share had shrunk to 67.4%, while that of China rose sharply to 14.8%, a rather dramatic 10.5% shift within one decade (Chart 14).

Second, there have also been significant geographical shifts in the composition of banking assets in the post crisis period. Banking assets have increased faster than shadow banking assets in the US, whereas these have shrunk relative to shadow banking in both the United Kingdom and the Euro Area. Like the Euro Area, the UK also witnessed a spurt in shadow banking following the crisis, but this has declined in recent years. As pointed out earlier, the likely reason for these shifts is the aggressive action taken by the US to shore up its banking system, even as Europeans have faltered and have been more focused on reining in the financial system, including banks.

Third, almost all the growth in shadow banking outside the Euro area in the post crisis period is in China and the Cayman Islands. The US's share in shadow banking assets (OFIs, or the broad measure of shadow banking) has fallen sharply by about 23%, from 49.3% in 2002 to 26.3% in 2017. This share has been ceded to the Euro area (7%, with the Euro area now accounting for 32% of shadow banking globally) and to China (Canuto 2019) and the Cayman Islands that have seen their shares in global shadow banking assets rising from practically nil to 10% and 6% respectively within the last decade (Chart 15). By the narrow measure of shadow banking however the US still has the largest share of shadow banking (29%, compared of 23% in the Euro area and 16% in China).

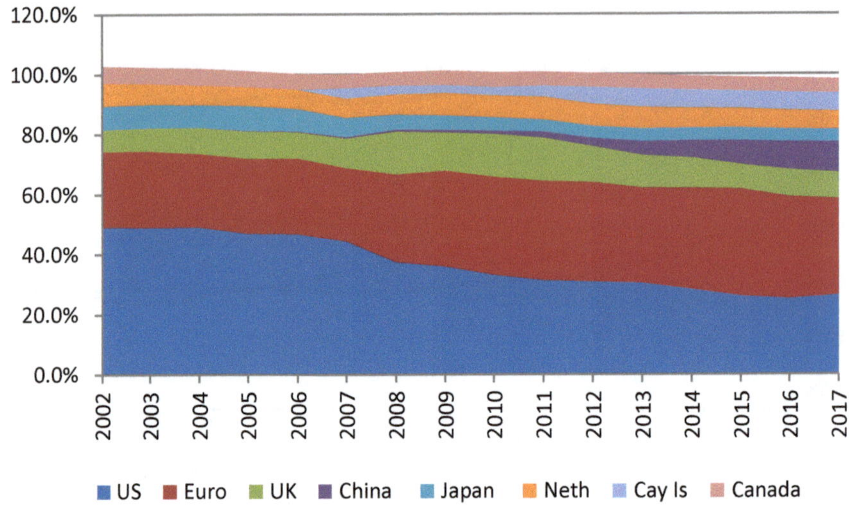


**Chart 15** Geographical distribution of shadow banking. *Source* Financial Stability Board (2019)

## *4.6 Compounding the Too Big To Fail Problem*

While views were sometimes expressed prior to the Global Financial Crisis that big financial institutions reduced financial risk (Beck et al. 2003), one of the seminal lessons of the crisis was that the existence of financial institutions considered too big to be allowed to fail created moral hazards that might actually encourage excessive risk taking as bail out by governments was assured in the event of bets going horribly wrong. One of the objectives of financial regulatory reform in the wake of the crisis was to mitigate this risk. Ironically, the too big to fail problem has been magnified in the wake of the crisis. The crisis saw a major shakeout in the management of big financial corporations. All the big global investment banks suffered huge losses, and either collapsed (Lehman Brothers) and/or were taken over by other institutions. This has led to increasing concentration in Financial Institutions and creation of even bigger banks. While the top 20 institutions accounted for 38% of financial assets in 2008, this share increased to 42% in the post crisis period (2016) (Bank of International Settlements 2018).

With American Banks bouncing back strongly it is unsurprising that this asset concentration has tilted in favour of American Banks and away from European ones. According to the latest (November 2018) list of 30 globally systemically important banks (G-SIBs), the five of the top dozen banks, including the biggest two (JP Morgan Chase and Citigroup), are now American. While European Banks also show the same concentration traits European banks have retreated, with the space vacated being filled by their American counterparts. European banking is set to weaken further in the event of Brexit (see Financial Stability Board 2018a; Onaran 2017; Arnold 2018; Schildbach 2018; True Economics 2013; Robinson et al. 2018).

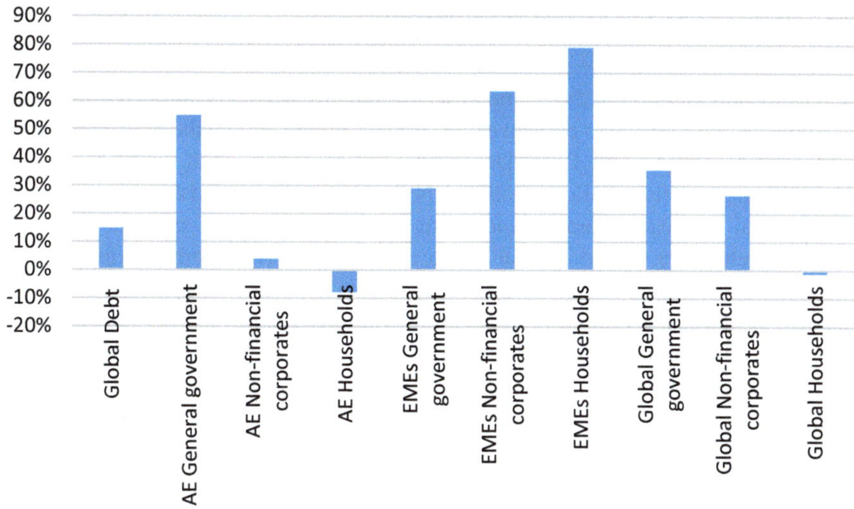


**Chart 16** Debt/GDP Growth 2007–17. *Source* Bank of International Settlements (2018)

## *4.7 The Rise and Rise of Leverage*

Global debt rose from $ 110 trillion at the end of 2007 to US $ 174 Trillion at the end of 2017, an increase of 58%. Even when controlled for GDP growth, the increase in leverage of 15% over a decade is significant, considering that excessive leverage was a contributing factor of the GFC. Leverage in AEs continued to increase mostly on the back of fiscal expansion, even as private debt has not grown, and households have indeed deleveraged (Chart 16). Gross public debt rose from 86.9% of the GDP in 2009 to 106.1% in 2018 in the US. In the Euro Area, where the fiscal stimulus was much less, and rollback more aggressive, the corresponding increase was more modest, from 79.2 to 84.4%[23] Such a sharp increase in public debt over a decade has raised the prospect of fiscal dominance that might make exit from easy monetary policies more difficult.

EMDEs used the low interest rates to borrow more, with governments, Corporates and households sharply increasing their debt as a proportion of GDP, in that order. Unlike in advanced economies, the increase in debt in EMDEs was mostly in the private sector (Chart 16). Governments increased their debt from 37% of GDP to 48%, Non-financial Corporates from 57 to 93% and households from 19 to 35%.

[23]The central bank balance sheet data is from the data publicly available on the Federal Reserve and ECB websites. The fiscal numbers are from IMF's Fiscal Monitor (2009).

## 4.8 *Reform of Financial Regulation*

Increasing deregulation of the financial sector that progressively chipped away at the mechanisms put in place to prevent excessive risk taking and financial instability put in place in response to the Great Depression has shared much of the blame for the Global Financial Crisis. Following the crisis, the G 20 spearheaded a number of global initiatives to repair this damage and make the financial system safer. Its approach was comprehensive, spanning four broad areas, regulatory reform to improve the resilience of the financial system to shocks, putting in place orderly resolution structures for systemically important financial institutions deemed too big to be allowed to fail to avoid taxpayer bailouts, improving regulatory co-operation and supervisory oversight of systemically important financial jurisdictions, and mechanisms for periodic risk assessment and review of implementation of the new standards in major financial jurisdictions. There is also a new recognition of the need for macroprudential regulation that has expanded the perimeter of risk assessment from individual institutions to entire markets.[24]

The broad objective of the core reforms was to make commercial banking safer by upgrading its regulatory framework from the procyclical Basel II to the countercyclical Basel III, and to insulate it from the activities of shadow banking that was the source of instability in financial markets in the lead up to the financial crisis. The Basel III framework, which has increased both the quantum and quality of capital that commercial banks are required to hold, with countercyclical buffers, additional requirements for systemically important banks (SIBs), and new liquidity coverage, leverage and net stable funding ratios to disincentivize excessive debt and incentivize stable sources of funding, is in place. Resolution frameworks for SIBs are also being put in position to obviate taxpayer bailouts in cases where they fail despite these additional safeguards.

While the Glass Steagall Act has not been reinstated, national legislations (the Volcker Rule in the USA, the Liikanen and Barnier in the European Union and Vickers in the UK) to ring fence the core commercial activities of banks from its trading ones are at various stages of enactment and implementation. The oversight of shadow banking, at the centre of the financial panic in 2007–08, has also improved even though it still remains outside the regulatory perimeter. Securitization is being made safer through mandatory retention of some skin in the game by minimum mandatory credit risk retention on the balance sheet. Derivatives trading is being nudged towards centralized clearing systems from over the counter trading through higher capital and margin requirements. The International Organization Of Securities Commissions (IOSCO) has made recommendations to reduce the risk of Money Market Funds—the most dynamic element of shadow banking in the post crisis period—to runs. The LIBOR benchmark that was found susceptible to manipulation has been reformed and might be phased out altogether by 2021.

[24]For a detailed assessment of financial regulatory reform after the Global Financial Crisis (see Sheel and Ganguly (2016)). For an update on the current status of implementation of these reforms see Financial Stability Board (2018b).

There is also now greater harmonization, supervisory cooperation and exchange of information between regulatory authorities in systemically important financial jurisdictions who worked together in developing the G 20 financial regulatory reforms. This can be expected to provide a level playing field and reduce regulatory arbitrage going forward, which should be conducive to greater financial stability. While most these reforms have been enacted, implementation across the 29 systemically important jurisdictions remains work in progress.

## 5 Concluding Remarks: Prospects and Risks Going Forward

A decade after the Global Financial Crisis broke the proximate risks arising from the two interrelated factors usually identified as the ultimate villains of the piece, namely a run-away financial system and global imbalances, have been significantly attenuated. The financial system is now better regulated, its runaway growth arrested, and its riskiest components in retreat. External imbalances have declined. Despite this it is still too early to say whether this was just another crisis that has punctuated the modern world from time to time or whether it has changed the world forever going forward.

A number of pre-crisis trends have been carried forward into the recovery, such as the decline in trend growth in advanced economies, falling labour participation and labour intensity of output, the downward pressure on consumer price inflation despite full employment and high levels of liquidity that inflate asset prices but not consumer prices, as well as growing inequality. Indeed, the latter may well have been exacerbated by policies deployed to combat the crisis.

The continuing inability of policy makers in advanced economies to address these deep-rooted structural problems is undermining the liberal democratic consensus in these societies that is being increasingly challenged with equal vehemence from both the left and the right ends of the political spectrum (Kagan 2019). The more worrying problem is that beyond rhetoric neither contender has been able to come up with persuasive, realistic corrections. This could presage growing instability going ahead. The left solutions could further pressure an overstretched fisc and further undermine animal spirits,[25] while the right solutions might exacerbate existing fault lines.

What then has changed?

The Great Depression of the 1930s is etched in the collective memory for the birth of macroeconomic policies and the rise of Keynesianism. The Great stagflation of the 1970s is best remembered for the relative decline of Keynesianism and the

[25]Some of the left corrections, such as higher taxes on extreme incomes and wealth and universal basic incomes that involve rewriting social contracts could possibly have been attempted during the boom. These are now much more difficult with stalling growth, absence of animal spirits, and bloated central bank and Treasury balance sheets.

ascendance of monetary policy conducted by independent central banks. Will the Great Financial Crisis be remembered for the signal success of macroeconomic policies that pulled the global economy back from an abyss similar to the 1930s, for their inability to exit from such policies designed to be temporary countercyclical tools, for reining in global finance, the root of the instability resulting in the crisis, and the comeuppance of EMDEs?

Sovereigns had long responded to financial crises as they presaged economic apocalypse of their domain. Indeed, the birth of central banks itself can be ascribed to such response. The rise of macroeconomic policy on the other hand was predicated on the belief that the State should not be a bystander of business cycles, or fluctuations in economic activities occasioned by periodic shocks. They were designed as short-term tools to nudge these cycles in a manner that the economy operates at full potential. Fiscal policy was the original policy tool of first resort, perhaps because it was within the control of the political executive and because the imperatives of the gold standard constrained monetary intervention. The unpleasant monetarist arithmetic arising out of fiscal expansion however soon undermined the gold standard and culminated in the Great Stagflation.

The ascendancy of central banks following the Great Stagflation was in essence a grand bargain where the political executive ceded authority to rules bound independent—bureaucratic—central banks in exchange for price stability. Following Paul Volcker's use of monetary policy as a blunt tool to bludgeon hyperinflation at the cost of growth, a long period of price stability followed in the form of the Great Moderation. The tension between the Treasury and the central bank was palpable, with the former leaning towards growth and the latter towards price stability, but the grand bargain held.

In hindsight it is not clear whether the Great Moderation was the triumph of central bankers or the outcome of a puzzling decline of consumer price inflation that fell across the board, in developed and developing countries alike. It stayed low despite monetary policies that were accommodative by the yardstick of the Taylor Rule (Taylor 2010a, b). Indeed, it was ceasing to be the canary in the gold mine that divined business cycles. By the turn of the twenty first century deflation was a greater concern than inflation for central bankers in advanced economies. Despite innovative new instruments central bankers have found it more difficult to slay the dragon of disinflation than the monster of inflation. Japan has been stuck with the lower zero bound and deflation for two decades, and the Euro Zone since the Global Financial Crisis. In the post crisis period while growth and employment have returned to potential, central banks are finding it difficult to meet their inflation targets.

Meanwhile, in sharp contradistinction to consumer prices, asset price inflation was touching new highs, assisted by loose monetary policy and dismantling of the financial regulatory structure put in place since the Great Depression. In their single-minded pursuit of macroeconomic stability central banks lost sight of their original mandate, financial stability. The tools for ensuring macroeconomic stability were moreover considered too blunt to deal with asset bubbles. Central bankers, in advanced economies at least, were of the view that it was not the job of central banks to call and prick asset bubbles.[26] Their task was to clean up the mess that followed and return the economy to full potential.

With central banks focused on macroeconomic stability, and regulators in the financial sector overseeing individual institutions, there was no constituency to assess risks building up in the financial system as a whole and make midcourse corrections to 'irrational exuberance' and hubris in financial cycles. While central banks were able to clean up after the dotcom bubble in the nineties and the Asian Financial crisis with liquidity injections, the cost of inaction on the financial bubble inflated in the run up to the Great Financial Crisis is now considered unacceptably high. The debate as the financial crisis was brewing was whether it was time that central banks started making financial stability an objective of monetary policy (Sheel 2007). Ironically, this debate appears to have petered out even as the jury is still out on the ability of central banks to clean up after the mess and exit from extraordinarily accommodative monetary policy. Despite the ostensible recovery, advanced economies continue on life support, with the extraordinary monetary and fiscal stimulus still largely in in place.

Whereas the original criticism of central banks was that they were not expansionary enough, privileging price stability above economic growth, in the post crisis period the criticism is that they are far too expansionary, endangering financial stability. The arm's length distance between monetary and fiscal authorities is also being undermined by the greater cooperation required between the two to keep deflationary forces at bay. The grand bargain underlying the independence of central banks could well be breaking down. Might the crisis spell the decline of monetary policy and the doom of central bank independence? The central banker once at the helm of crisis management, Ben Bernanke, certainly seems to consider this within the realms of possibility (Bernanke 2017) (Chart 17).

Fiscal policy was criticized for its easy rollout and difficult exit because it was captive to the political executive. But now the same fate appears to have befallen monetary policy conducted by 'independent' central banks. The Taylor Rule has broken down in a low inflation environment. Unconventional policies might well be here to stay on account of lower inflation and nominal interest rates (Bernanke 2017). In these circumstances, the balance sheet and interest paid on reserve might eclipse the Feds Funds Rate as the primary instrument of monetary policy. The monetary policy independence of central banks is also being undermined by the return of fiscal dominance. Fiscal balances in advanced economies were already

[26]"Certainly prices of goods and services now being produced--our basic measure of inflation--matter. But what about futures prices or more importantly prices of claims on future goods and services, like equities, real estate, or other earning (financial) assets? Are stability of these prices essential to the stability of the economy? Clearly, sustained low inflation implies less uncertainty about the future, and lower risk premiums imply higher prices of stocks and other earning assets. We can see that in the inverse relationship exhibited by price/earnings ratios and the rate of inflation in the past. But how do we know when irrational exuberance has unduly escalated asset values, which then become subject to unexpected and prolonged contractions as they have in Japan over the past decade? And how do we factor that assessment into monetary policy? We as central bankers need not be concerned if a collapsing financial asset bubble does not threaten to impair the real economy, its production, jobs, and price stability" (The Federal Reserve Board 1996).

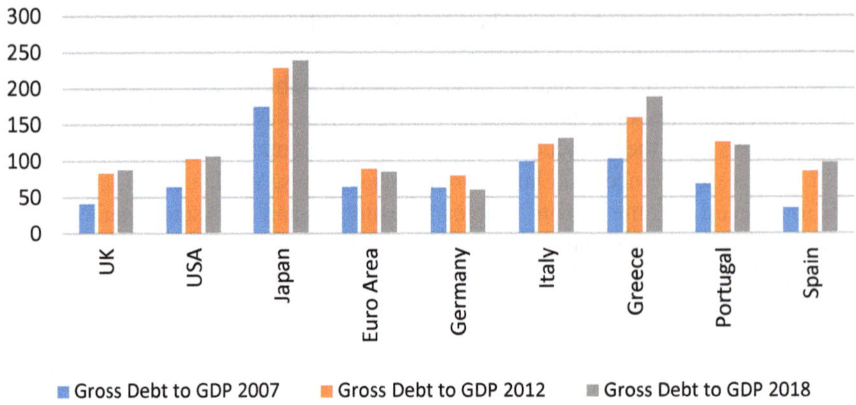


**Chart 17** Sovereign gross debt. *Source* IMF Fiscal Monitor Database

under pressure prior to the crisis on account of structural headwinds emanating from ageing, slowing trend growth and unsustainable welfare state models, with Euro zone countries struggling to keep both fiscal deficits and public debt within the Maastricht norms of 3% and 60% of GDP respectively. The protracted recovery from the crisis elevated public debt to much higher levels, servicing which might require greater coordination with central banks in keeping policy rates low and staggering the roll back of their bloated balance sheets. With the decline in external surpluses, the foreign demand for Advanced economy safe assets has also reduced (Chart 7), further queering the pitch for rolling back central bank balance sheets. The fiscal costs that the corrections some of the left critiques of liberal democracy entail might also constrain rollback of the balance sheet, if not indeed further expansion. It is therefore possible that in these circumstances the rollback might not occur at all, and current levels are simply normalized over an extended period as a share of GDP through economic growth.

Might the same logic work for high levels of public debt? Both Lawrence et al. 2019) and Olivier Blanchard (2019) would appear to think so since risk free interest rates continue to, and are projected to, remain below nominal GDP growth. The stock of public debt could therefore diminish as a proportion of the national income over time. Olivier Blanchard argues that this is nothing unusual as this has indeed been the case on average over the past in the US. But this could also be another way of saying that Governments have mostly inflated their way out of debt, preferring to take recourse to the inflation tax than the politically more difficult path of raising tax rates. Such outcomes are consistent with fiscal dominance of monetary policy and in no way invalidates unpleasant monetary arithmetic. Be it as it may, monetary policy would need to remain accommodative to achieve fiscal rollback without tightening fiscal policy. The downward pressure on consumer price inflation, evident long before the Global Financial Crisis, might work in favour of such an outcome.

The absence of rollback of easy monetary and fiscal policies raises two questions. First, is the monster of inflation lurking in the shadows? Second, is any policy space left to respond to the monster or any other major crisis? Trends in asset price movements indicate that high levels of liquidity are already inflating bubbles just as they did prior to the crisis. The financial cycle in the post crisis period has however been kept in check by deleveraging.[27] While the new regulatory structure appears to have made the financial system more resilient to withstand shocks,[28] past experience indicates that regulatory reforms are not set in stone. As the memory of Crisis recedes, and irrational exuberance returns to financial markets, reforms can be diluted and even rolled back over time. Already bank managements have pushed back against the mitigation of moral hazards in their compensation practices that nudge them towards excessive risk taking. The Volcker Rule is being diluted, despite it being a weak substitute for the Glass Steagall Act in insulating regulated commercial banks from the risky practices of unregulated shadow banking. US President Trump has called for a review of the Dodd-Frank Act itself. Shadow banking has rebounded more strongly than commercial banks in the post crisis period. While it has by and large eschewed the riskier instruments that triggered panic during the crisis, new innovations and new risks are emerging, especially those emanating from new financial technologies. Shadow banking is also expanding rapidly to EMDEs, particularly China, which never had a financial crisis, and where policy is biased towards greater liberalization than regulation. If the left critique of liberal democracy entails fiscal expansion and monetary accommodation, the right critique entails further financialization of the economy that rewards owners of capital at the cost of labour.

It is therefore arguable whether the financial system will fundamentally change in the post crisis period, the regulatory overhaul notwithstanding. The effectiveness of the extant overhaul is still untested. This will only happen at the time of the next crisis. While the failure to address the real fault lines in the financial system will be palpable, success is likely to remain invisible, because it is designed to prevent the buildup of risks in the financial system, and financial crises themselves.

In the immediate aftermath of the crisis EMDEs were critical of easy monetary policies in advanced economies as these sent a tsunami of destabilizing capital flows in their direction. They are now wary of their withdrawal at a time they are struggling with falling growth, as monetary tightening in advanced economies spills over as external shocks in the form of sudden capital stops and reversals, with a negative fall

---

[27] Financial cycles are driven by both equity and debt. The period in the run up to the Global Financial Crisis witnessed a financial super cycle in Advanced Economies because it was driven by a boom in both asset prices and leverage, whereas in the post crisis period the financial cycle is basically driven by only a boom in equity prices.

[28] There are however at least three notable omissions in the post crisis regulatory rejig of the financial system. First, while the new leverage ratio under Basel III puts some roadblocks in the way of runaway leverage, the tax structure continues to favour debt over equity. Second, banks have been left with the option of determining their own risk weights, leaving them free to game their capital requirements. Third, while some steps have been taken to insulate MMFs from runs, the 'mark to market' model that according to Bair (2010), former chairperson of the US Federal Deposit Insurance Corporation, biases markets towards underestimating capital requirements during boom times, and can lead to fire sales during panics, has been left untouched (see also Forbes 2010).

out on growth. These flows have already declined sharply. EMDE Corporates took advantage of low rates to borrow in international markets. In these circumstances a rise in interest rates and currency depreciation will dent their balance sheets further. Thus far, the monetary tightening in the US has been countervailed by continuing easy monetary policy in Europe (including the UK) and Japan. Were monetary tightening to extend to Europe as well, EMDEs could find themselves in the all too familiar, if unpleasant, grip of the impossible trinity, with low growth compelling them to keep monetary conditions easy on one hand, but capital flight compelling them to tighten on the other. While they can draw upon their accumulated stockpile of FX reserves to cushion the shock, experience in countries like Korea indicates that "their deployability may be smaller than their size may suggest, as markets can become nervous once the buffer shrinks. And the evidence suggests that macroprudential tools are more effective in building up buffer than in cushioning against busts" (Bank of International Settlements 2018, Chap. IV).

The period prior to the crisis, and its immediate aftermath was a period of accelerated income convergence between Advanced Economies and EMDEs, creating geopolitical space for major developing countries in a world long dominated by the G7 countries. Despite their often mutually incongruent and even conflicting interests the BRICS platform rapidly developed into an influential global forum alongside the G7. The major EMDEs longstanding demand for greater voice and share in the institutions of global economic governance, such as the Bretton Woods twins the World Bank and the IMF, began to be taken more seriously on account of changing weights in the global economy. It was no coincidence that when the crisis broke the global leadership and coordination in addressing it was provided by the only compact global forum comprising the G7 and BRICS, namely the G 20, which eclipsed the G7 as the premier institution for global economic governance. The EMDE members of the G 20 were also inducted to the high table of major standard setting bodies like the Financial Stability Board.

The relatively stronger recovery in Advanced economies relative to EMDEs, that has gone hand in hand with the decline in trade and external imbalances, has exposed the continuing dependence of EMDEs on demand in Advanced Economies after a brief 'decoupling' euphoria. If EMDEs are to escape the Arthur Lewis, and Middle Income, trap, they would need to consume more. If they are to simultaneously protect investment, they might need to run current account deficits and import, rather than export, savings. For this to occur Advanced Economies would need to consume less and save more, as there is only so much global commons available for growth. Global imbalances may not themselves be destabilizing; what is destabilizing is their financialization, or a savings glut by which excess savings find their way into financial markets rather than into investment in the real economy.

The decline in the rate of income convergence has dented the new found geopolitical space of EMDEs. The G 20 has diminished in importance, ceding space to growing nationalism and bilateralism that is undermining the rules based international order put in place mostly by the efforts of advanced economies. The constituency for the rules based international order and globalization has shifted from advanced economies to EMDEs in the wake of the crisis. This shift is the likely result of the inability of policies to address the pre-crisis structural problems deriving from stagnant real wages, growing inequality and falling labour participation rates in advanced economies that is fueling the spread of of protectionism and nationalism.

The United States, China and Germany[29] have been the biggest beneficiaries of the emerging new order. These economies have not only recovered more robustly than the others, but are also becoming regional hegemons, while the crisis has underscored the economic strength of the US as the global hegemon. The crisis has however bared structural weaknesses of both the regional hegemons, while uncovering hidden strengths of the global hegemon.

Germany, the other regional hegemon, finds itself increasingly vulnerable to internal centrifugal forces within the Eurozone deriving from the market discovery of an intrinsically unstable monetary union during the Eurozone debt crisis, an impending Brexit that could induce others to exit the union, and the imminent exit of German Chancellor Angela Merkel, a universally respected unifying force. The crisis has bared the Achilles heel of the European Monetary Union, and of its primary gatekeeper, which might keep it hostage to markets from time to time until the flaw is addressed to the latter's satisfaction.

A long period of hypergrowth has increased China's geopolitical profile as it now the biggest economy in the world when measured at purchasing power parity, and the second biggest at market exchange rates. It is also using its new found wealth to put in place an alternative regional financial architecture through the Belt Road Initiative (BRI), a new 'BRICS' development bank and a multilaterlized Chiang Mai Initiative. China's growth model has however been found to be unsustainable, and the attendant shift has weakened its growth impulse. While its large foreign exchange reserves and domestic savings provide a good cushion against external shocks, the sharp increase in debt, especially in the shadow banking sector, and non-performing loans further threatens growth,[30] and an overextended BRI, makes it look vulnerable to a financial crisis going forward. The second largest EMDE, and now the third biggest economy when measured at purchasing power parity, looks equally vulnerable, and for similar reasons.

It was long known that while the US dollar was the US currency it was the problem of other countries.[31] The Global Financial crisis showed that even a financial crisis emanating from the US was the problem of other countries. Not only did the dollar strengthen as a result of a flight to safety, but it was the US Federal Reserve that bailed out other countries, rather than the IMF, the traditional lender of last resort. This strength ultimately derives from the special role of the US dollar as the de facto global reserve currency. The seemingly bottomless global appetite for the dollar allows it to fund levels of domestic and external deficits that would normally be

[29]In a recent article in Financial Times, Rachman (2019), chief Foreign Affairs commentator, sees the globalized world yielding to a two bloc world dominated by the US and China.

[30]Cross country evidence indicates a fairly strong negative correlation between non-performing loans and economic growth (Balgova et al. 2016).

[31]It was at a G-10 meeting in Rome in 1971 that the US Treasury Secretary John Connally made what was then considered an astonishing statement to his counterparts "the dollar is our currency, but it's your problem."

penalized by markets elsewhere. It also gives it the economic clout to discipline other countries—through sanctions without calling upon its deep military strengths.

The contours of a new global economic order in the wake of the global financial crisis are still unclear, but they have nevertheless begun to take shape. The policy mix of how this new order will grapple with the continuing pre-crisis trends of stagnant wages, falling labour participation rates, growing inequality and stalling growth that is creating geopolitical instability and a backlash against globalization in advanced economies, is less clear.

## References


Akin, C., & Kose, M. A. (2007, December 1). *Changing nature of North-South linkages: Stylized facts and explanations*. IMF Working Paper WP/07/280. http://www.imf.org/external/pubs/cat/longres.aspx?sk=21423.

Arnold, M. (2018, September 17). How US Banks took over the financial world. *Financial Times*. https://www.ft.com/content/6d9ba066-9eee-11e8-85da-eeb7a9ce36e4.

Bair, S. C. (2010). *Statement of Sheila C. Bair, Chairman, Federal Deposit Insurance Corporation on the Causes and Current State of the Financial Crisis before the Financial Crisis Inquiry Commission*, January 14, 2010. https://www.fdic.gov/news/news/speeches/archives/2010/spjan1410.html.

Balgova, M., Nies, M., & Plekhanov, A. (2016, October). The economic impact of reducing non-performing loans. *European Bank for Reconstruction and Development*. Working Paper #193. https://www.ebrd.com/publications/working-papers/economic-impact.html.

Bank of International Settlements (2018, June 24). Annual Economic Report 2018. https://www.bis.org/publ/arpdf/ar2018e.htm.

Beck, T., Demirgüç-Kunt, A., Levine, R. (2003, August). *Banking concentration and crises*. NBER Working Paper 9921. http://www.nber.org/papers/w9921.

Bernanke, B. S. (1994). The macroeconomics of the great depression: A comparative approach. NBER Working Paper 4814, August 1994. https://www.nber.org/papers/w4814.pdf.

Bernanke, B. S. (2003). *Speech at the Japanese Society of Monetary Economics, Tokyo, Japan*, August 1994. https://www.federalreserve.gov/boarddocs/speeches/2003/20030531/default.htm.

Bernanke, B. S. (2002). https://www.federalreserve.gov/BOARDDOCS/SPEECHES/2002/20021108/. Remarks at a conference, University of Chicago, Illinois, November 8, 2002.

Bernanke, B. S. (2005). *The Global Saving Glut and the U.S. Current Account Deficit*, Remarks at the Sandridge Lecture, Virginia Association of Economists, Richmond, Virginia, March 10, 2005. https://www.federalreserve.gov/boarddocs/speeches/2005/200503102/default.htm.

Bernanke, B. S. (2007). *The Sub-Prime Mortgage Market*, Speech at the Federal Reserve Bank of Chicago's 43rd Annual Conference on Bank Structure and Competition, Chicago, Illinois, May 17, 2007. https://www.federalreserve.gov/newsevents/speech/bernanke20070517a.htm.

Bernanke, B. S. (2010). *Monetary Policy and the Housing Bubble*, Speech at the Annual Meeting of the American Economic Association, Atlanta, Georgia, January 3, 2010. https://www.federalreserve.gov/newsevents/speech/bernanke20100103a.htm.

Bernanke, B. S. (2015). *Why are interest rates so low, part 3: The Global Savings Glut*, Brookings, April 1, 2015, https://www.brookings.edu/blog/ben-bernanke/2015/04/01/why-are-interest-rates-so-low-part-3-the-global-savings-glut/.

Bernanke, B. S., Reinhart, V. R., Sack, B. P. (2004). *Monetary policy alternatives at the Zero bound: An empirical assessment*, Staff Working Paper # 48, Finance and Economics Discussion Series, Federal Reserve, Washington, D.C. https://www.brookings.edu/wp-content/uploads/2004/06/2004b_bpea_bernanke.pdf.

Ben S. Bernanke, *Monetary Policy in a New Era*, Brookings Institution, October 2, 2017. file:///D:/dropbox/Dropbox/ongoing/bernanke_rethinking_macro_final_monetary%20policy%20in%20the%20new%20era.pdf.

Bhattacharya, J., & Haslag, J. H. (1999). *Monetary policy arithmetic: Some recent contributions*, Federal Reserve Bank of Dallas, Economic and Financial Review, Third Quarter 1999. http://citeseerx.ist.psu.edu/viewdoc/download?doi=10.1.1.199.4767&rep=rep1&type=pdf.

Blanchard, O. (2019). *Public debt and low interest rates*, American Economic Association Presidential Lecture, Peterson Institute for International Economics and MIT, January 2019. https://www.aeaweb.org/aea/2019conference/program/pdf/14020_paper_etZgfbDr.pdf.

Blanchard, O., & Summers, L. (2017). *Rethinking stabilization policy: Back to the future,* Petersen Institute for International Economics, October 8, 2017. https://piie.com/system/files/documents/blanchard-summers20171012paper.pdf.

Bradford De Long, J., & Lawrence, H. (2012). Summers, *Fiscal Policy in a Depressed Economy*, March 20, 2012, https://delong.typepad.com/20120320-conference-draft-final-candidate-delong-summers-brookings-fiscal-policy-in-a-depressed-economy-1.32.pdf.

Brown, E. C. (1956). Fiscal policy in the thirties: A reappraisal, *The American Economic Review*, 46(5), December 1956. http://static.stevereads.com/papers_to_read/fiscal_policy_in_the_thirties_a_reappraisal.pdf.

Canuto, O. (2019). *China's growth rebalance with downslide,* Academia.edu, March 2019. https://www.academia.edu/38477037/China_s_Growth_Rebalance_with_Downslide?email_work_card=title.

Christiano, L. J., Motto, R., & Rostagno, M. (2004). *The great depression and Friedman-Schwartz hypothesis*. NBER Working Paper 10255, National Bureau of Economic Research, Cambridge, USA. http://www.nber.org/papers/w10255.

Conference Board. (2018). *The conference board total economy database*™, March 2018. https://www.conference-board.org/data/economydatabase/index.cfm?id=27762.

Correia, I., Farhi, E., Nicolini, J. P., & Teles, P. (2012). *Unconventional fiscal policy at the zero bound*. Federal Reserve Bank of Minneapolis Research Department, Working Paper 698. https://www.minneapolisfed.org/research/wp/wp698.pdf.

Dotsey, M. (1994). *Some Not So Unpleasant Monetarist Arithmetic,* Federal Reserve Bank of Richmond, Working Paper 95-02, June 1994 (Revised March 1995). Retrieved from https://www.richmondfed.org/~/media/richmondfedorg/publications/research/working_papers/1995/pdf/wp95-2.pdf.

Eggertsson, G. B. (2005). *Great Expectations and the End of the Depression*. Federal Reserve Bank of New York, Staff Report no. 234 December 2005, https://www.newyorkfed.org/medialibrary/media/research/staff_reports/sr234.pdf.

Eggertsson, G. B., Mehrotra, N. R., Summers, L. H. (2016). *Secular Stagnation in the Open Economy*. NBER Working Paper # 22172, April 2016. https://www.nber.org/papers/w22172.pdf.

Eichengreen, B. (1986). *The Political Economy of the Smoot-Hawley Tariff*, NBER Working Paper No. 2001, National Bureau of Economic Research, Cambridge, USA; also available at https://www.nber.org/papers/w2001.pdf.

Eichengreen, B. (2010). Lessons of the crisis for emerging markets. *International Economics and Economic Policy*, 7(1). https://link.springer.com/article/10.1007/s10368-010-0149-9.

Eichengreen, B., O'Rourke, K. (2012). *A tale of two depressions redux*, VOX, CEPR Policy Portal, March 6, 2012, https://voxeu.org/article/tale-two-depressions-redux.

Financial Stability Board. (2017). *Assessment of shadow banking activities: risks and the adequacy of post-crisis policy tools to address financial stability concerns*, May 3, 2017. http://www.fsb.org/2017/07/assessment-of-shadow-banking-activities-risks-and-the-adequacy-of-post-crisis-policy-tools-to-address-financial-stability-concerns/.

Financial Stability Board. (2018a). List of global systemically important banks (G-SIBs), November 16, 2018. http://www.fsb.org/wp-content/uploads/P161118-1.pdf.

Financial Stability Board. (2018b). Implementation and Effects of the G20 Financial Regulatory Reforms 28 November 2018 4th Annual *Report*, http://www.fsb.org/2018/11/implementation-and-effects-of-the-g20-financial-regulatory-reforms-fourth-annual-report/.

Financial Stability Board. (2019). *Report on Non-Bank Financial Intermediation 2018*, February 4, 2019. http://www.fsb.org/2019/02/global-monitoring-report-on-non-bank-financial-intermediation-2018/.

Fishback, P. V. (2010). U.S.Monetary and Fiscal Policy in the 1930s, NBER Working Paper 16477, National Bureau of Economic Research, Cambridge, USA. Retrieved from http://www.nber.org/papers/w16477.

Forbes, S. (2010). Transcript: Shiela Bair. *Forbes Magazine*, August 2, 2010. https://www.forbes.com/2010/07/30/bair-lehman-bank-failure-intelligent-investing-fdic.html#99add6d454b3.

Friedman, Milton. (1963). *Inflation causes and consequences*. New York: Asian Publishing House.

Greenspan, A. (2002). '*Opening Remarks*', in Rethinking Stabilization Policy, A Symposium sponsored by the Federal Reserve Bank of Kansas City, Kansas City, August 29–31, 2002. https://www.kansascityfed.org/publicat/sympos/2002/pdf/S02Greenspan.pdf.

Hakkio, C. S. (2013). The Great Moderation 1982–2007, Federal Reserve History, Richmond, USA. https://www.federalreservehistory.org/essays/great_moderation.

IMF Fiscal Monitor July 2009. *IMF Fiscal Affairs Department database*. https://www.imf.org/en/Publications/FM/Issues/2018/10/04/fiscal-monitor-october-2018.

International Monetary Fund (IMF). 2018. *World economic outlook: Challenges to steady growth*, IMF, Washington D.C. Retrieved from https://www.imf.org/en/Publications/WEO/Issues/2018/09/24/world-economic-outlook-october-2018.

Irwin, D. A. (1996). *The Smoot-Hawley Tariff: A quantitative assessment*. NBER Working Paper No. 5509, National Bureau of Economic Research, Cambridge, USA. Retrieved from https://www.nber.org/papers/w5509.pdf.

International Institute for Labour Studies (IILS). (2011). *A Review of Global Fiscal Stimulus*, EC-IILS Joint Paper Discussion, Series 5, International Labour Organization. https://www.ilo.org/wcmsp5/groups/public/—dgreports/—inst/documents/publication/wcms_194175.pdf.

Kagan, R. (2019). *The strong men strike back*, The Washington Post, March 14, 2019. https://www.washingtonpost.com/news/opinions/wp/2019/03/14/feature/the-strongmen-strike-back/?utm_term=.6f07a8932ae3.

Krugman, P. R. (1998). *It's Baaack: Japan's Slump and the Return of the Liquidity Trap*, Brookings Papers on Economic Activity, No. 2. Retrieved from https://www.brookings.edu/wp-content/uploads/1998/06/1998b_bpea_krugman_dominquez_rogoff.pdf.

Kuttner, K. N., Posen, A. S. (2002). Fiscal Policy Effectiveness in Japan. *Journal of the Japanese and International Economies* 16, 536–558. Retrieved from http://citeseerx.ist.psu.edu/viewdoc/download?doi=10.1.1.612.68&rep=rep1&type=pdf.

Lewis, A. (1979). "*The Slowing Down of the Engine of Growth*", 1979. http://www.nobelprize.org/nobel_prizes/economic-sciences/laureates/1979/lewis-lecture.html.

Mishel, L., Gould, E., & Bivens, J. (2015). Wage stagnation in nine charts. *Economic Policy Institute*, January 6, 2015. https://www.epi.org/publication/charting-wage-stagnation/.

Mislinki, J. (2019). *Adviser Perspectives, January 23, 2019*. https://www.advisorperspectives.com/dshort/updates/2019/01/23/fhfa-house-price-index-house-prices-up-0-4-in-november.

OECD (Year). *Trade in Value Added (TIVA) database*. http://www.oecd.org/sti/ind/measuring-trade-in-value-added.htm#access.

Onaran, Y. (2017). *Too Big to Fail*, Bloomberg December 9, 2017. https://www.bloomberg.com/quicktake/big-fail.

Pew Research Centre, August 7, 2018. http://www.pewresearch.org/ft_18-07-26_hourlywage_feature/.

Rachman, G. (2019). The US, China and the return of a two-bloc world. *Financial Times*, March 11, 2019. https://www.ft.com/content/35accdc0-43de-11e9-a965-23d669740bfb.

Reinhart, C. M., & Rogoff, K. S. (2014). Recovery from financial crises: Evidence from 100 episodes. *American Economic Review*. Papers & Proceedings 2014, 104(5): 50–55. http://dx.doi.org/10.1257/aer.104.5.50.

Robinson, E., Nguyen, L., & Onaran, Y. (2018). On the Eve of Brexit, U.S. Banks Are Set to Conquer Europe. *Bloomberg Quint*, December 13, 2018. https://www.bloombergquint.com/global-economics/on-the-eve-of-brexit-u-s-banks-are-set-to-conquer-europe#gs.GJUklikK

Romer, C. D. (1993). The nation in depression, *Journal of Economic Perspectives*. 7, Number 2-Spring 1993-Pages 19-39, https://eml.berkeley.edu/~cromer/Reprints/The%20Nation%20in%20Depression.pdf.

Romer, C. D. (2011). *What do we know about the effects of fiscal policy?* Hamilton College, USA, November 7, 2011. https://docplayer.net/63271167-What-do-we-know-about-the-effects-of-fiscal-policy-separating-evidence-from-ideology.html.

Romer, C. D. (1991). *What ended the great depression?* NBER Working Paper No. 3829, National Bureau of Economic Research, Cambridge, USA; also available at https://www.nber.org/papers/w3829.pdf.

Sanchez, J. M., & Kim, H. S. (2018). *Why is inflation so low, regional economist*, Federal Reserve Bank of St Louis, USA; also available at https://www.stlouisfed.org/publications/regional-economist/first-quarter-2018/why-inflation-so-low.

Sargent, T. J., Wallace, N. (1981). Some unpleasant Monetarist arithmetic, *Federal Reserve of Minneapolis Quarterly Review*. Retrieved from https://www.minneapolisfed.org/research/qr/qr531.pdf.

Schildbach, J. (2018). Fitness programme continues: European banks become leaner, but stronger. *Deutsche Bank*, July 11, 2018, https://www.dbresearch.com/servlet/reweb2.ReWEB?rwsite=RPS_EN-PROD&rwobj=ReDisplay.Start.class&document=PROD0000000000472373#.

Sheel, A. (2007). Sub-prime and monetary policy, *Business Standard*, New Delhi, September 14, 2007. https://www.business-standard.com/article/opinion/alok-sheel-sub-prime-and-monetary-policy-107091401028_1.html.

Sheel, A. (2011). Eurozone's impossible trinity, *Business Standard*, New Delhi, November 24, 2011. https://www.business-standard.com/article/opinion/alok-sheel-euro-zone-s-impossible-trinity-111112400047_1.html.

Sheel, A. (2013). *Growth or Austerity: The Policy Dilemma* (with C. Rangarajan), *ICRA Bulletin, Money and Finance*, February 2013.

Sheel, A. (2014). *"G 20 and the Policy Response to the Global Financial Crisis" in* (eds.) Callaghan, M., Ghate, C., Pickford, S., & Rathinam, F. Global Cooperation Among G20 Countries: Responding to the Crisis and Restoring Growth (Springer, New Delhi, Dordrecht, Heidelberg, London, New York 2014) Part VI. Austerity and Growth, pp. 241–80.

Sheel, A., & Ganguly, M. (2016). Financial Regulatory Reform: A Mid-Term Assessment from an Emerging Market Perspective. In (Eds.). Rajat Kathuria & Neetika Kaushal Nagpal, *Global Economic Cooperation*. Views from G 20 Countries. Springer, 2016, Chapter 10.

Stiglitz, J. E. (2009). Capitalist fools. *Vanity Fair*, 51(1); also available at https://www.vanityfair.com/news/2009/01/stiglitz200901.

Summers, L. H. (2018). Secular Stagnation has not gone away, Financial Times, May 6, 2018, https://www.ft.com/content/aa76e2a8-4ef2-11e8-9471-a083af05aea7.

Summers, L. H., & Rachel, L., On falling neutral real rates, fiscal policy and the risk of secular stagnation. In *Brookings Papers on Economic Activity BPEA Conference Drafts, March 7-8, 2019*. https://www.brookings.edu/wp-content/uploads/2019/03/On-Falling-Neutral-Real-Rates-Fiscal-Policy-and-the-Risk-of-Secular-Stagnation.pdf.

Taylor, J. B. (2010a). The fed and the crisis: A response to Ben Bernanke. *The Wall Street Journal*, January 11, 2010. Retrieved from https://web.stanford.edu/~johntayl/2010_pdfs/Fed-Crisis-A-Reply-to-Ben-Bernanke-WSJ-Jan-10-2010.pdf.

Taylor, J. B. (2010b). Macroeconomic lessons from the great deviation. Remarks at the 25th NBER macro annual meeting, May 2010. https://web.stanford.edu/~johntayl/NBERMacroAnnualTalkFinal.pdf.

The Economist (2008). Emerging markets. *The Decoupling Debate*, March 6, 2008. http://www.economist.com/node/10809267.

True Economics (2013). *IMF assessment of the Euro Area banking sector risks - part 3,* March 15, 2013. http://trueeconomics.blogspot.com/2013/03/1532013-imf-assessment-of-euro-area_5878.html.

The Economist (2017). *A decade after the crisis, how are the world's banks doing*?, Special Report, May 6, 2017. https://www.economist.com/special-report/2017/05/06/a-decade-after-the-crisis-how-are-the-worlds-banks-doing.

The Federal Reserve Board (1996). *Remarks by Chairman Alan Greenspan at the Annual Dinner and Francis Boyer Lecture of The American Enterprise Institute for Public Policy Research, Washington, D.C*, December 5, 1996. https://www.federalreserve.gov/boarddocs/speeches/1996/19961205.htm.

Uribe, M. (2016). *Is the monetarist arithmetic unpleasant?* NBER Working Paper 22866, National Bureau of Economic Research, Cambridge, USA. Retrieved from https://www.nber.org/papers/w22866.pdf.

US Government Accountability Office, 2011, Report to Congressional Addressees, Federal Reserve System, July 2011. https://www.gao.gov/new.items/d11696.pdf.

# Part II
# Trade, Investment and the Multilateral Process

# Chapter 4
# Where Is US Trade Policy Headed Under the Trump Administration?

**Anwarul Hoda**

**Abstract** The anti-globalisation rhetoric of candidate Donald Trump's election campaign has shaped the trade policy of the new Administration. Bilateralism is the favoured approach but unilateral measures have also been taken to pursue the protectionist agenda. A number of trade policy actions have focused on China, inducing a trade war. The unrelenting opposition by the US to appointments to vacancies in the Appellate Body has caused a crisis in the WTO and given rise to doubts on its commitment to the rules based multilateral trading system.

## 1 Introduction

During his election campaign, Donald Trump lamented the loss of manufacturing jobs in the USA and put the blame on his predecessor administrations for two trade agreements responsible for the loss, namely the North American Free Trade Agreement (NAFTA) and the World Trade Organization. In an election speech on June 28, 2016, in Monessen, Pennsylvania, he charged that 'China's entrance into the World Trade Organization has enabled the greatest jobs theft in history.'[1] Throughout his campaign speeches, the future President Trump spoke in this vein, blaming his rival presidential candidate for disappearing jobs and upbraiding politicians in general for supporting the policy of globalisation. In the light of the success of the anti-globalisation approach in getting him elected, it was inevitable that US trade and economic policy would turn inwards once he was in the White House. Increased protection of domestic manufacturing by raising tariffs became the dominant objective of US trade policy after the new Administration was sworn in on January 20, 2017.

This paper attempts a brief overview of trade policy developments during the first two years of the Trump Administration. Section 2 describes the new Administration's

[1] https://www.politico.com/story/2016/06/fulltranscript-trump-job-plan-speech-224891.

A. Hoda (✉)
ICRIER-Trade Policy and WTO Research Programme, New Delhi, India
e-mail: ahoda@icrier.res.in



R. Kathuria and P. Kukreja (eds.), *20 Years of G20*,
https://doi.org/10.1007/978-981-13-8106-5_4

preference for bilateralism, Sect. 3 analyses the unilateral actions to raise tariffs on various products, Sect. 4 examines the initiatives to deal with the rise of China, Sect. 5 evaluates the crisis in the Appellate Body and Sect. 6 concludes.

## 2 Bilateralism Gains Ascendency

To advance the protectionist agenda, bilateralism became the favoured approach in US trade policy, and a corollary of this approach was the dislike for multiparty agreements. When there are several members, everyone starts expecting the US to assume leadership and the environment inevitably emerges that constrains trade policy officials in pursuing their narrow interests in the negotiations. What is more, the detailed rules of engagement that are drafted initially prevent dominance of the hegemon during ensuing negotiations. On the other hand, when the number of negotiating members is only two or three, there is opportunity for the big player to gain advantage by arm-twisting the weaker partner. In January 2017, President Trump declared to Republican lawmakers, “believe me, we’re going to have a lot of trade deals. But they’ll all be one-to-one. There won’t be a whole big mash pot” (Gertz 2017).

One of his first acts on getting elected was for President Trump to withdraw from the Trans-Pacific Partnership (TPP), which the United States itself had proposed and for which President Obama had worked so hard during his second term in office. And then he browbeat partner nations to agree to renegotiate the FTA agreements: the NAFTA Agreement (renamed the USMCA) and the Korea-US (KORUS) Agreement. The revised KORUS FTA agreement entered into effect on January 1, 2019, and its text has been published. While ratification of the USMCA is not a done deal as yet as it is still to be approved by the Congress in both countries, its negotiation has been completed and details are known from the fact sheet made available on the USTR’s official website.

In the USMCA, the US has had some amount of success in pulling back concessions, which had resulted in manufacturing migrating to other countries. In the automobile sector, there are two key gains: first, the threshold of regional (North American) content has been raised from 62.5 to 75%, and second, a new labour value content rule has been created, requiring 40–45% of the content to be made by workers earning at least USD16 per hour. In textiles and apparel also there are material changes, albeit of lower trade significance. The use of non-NAFTA input has been restricted by requiring that sewing thread, pocketing fabric, elastic bands and coated fabrics used in the finished products must be made in the region in order to qualify for the duty-free benefit. The US has also wrested from Canada concessions in agriculture that will expand trade in dairy and poultry products.

In the revised KORUS Agreement too, the main concession obtained in manufacturing is not for liberalising but restricting trade. The original KORUS FTA had eliminated the duty of 2.5% on US imports of cars but allowed it to delay liberalisation of the 25% tariff on light trucks up to 2018 and eliminate it by 2021. The new

Agreement allows the US to maintain the tariff on light trucks at 25% for 20 years more (up to 2041). The US succeeded in postponing liberalisation of the light truck segment of the auto industry and retained the right to maintain the tariff at the rather high level of 25%. The bilateral approach has clearly enabled the US to roll back liberalisation agreements entered into earlier with smaller trading partners.

The bilateral approach in trade adopted in the US trade policy has not led to quick success vis-à-vis bigger trading partners. Negotiations on the Transatlantic Trade and Investment Partnership (T-TIP) Agreement launched in 2013 for closer economic co-operation between the US and the EU had petered out in 2016 after intense initial activity. The US-EU trade relations tended to worsen sharply in March 2018, following the imposition of tariff on steel and aluminium under Section 232 of the US Trade Expansion Act, 1962, and the retaliatory response by the EU for national security reasons and the commencement of investigations on automobiles under the same provision (see Sect. 3 for details). At this stage, President Juncker of the EU visited Washington to repair political relations and the two sides agreed to hold bilateral trade negotiations again. But there is a wrangle on the precise scope of the resumed dialogue. The US is keen on the talks including agricultural products but the EU is adamantly opposed to the suggestion and the situation appears to be one of a stalemate. Success with the bilateral approach may not be come easily when the opposite number has the strength to withstand intimidatory tactics.

Initially, Japan responded coldly to the US invitation to bilateral trade negotiations. Its preference was for the US to re-enter the Trans-Pacific Partnership (TPP), which the new Administration had chosen to jettison. However, perseverance paid off and, in September 2018, Japan agreed to enter into formal bilateral negotiations, focused more or less on trade in goods. The general assessment is that Japan softened its response in the light of the commencement of investigation in the US under Section 232 for the levy of tariff on cars for national security reasons. Japan has a large stake in the US import market for automobiles and the agreement to begin talks has enabled Japan to obtain a tacit agreement that tariff would not be imposed while the talks are going on. One other point at issue in the bilateral talks will be whether Japan can go beyond the TPP in liberalising agricultural products.

## 3 Unilateral Action to Raise Tariffs

### *3.1 Tariffs on Steel and Aluminium*

In order to provide increased protection to manufacturing, the new Administration looked at possibilities offered by existing domestic trade laws to raise tariff. The anti-dumping legislation has been a favoured tool for protection but it cannot be used across the board to cover a large segment of manufacturing. The safeguard legislation is available to raise tariff on any sector, but there are many restrictions on safeguard action in the WTO rules. The US Administration saw many advantages in using Section 232 of the Trade Expansion Act, 1962, for raising tariff on some critical sectors of industry, ostensibly to safeguard national security.

On March 8, 2018, the US issued two presidential proclamations under Section 232 of the Trade Expansion Act of 1962, imposing a 25% tariff on imports of steel and a 10% tariff on imports of aluminium.

On steel, the US government declared that the increase in imports and the situation of global excess capacity for the production of steel threatened the closure of domestic steel producing capacity, thus weakening the ability to 'meet [steel] demands for national defense and critical industries in a national emergency'. On aluminium, the US authorities averred that the United States was 'at risk of becoming reliant on foreign producers of high-purity aluminum that is essential for key military and commercial systems.'

GATT 1994, which is one of the multilateral trade agreements on trade in goods embodied in the WTO Agreement, provides for security exceptions, under which all government actions taken to protect a country's essential security interests fall outside the purview of its rules. The intention is to cover actions 'taken in times of war or other emergency in international relations' and actions relating to 'arms, ammunition and implements of war' as well as military supplies. Use of the provision to increase protection on any product is overstretching the possible coverage of the provision on security exception beyond credible limits.

Since the entry into force of the WTO Agreement, no question had arisen earlier on the interpretation of the provision relating to the security exception. However, during the GATT 1947 days, an understanding prevailed that the member concerned was the best judge of what was in its security interest. Relying on this understanding, the USA is taking the stand that the right to take any trade action cannot be subject to review by the WTO panel.

In 2017, the year before the presidential proclamations were issued, Canada, Brazil, South Korea and Mexico were the top exporters of steel to the USA, with Russia, Turkey, Japan, Germany and Taiwan coming next in order. In the case of aluminium, Canada, China and Russia were the top suppliers, followed by Mexico, Germany, Japan, France and Italy. A significant feature of the US invocations of the security exception is that they have come at a time when there is no emergency in international relations among the countries involved. In fact, it is also noteworthy that since 1949, the USA has been tied with Canada, Germany, France and Italy in a military alliance, the NATO; Turkey too joined it in 1952. The use of the security exception to raise barriers against imports from long-standing allies does not stand scrutiny as a justifiable or reasonable action.

The US action also raises some fundamental questions about the viability of the WTO as an international agreement. WTO members have participated in several rounds of negotiations since the General Agreement on Tariffs and Trade, 1947, was established and they have all made the commitment that they would not raise the agreed level of tariff except after entering into renegotiations. If the security exception is used to get out of a commitment, all past efforts at liberalisation will be set at nought. What is more, the use of the security exception by one member raises the possibility that other members will take the cue and take protective action on a host of products that can be deemed to have the remotest connection with the defence of the country, and then use the security exception, as the US has done in this case, to claim the sole right to determine what is in its security interest. In such a situation, the WTO framework of rules and disciplines for the conduct of world trade among members in general and on the use of tariff measures for regulating trade in particular will fall apart.

The US action has predictably generated a chain of disputes. To start with, the EU, China, Russia, Canada, Mexico, Norway, Turkey, India and Switzerland have raised disputes against the USA for imposing tariffs on steel and aluminium. The USA tried to block the complaints by challenging the jurisdiction of WTO panels to review a matter involving national security. Indeed, disputes have multiplied as China, Canada, the EU, Mexico and Turkey have imposed countermeasures on imports from the USA, contending that the US measures are in reality safeguard measures taken for economic and commercial reasons and the US has raised its own disputes on the countermeasures imposed by these members. If the sequence of disputes results in a verdict against it, is it likely that the US, which is the world's largest economy, will withdraw from the WTO Agreement and push it into irrelevance? If, on the other hand, it results in a verdict in favour of the US, will not the proliferation of similar measures by other WTO members also cause havoc for the multilateral trading system? Seen against the background of the attack on the Appellate Body (which we consider in Sect. 5), is it possible that the proximate aim of US trade policy is to destroy the system from within, and the ultimate goal is to rely on bilateral agreements to govern international trade among nations?

While the US action and the countermeasures resorted to by its trading partners have got increasingly embroiled in WTO disputes, what has been the effect of the measures on the US economy? The US steel and aluminium industries have no doubt made gains from the price increase and capacity utilisation has increased in the industries but downstream industries have certainly suffered from what was a self-inflicted wound. FTI Consulting reported in August 2018 that the three US major automobile manufacturers lowered their profit outlook for the year on account of higher aluminium and steel prices. In fact, some other industries suffered more as a result of retaliatory countermeasures taken by other countries. US farmers were hit by the a 91% fall in China's imports of US soybeans in 2018 (NY Times op-ed by Hillman 2018) and by a fall of around 40% since 2014 in the spot market prices on US cheese and whey due to retaliatory tariffs imposed by Mexico and China (Haddon 2018).

The loss suffered by farmers is a political minefield for the leadership of both the Republicans and Democrats. To save the day, both parties have joined to vote for the 2019 Farm Bill, which will inter alia compensate the farmers for the losses suffered on account of the decline in prices resulting from the trade war. Even earlier, on August 27, 2018, the US Department of Agriculture had announced an initial amount of USD4.7 billion against the total package of USD12 billion as aid against retaliation (Daniels 2018).

## 3.2 *Investigation for Imposing Tariffs on Automobiles and Auto Products*

The tariffs on two widely traded metals stirred a huge conflict in international trade relations but the next move in US trade policy caused an even deeper shock in world trade. On May 23, 2018, the US president ordered an investigation on whether the imports of automobiles and auto components were causing or threatening impairment of national security. This sector was the prime mover in the rapid industrialisation of the US early in the 20th century but in recent decades, the US industry has lost ground not only to Japan, Germany and South Korea, but also to its regional trading partners, Mexico and Canada. We have seen that in the USMCA, one of the main outcomes was to roll back liberalisation of automobiles and auto components within the region. In the revised KORUS Agreement, the liberalisation of light trucks was deferred by 20 years. The plan is obviously to increase tariffs further on products imported from both regional and non-regional partners. Imports of USD95 billion have already been covered by the tariff increases on steel and aluminium and now, the idea is to extend protectionist action to cover imports of automobiles and auto components valued at an additional USD361 billion. If Section 232 tariffs are actually imposed on these products, the total coverage of tariffs under the security exception will be as much as 20% of total US imports.

The investigation has been completed and the report submitted on February 19, 2019, to the Department of Commerce, but the conclusions and recommendations had not been made public till the date of writing (March 26, 2019).

The world automobile industry is highly globalised and manufacturers, including those in the USA are interconnected, relying extensively on the use of parts and components from supply chains at home and abroad. A compilation made by Price Waterhouse Coopers (2017) of the top global OEMs (original equipment manufacturers) of components lists 100 global suppliers of components used by automobile manufacturers world-wide, demonstrating the diversity of the origins of these components.

A study by Shultz et al. (2019) published by the Center for Automotive Research (CAR) estimates that the US imported 48% of its sales of light vehicles in 2017, the main source countries being Mexico (14%), Canada (11%), Japan (11%), South Korea (5%) and Germany (3%). Although 52% of the US sales of light vehicles were US produced vehicles, only 29% was accounted for by US firms and the remaining 23% was produced by foreign firms.

Taking the globalised nature of the automotive industry into account, an analysis made by Lovely et al. (2018) has come to the conclusion that foreign cars assembled in the USA sometimes have more domestic content than comparable vehicles bearing US names. More significantly, they conclude that if the US were to impose 25% tariff on all automotive products and parts, there would be a significant consumer price increase even without any retaliation from the US trading partners, causing production of the motor vehicles industry in the country to fall by 1.5% and employment by 1.9%. The study by Shultz et al. (2019) referred to above envisages different scenarios, depending upon the major source countries to which a Section 232 tariff of a possible 25% would be applied, and comes to the conclusion that "the US light vehicle sales would still decline and consumer prices would still rise under every scenario".

The increase in price due to the imposition of tariff on imports will hit foreign suppliers adversely no doubt, but it will cause considerable harm to US manufacturers as well. It is obvious that tariffs on imported components will make US built vehicles less competitive in foreign markets. The tariff increase could have an economic effect just the opposite of the intended increase in manufacturing output and jobs sought to be achieved. The integrated nature of the global supply chain will rob domestic industry of any clear gains. The main purpose of the Section 232 initiative could be to intimidate trading partners and wrest concessions in the course of bilateral negotiations.

## 4 Dealing with China

With its pre-eminence as the world's largest economy obviously imperilled by the rise of China as an economic super-power, the US has been active to deal with the threat.

### *4.1 Trilateral Co-operation to Curb Non-market Oriented Policies and Practices*

Ministers of the US, the EU and Japan have been involved in trilateral diplomacy for decades to deal with important international economic issues. In the last two years or so, their meetings have focused on issues that have a bearing on China, without mentioning the name of the country. A joint statement, issued after a meeting of the three trade ministers at New York on September 25, 2018, pointedly refers to 'their concern with and their shared objective to address non-market oriented policies and practices of third countries'.[2] The ministers go on to express the belief that these policies and practices 'lead to severe overcapacity, create unfair competitive conditions for their workers and businesses, hinder the development and use of innovative technologies, and undermine the proper functioning of international trade, including where existing rules are not effective'.

In the joint statement, the ministers have spoken of their objective to draw up new rules in industrial subsidies and state-owned enterprises and to work together to make existing WTO disciplines more effective. They have deplored policies and practices that induce forced technology transfer.

[2]https://www.meti.go.jp/English/press/2018/09/20180925004/20180925004-2.pdf.

The ministers also made a particular mention of the agreement among them to co-sponsor a transparency and notification proposal in the Goods Council of the WTO to improve its monitoring and surveillance function. Subsequently, a paper titled 'Procedures to enhance transparency and strengthen notification requirements under WTO Agreements' was submitted jointly by Argentina, Costa Rica, the European Union, Japan and the United States (WTO 2018).

## *4.2 Unilateral Tariffs Under Section 301*

In the Trump Administration, there was impatience from the outset on the issue of forced transfer of technology and, on August 18, 2017, the US Trade Representative (USTR) initiated investigations under Section 301 into "China's acts, policies, and practices relating to technology transfer, intellectual property and innovation".

As a member of the WTO, the US has the obligation to seek redressal of disputes only in accordance with the procedures laid down in the Dispute Settlement Understanding (DSU) of the WTO. Unilateralism, as envisaged in Sect. 301 of the US Trade Act, 1974, was an issue in the Uruguay Round and there was a specific agreement, incorporated in Article 23 of the DSU, prohibiting recourse to unilateral action. In authorising unilateral action, the President overlooked the multilateral commitments of the United States.

The investigations ended on March 22, 2018, with the finding that China uses foreign ownership restrictions to require technology transfer from US companies and that these companies are also induced to licence technologies to Chinese entities on non-market based terms. One other conclusion reached was that "China directs and unfairly facilitates the systematic investment in, and acquisition of, US companies and assets by Chinese companies to obtain cutting-edge technologies and intellectual property and generate the transfer of technology". The most serious charge against the Chinese authorities contained in the report is abetment of theft of sensitive commercial information from the computer networks of US companies.

On the basis of these findings, the US imposed a 25% duty on imports of USD50 billion from China. On April 3, 2018, the USTR first announced the proposed list of products but by the time the list was finalised after hearings and consultations, it was already June 15, 2018. A trade war followed. China retaliated and imposed tariffs on imports into China from the USA. In September 2018, the US imposed 10% tariff on Chinese goods valued at a further USD200 billion, and threatened to raise the level to 25% in January, 2019. China also threatened to impose retaliatory tariff on a further USD60 billion worth of imports from the USA. Fortunately, at the Buenos Aires G20 Summit (December 1, 2018), there was agreement on a 90-day pause, before considering further escalation. In the US-China talks that have taken place in the interim, although there is lack of clarity on whether there is progress in the resolution of US grievances, the deadline of March 2, 2019, has been extended by President Trump.

The US finally took the first step required by the DSU and asked for consultation with China through a WTO notification on March 23, 2018, seven months after initiating action under Section 301 (WT/DS542/1 China-Certain Measures Concerning the Protection of Intellectual Property Rights). The only explanation for this is that the Administration was in a protectionist hurry to raise barriers. The EU too has raised a dispute (WT/DS549/1-China- Certain Measures on Transfer of Technology) on the same issue but it has done so without raising any impediments to China's trade. While the US introduced the retaliatory measure first and then raised a dispute, the EU raised a dispute first and is waiting for the decision before possibly taking such measures.

The message that comes out from the Section 301 action against Chinese goods is that US trade policy actions will not be constrained by the existing disciplines of multilateral rules, no matter how recently they have been renegotiated and reaffirmed.

## 4.3 China's Status as a Market Economy

During the negotiations for China's accession to the WTO, its status as a market economy was a major source of worry for WTO members. The main concern was the existence of hidden trade-distorting subsidies or pricing practices as a result of state ownership of industrial enterprises. To take care of this concern, other importing members were given flexibility in the methodology for making price comparisons to determine the existence of dumping. The standard methodology in the WTO Agreement to determine dumping is to compare the export price of the product with the home market price or with a third country price. If there are difficulties in determining both home market and third country prices, the rules allow the use of "constructed value" or of alternative procedures "on such reasonable basis as the authorities may determine". The practice in the USA has been to calculate dumping margins on products from China using prices and costs from a market economy country at the same level of industrial development in place of Chinese producers' input costs and prices. This gives greater latitude to the authorities to determine the margin of dumping.

A provision in the Protocol on the Accession of China[3] required the producers under anti-dumping investigations to clearly demonstrate that market economy conditions prevailed in the industry under investigation. If market economy conditions were not clearly shown, the importing member could depart from the primary requirement to use Chinese costs or prices for the purpose of price comparability. However, the protocol also stipulated that the provision "shall expire 15 years after the date of accession". Since China acceded to the WTO on December 11, 2001, after December 11, 2016, the language of the protocol appears to require members to treat China as a market economy country to calculate the dumping margin. However, the issue has become contentious as a contrary legal view has also been taken that 'ME treatment is reserved for when China earns ME status by completing its economic transformation' (Miranda 2016). The US has taken a formal decision internally to treat China

[3]WTO Document WT/L/432.

as a non-market economy and China has filed a complaint in the WTO against the US (DS 515). The dispute has not proceeded beyond the stage of consultations.

## 5 Crisis Over the Appellate Body of the WTO

President Trump has never looked kindly at the WTO, always using strong words, calling the institution a disaster or a catastrophe. He has frequently threatened that the US would leave the WTO. But it is now becoming increasingly clear that what the US is aiming at is to weaken the WTO from within, take it backwards and convert it into a platform for bilateral or multilateral negotiations. That is what GATT 1947 was before the Uruguay Round transformed it into a strong institution with an almost automatic procedure for dispute settlement.

It is ironic that the weakening of the WTO's dispute settlement machinery is being sought by the very nation that had taken the initiative to strengthen it during the negotiations in the Uruguay Round (1986–1994). The dispute settlement machinery of GATT 1947 was improved considerably during its 47 years of operation, but it was still riddled with inadequacies, mainly on account of the requirement of consensus in decision-making. All important decisions, be it for the establishment or composition of a panel, the adoption of a panel report or the authorisation of retaliatory suspension of concessions could be blocked by individual contracting parties. Thus, dispute settlement remained primarily a negotiating process and the prescribed procedures merely gave some opportunity for diplomatic pressurisation.

During the negotiations for the WTO Agreement, it was the US that led the effort towards greater judicialisation of the dispute settlement procedures and the most important change that was brought about was the introduction of the rule of negative consensus. This rule implies that the request by a member for the establishment of a panel is accepted or the report of a panel adopted unless the Dispute Settlement Body (DSB) decides by consensus not to do so. Two other major improvements introduced in the WTO were that time limits were stipulated for each stage of dispute settlement and provision was made for review by the appellate body (AB). The DSB is required to set up a Standing Appellate Body, composed of seven persons, three of whom are to serve on any one case. Individual experts serve for a term of four years but each person may be reappointed once.

The process of appointment/reappointment of AB members from time to time was uneventful until 2011, when a US nominee was not proposed for reappointment, and it was widely suspected that the US government was not pleased with the rulings in which she was involved. A more overt intervention was made by the US in 2016, when it opposed the reappointment of a South Korean member of the AB while alleging that there was judicial overreach in the appeals in which he was involved. Denial of reappointment of members of the AB was clearly aimed at impairing the independence of AB members. But things have got worse after the change of Administration in 2017 in the US. Now, the US representative is obstructing in a routine manner the process of selection to fill up vacancies in the Appellate Body and the number of AB members in position is already down to the minimum of three required to hear appeals.

The US has raised a number of issues regarding the functioning of the AB, which they would like to see resolved before they can allow the selection procedures for filling up vacancies to proceed. Should the AB report bear the name of a member who participated in the decision but has demitted office before its submission? What is the legal status of an AB report that has not been submitted within the mandatory time limit of 90 days? Should the AB reports contain advisory opinions? Should the AB examine a member's domestic legislation as a matter of law or treat it as a matter of fact? Should the AB rulings be treated as a precedent in future cases?

All the points raised by the US are legitimate issues. But what is unjustifiable is to link the resolution of these issues to the process of filling up the vacancies in the AB. What makes the US position untenable is that it has found fault with every suggestion made by members to resolve the issues, while not submitting any proposal on its own behalf. In the meantime, December 2019 is approaching fast, when two more AB members will retire and the AB will become non-functional. Once that happens, the process of dispute settlement will not advance any further in a case in which a party notifies its decision to appeal against a panel report as there will be no AB to consider the matter further. In that eventuality, the WTO will revert to the GATT era of resolving disputes essentially by means of negotiations and diplomatic pressures. In the absence of a credible dispute settlement machinery, the rules based multilateral trading system will weaken, giving the stronger trading nations the upper hand in the governance of international trade. Is this what US trade policy is aiming at?

## 6 Conclusions

- During the electoral campaign in 2016, as a presidential candidate, Donald Trump had adopted a strong anti-globalisation stance and it was inevitable that on being elected, he would maintain a protectionist approach in trade policy, contrary to the past record of the Republican Party.
- In dealing with partner nations over trade matters, the Trump Administration has declared its preference for bilateral agreements over multi-party ones. Bilateral agreements help the US in wresting concessions from trading partners lacking in comparable economic clout, as can be seen in the KORUS Agreement and USMCA. However, the jury is open on whether bilateral negotiations will also bring results when bigger trading nations like the EU and Japan are involved.
- The US measures on steel and aluminium under Section 232 of the Trade Expansion Act (1962) have disrupted world trade and triggered a chain of WTO disputes. The investigation under the same provision on automobiles and auto components has also caused major uncertainty for supply chains on which the internationally integrated industry is particularly dependent. At the same time, no overall advantage to the US industry is discernible from measures taken or proposed to be taken. The question arises if the real objective of the Administration is to intimidate trade

partners so that it is easier for the US to wrest concessions during ongoing or future bilateral negotiations.

- The obstruction of the selection process for the AB members was initially thought to be linked to the procedural improvements sought by the US in the working of the AB. But when the US has shown no inclination to engage in the negotiations to resolve the issues raised, suspicion has arisen that there is a deeper game to take back the dispute settlement procedures to the ineffective and inefficient system that existed in the GATT 1947 era.
- Some trade policy actions of the US, such as the use of Sect. 301 against China, have been particularly disruptive as they have instigated a trade war and generated fears of a worldwide recession if they continued for a long time. However, the fact that the two powers have entered into a dialogue after the Buenos Aires G20 Summit has raised some hope.
- The major trade policy actions of the Trump Administration, taken in their totality, have created ambivalence about the US commitment to the rules based multilateral trading system.

## References


Daniels, J. (2018). Trump is giving farmers a $6 billion bailout so they can weather his trade war. CNBC, Retrieved March 28, 2019 from https://www.cnbc.com/2018/08/27/trump-farm-bailout-to-provide-6-billion-dollars-in-initial-relief.html.

Gertz, G. (2017). What will Trump's embrace of bilateralism mean for America's trade partners? [Blog post]. February 8. Retrieved March 27, 2019 from https://www.brookings.edu/blog/future-development/2017/02/08/what-will-trumps-embrace-of-bilateralism-mean-for-americas-trade-partners/.

Haddon, H. (2018). America can't move its cheese. *The Wall Street Journal*. December 17. Retrieved March 27, 2019, from https://www.wsj.com/articles/america-cant-move-its-cheese-11545042600.

Hillman, J. A. (2018). How to make the trade war even worse (Opinion), *The New York Times*, December 17. Retrieved March 27, 2019. https://www.nytimes.com/2018/12/17/opinion/trade-war-china-wto.html.

Lovely, M. E., Cohen-Setton, J., & Jung, E. (2018). *Vehicular assault: Proposed auto tariffs will hit American buyers' wallets*, *Policy Brief* No. 18–16 July, Peterson Institute of International Economics, 1750 Massachusetts Avenue, NW Washington, DC.

Miranda, Jorge. (2016). More on why granting China market economy status after December 2016 is contingent upon whether china has in fact transitioned into a market economy. *Global Trade and Customs Journal, 11*(5), 244–250.

Price Waterhouse Coopers (2017). Top suppliers: North America, Europe and the World. *Supplement to Automotive News*, June 26, 2017. Retrieved from https://www.magna.com/dics/default-source/2017-press-releases/automotive-news-top-suppliers-6–26-2017.pdf?sfvrsn=2 Accessed March 28, 2019.

Schultz, M., Dziczek, K., Chen, Y., and Swiecki, B. (2019). U.S. Consumer & Economic Impacts of U.S. Automotive Trade Policies. Center for Automotive Research, Ann Arbor, MI.

WTO (2018). Procedures to enhance transparency and strengthen notification requirements under WTO Agreements. General Council and Council for Trade in Goods. Documents JOB/GC/204 JOB/CTG/114 dated 1 November 2018.

# Chapter 5
# Trade, Investment, and the Multilateral Trading System

**Sugandha Huria and Manoj Pant**

**Abstract** The world economy now trades not in final goods or services, but components, parts, tasks and activities and this variety of trade occurs not between countries but companies/firms, the majority of which are foreign affiliates of different multinationals. This increasing inseparability between trade in goods, services, and investment overtime or the so-called *trade-services-investment nexus* calls for a common set of norms that guide their trade volumes at the multilateral level, which is presently not existing. Recent attempts by some of the world's largest trading countries to instigate protectionist policies seem to have furthered the extent of uncertainty involved in establishing a multilateral trading/investment system. To this end, the chapter emphasises on the role of bilateral/plurilateral or regional trade agreements, which have the WTO rules as their foundations, in (at least) paving a way towards multilateralism.

**Keywords** Trade · Investment · WTO · Multilateral trading/investment system

## 1 Introduction

John Stuart Mill, in his 1848 text on *Principles of Political Economy with Some of their Applications to Social Philosophy*, emphasised the role of commerce and industry in rendering the inter-country wars obsolete by strengthening and multiplying the inter-connectivity between them. The author underlined the idea that an increase in the international exchange of goods across different economies can serve as a principal guarantee for maintaining peace in the world. In a literal sense, this is precisely because gains from trade in one country are well connected to the other, and hence, trade enhances integration/interdependency amongst these trading economies and reduces the risk of conflicts. His remarks could be construed as less relevant at the

S. Huria (✉)
Jawaharlal Nehru University, New Delhi, India
e-mail: sugandhahuria@hotmail.com

M. Pant
Indian Institute of Foreign Trade, New Delhi, India
e-mail: mpant101@gmail.com; diroffice@iift.ac.in

 
R. Kathuria and P. Kukreja (eds.), *20 Years of G20*,
https://doi.org/10.1007/978-981-13-8106-5_5

time when they were made, since in less than a century, the world economy experienced three major economic downturns—the Great War (or WWI, 1914–18), the great depression of 1929 and another world war (WWII, 1939–45). However, their relevance is well evidenced post the negotiation and implementation of the *General Agreement on Tariffs and Trade* (or GATT) in 1948.

As an early step towards economic globalisation, GATT was formulated as a response to these crises in order to boost economic growth and recovery via regulating trade and commerce at least amongst its member countries. The basic idea was to establish a code of conduct that would progressively institute a shift from autonomous/unilateral to negotiated liberalisation by reducing/eliminating trade barriers on a Most Favoured Nation (or, MFN) basis and promoting what is popularly referred to as multilateralism. While the agreement could cover and regulate cross border trade in goods, the inability of GATT to expand its scope to trade in services and investment—two another propelling forces of liberalisation—led to the conclusion of the World Trade Organisation (WTO) following the Uruguay round of trade negotiations.

This was essential because by then, it was realised (both empirically and got established in theory as well (see, for example, Taussig 1931; Casas 1972; Batra 1973; Batra and Casas 1973, etc.)) that not all the stages of production are undertaken domestically in each trading country meaning thereby that trade and commerce are established by not only exchanging goods, particularly final goods, but intermediates as well. More so, the composition of trade baskets also changed for they no longer constituted only tangible commodities but services as well. Initially construed as non-tradable in nature, by then, it became quite evident that these services either get traded along with the goods in which they are embodied or in the form of direct services exports, both of which constitute a significant portion of the world trade today.[1] Lower tariffs, gradual decline in the costs of transportation and communication, rapid technological process and organisational innovations, also drastically reduced the coordination costs amongst countries (transport, logistics and supply chain services are particularly important in this regard) and accentuated the opportunities for complex international fragmentation of production activities. As a consequence, different stages of production are now located at different places in the world market. For instance, higher labour costs and heavy regulations in industrialised economies of the North have accelerated the shift through a wave of offshoring and outsourcing to countries in the South (Dadush 2015) and therefore, evidence the inter-linkages between trade in goods, services and investment as well.

The increasing association between the first two is also well documented in the relatively new and growing literature on servicification and the emergence of international supply/value chains. And, the inter-linkage between trade and investment (particularly, foreign direct investment) is what is symbolising the world trade

[1] As of 2016, trade in services constituted approximately 23% of total world trade. In fact, this share exceeded 30% in countries such as Singapore and even crossed 50% in some others such as Lebanon, Ireland, etc. (World Bank's World Development Indicators (WDI) database).

today—with a substantial portion of trade being conducted by the foreign affiliates of multinational corporations (in the form of intra-firm exchange).

Even though the establishment of the WTO marked the inclusion of services and investment related issues in the multilateral trading system via the general agreement on trade in services (or GATS) and agreements on trade related intellectual property rights, trade related investment measures (TRIPs and TRIMs, respectively), there does not (so far) exist any comprehensive (unified) multilateral framework that acknowledges and guides the link between the three.

As regards the world economy, it seems that the countries are trying to establish this by contracting more and more regional trade agreements (RTAs)—now that services trade and investment are becoming a part and path to almost all the newer trade arrangements being signed by the WTO members. However, these reciprocal trade agreements are not binding at the multilateral level. Moreover, even though the nature of trade has changed dramatically in the past few decades and so does the nature of the trade theories, now that not countries or industries but heterogenous firms trade with each other, the conventionally established 'free trade doctrine'[2] still seem to guide the formation of these agreements. But, no such theoretical anchor exists for promoting a multilateral arrangement on investment and thus, the case for such a treaty remains weak.[3] A very simple example that reveals this reality is that most of the international investment agreements (IIAs) that have been concluded so far are bilateral investment treaties (or BITs) most of which are not meant to promote but protect foreign investment and fewer than 15% are negotiated as part of other treaties, of which RTAs are one (UNCTAD Investment Hub).[4]

In spite of the fact that the WTO has taken multiple initiatives to smoothen the process of trade in goods, services and investment and also tries to ensure that countries do not resort to enormous trade-distorting practices, the recent attempts by some of the world's largest trading countries to instigate protectionist policies have furthered the extent of uncertainty involved in establishing a multilateral trading/investment system. This is precisely because the uncertainties do not only exist for the countries that are retaliating against each other, but the negative effects have started to spill over onto the other parts of the inter-connected world and have also raised doubts regarding the credibility of the rule-based WTO system. In the light of these concerns, this chapter discusses the role of RTAs and bilateral/plurilateral investment treaties as attempts to at least pave a way towards multilateralism, how far the world

[2]The popular 'Free Trade Doctrine' is guided by the assumptions of perfectly competitive product/factor markets, small open economies and the theory of the first best (For details, refer any textbook on trade theories such as Batra (1973) or Bhagwati et al. (1998)).

[3]This is because the very basis of international investment, particularly FDI, lies in the root of imperfect competition where one firm (the investor, in this case) has access to some specific asset (be it knowledge, managerial capability or some kind of specific machinery/equipment), which enables it to compete with the local firms in the host economy.

[4]This is because these RTAs are negotiated between regional groupings that involve more than just one partner, and, higher the number of partners, more difficult it is to settle on a common platform as regards investment related negotiations.

seems to have reached a consensus on this and, hence, deliberates on the future of the multilateral trading and investment system.

Subsequent sections of this chapter are organised as follows. Section 2 briefly establishes the link between goods, services trade and investment both theoretically and by citing certain empirical literature. Recognising the association between the three, the following section documents how the trade theory literature has guided the formation of bilateral and plurilateral trade and investment agreements and also attempts to verify their significance in promoting the formulation of a (unified) multilateral framework within the ambit of the WTO. The final section discusses the potential implications of the recent trade episodes on the future of the multilateral trading/investment system and concludes the chapter.

## 2 Trade in Goods, Services and Investment—*How Are They Linked*?

When trade theory started developing, majority of the trade was in final goods. Whether we talk about the Smithian variety of trade (1776), which was based on the concept of absolute advantage or the theories of comparative advantage as propounded by Ricardo (1921) or Heckscher (1919) and Ohlin (1933) that was later explained by Samuelson (1948) and Vanek (1968)—all these conventional theories portray that international exchange of commodities is mutually advantageous for all the trading economies in the world market. But this does not necessarily mean that trade benefits all. Obviously, there are both gainers and losers in any policy change (trade or rather, free trade in the present case) and if the gainers can more than compensate losers, then we call a policy change as (social) welfare enhancing in nature. Thus, we cannot neglect the role of the so-called *compensating principle* in devising the *free trade doctrine* as proposed by our classical and neo-classical trade theorists.

Nonetheless, one of the shortcomings of this literature was its assumption that all the stages of production are undertaken domestically within each economy. In other words, these theories inherently assumed existence of only non-tradable intermediate inputs and also could only explain what is known as inter-industry and not intra-industry trade. The past few decades, however, have witnessed a drastic transformation in the variety and structure of foreign trade being conducted between various economies (with trade in intermediates and the so-called two-way trade contributing a significant share in this new variety) and the structure of international production activities as well. The emergence of the internationally linked supply/value chains (or what are popularly referred to as global value chains (GVCs)) cannot be neglected in guiding this transformation. Rapid advancement in technologies, reduction in transportation and communication costs and the removal of political as well as economic barriers to trade have accentuated this process of international slicing of production activities. As a consequence, what we observe today is not trade in final goods or services but of components, parts, tasks or activities.

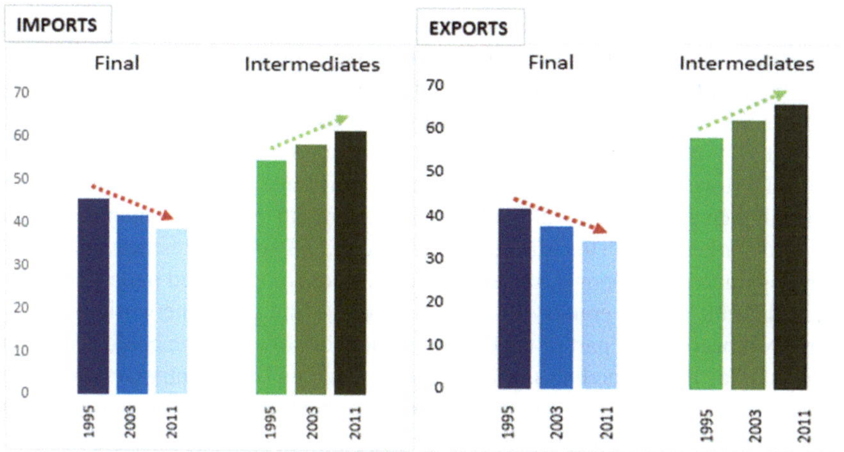


**Fig. 1** Gross imports and exports in final and intermediate goods, 1995–2011. *Source* OECD trade in value added database (2016 ed.), Authors' calculations. *Note* The calculations are done on the information available on three aggregates in the TiVA dataset viz. the OECD economies, non-OECD economies and the rest of the world

It is, however, very important to understand that GVCs or multi-stage trade in intermediates are not a new subject for trade theory/policy nor are they a concept for development of international trade. Rather, as posited by The National Board of Trade (2013), the term describes a new trade reality. In fact, the importance of this crucial association between tradable intermediate inputs and of final products, was identified by Taussig way back in 1931, and later also incorporated more systematically in trade theory models by Casas (*op. cit.*), Batra and Casas (*op. cit.*), Batra and Naqvi (1989) amongst others. But, it is only recently that statistics on trade in intermediates have become available to evidence their existence. Based on the Organisation of Economic Cooperation and Development's (OECD's) Trade In Value Added (or TiVA) database, both the left and right panels of Fig. 1 show how, in the past two decades, intermediate trade has dominated the total world trade (exports and imports).

Moreover, this increase in the network of trade is happening not between countries but companies/firms (Cusmano et al. 2010; Gereffi and Lee 2012), majority of which are foreign affiliates of different MNCs, and thus, it can be easily stated that trade and FDI are not two different activities.[5] In fact, they are becoming increasingly entwined over time with the international expansion of these supply chains, with about 80% of the world trade taking place through FDI only (World Economic Forum 2013). As it is, by its very definition, it is clear that foreign direct investment, as distinct from foreign portfolio investment, doesn't just include the transfer of foreign capital from the source to the host country, but also the transfer of know-how in the form of some advanced technology, managerial expertise, etc. An investor in the parent country, thus, decides to switch to domestic production in the other country (i.e., to

[5]See Chap. 8 of Pant and Srivastava (2015) for a survey of literature in this regard.

do FDI), when either the entry barriers like tariffs make its exports uncompetitive or when such a move becomes necessary to internalise these owner-specific advantages. Since the world economy has already been experiencing a gradual (global) average decline in the rates of tariffs post the conclusion of GATT and its successor, the WTO (see Sect. 3, Fig. 5), more or less, it is now the second motive that is triggering the rise in FDI flows over time. This means that even if trade is free, but FDI flows are restricted, then also it is very difficult for an economy to expand its integration with the world market today. This is because, absence of FDI not only restricts the flow of technology into this economy, but also affects its technology-based trade and makes it very difficult for the country to become a part of the global network of supply chains. Not becoming a part of the expanding network of exchange could also mean restricted trade in intermediates, which, in turn, could make a country comparatively less competitive in production of a commodity (or commodities) in which it used to enjoy comparative advantage earlier.

It, thus, seems reasonable to conclude that one cannot separate the analysis of trade from that of FDI. In fact, as per the Scandinavian school of thought, FDI is actually the last stage of involvement of an international firm as it moves from export (imports) to licensing of technology use to local firms to FDI. Hence, FDI is a composite consisting of trade in commodities, services and technology, and therefore, it seems necessary for even the economies around the world to harmonise their trade and FDI policies. Trade policy could indicate what corresponding FDI policies may need to be tweaked especially in the context of commodity and service exports. This will not only help in future economic policy adjustments but will also fuel greater involvement in the international supply networks. However, at the same time, it is equally essential to recognise the fact that this association is not very straight forward and could vary across economies, sectors, industries, markets, type of commodities/services and investment, etc. This is the reason why the existing literature debates on whether trade and FDI are complementary in nature or act as substitutes to each other.[6]

The other important relationship that requires attention is the rising trade in services and its growing association with trade in goods and investment. As noted by the WTO, over the past two decades, trade in services has become the most dynamic segment of foreign trade, growing more quickly in comparison to that of merchandise trade. Here, the role of developing countries in determining this rapid growth cannot be neglected, with their share in world trade rising from a quarter to over one-third during the period 2005–17 (Fig. 2).

Not only the direct services trade has gained momentum in these years, the indirect contribution of the sector as a key input in other downstream sectors' production and exports has played no less important role in organisation of the production process as value chains. This is evident from the fact that as per the gross trade data available in the International Monetary Fund-Balance of Payment Statistics (IMF-BOPs), the sector contributes to only about one-fifth to one-fourth of the total foreign trade, while its contribution based on the value-added statistics (OECD TiVA data, for example)

[6] See Pant and Srivastava (*op. cit.*).

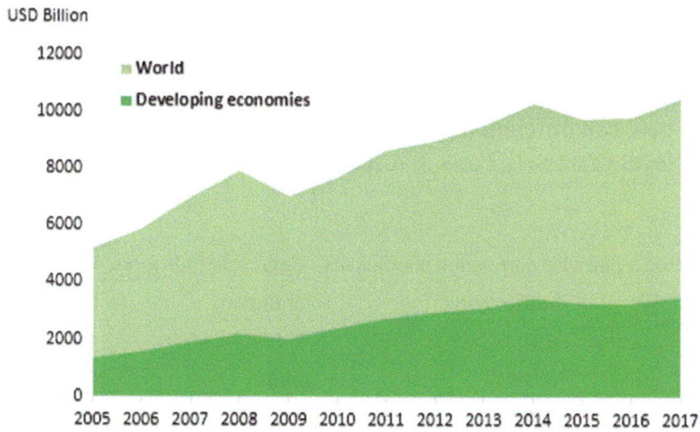


**Fig. 2** Share of developing countries in world services trade, 2005–2017. *Source* WTO-UNCTAD-ITC trade in services dataset

amounts to about 50% of the total world trade (Miroudot and Cadestin 2017). In a recent study, Lanz and Maurer (2015) also estimated that services value added account for about one-third of manufacturing sector exports in developed countries and around 26% of manufacturing exports from developing countries. In terms of total manufacturing demand as well, the contribution of services is no less than 30% on an average for the economies covered under the OECD TiVA dataset (OECD Stat 2015).

Transportation, communication, logistics and other related services are particularly important in this regard as they assume a coordinating role in managing the complex production networks. Similarly, the role of business services and other complex services as R&D in raising the productive efficiency of firms cannot be neglected. In fact, upgrading in manufacturing sector is now increasingly associated with what is popularly referred to as the process of *servicification*, where manufacturing units purchase, produce, sell and even export services.[7] A growing literature on this theme indicates that servicified firms are more productive, earn higher profits, export more and also have a higher probability of entering into the export markets vis-à-vis their non-servicified counterparts. More so, as argued by Taglioni and Winkler (2016), an increasing trend of foreign backward linkages of value added from abroad is also associated with a greater participation in global value chains. In other words, even imported services are linked to better international performance of the domestic firms.

Last, but not the least, the overlap between services trade and foreign direct investment is already well established as stated in the General Agreement on Trade In Services. FDI is mode-3 of supply of services in the WTO parlance, and, in fact, it accommodates majority of the services trade in the world market, reflecting its crucial

[7] See for example, Goldar et al. (2017), Hoekman and Shephard (2017), Miroudot and Cadestin (*op. cit.*) amongst others.

role in driving the global supply of services, transferring managerial and technical know-how and improving the capacity of economies to participate in GVCs (WTO).

For a quick empirical verification, we also compute Pearson's pairwise correlation coefficients between different trade and FDI indicators, both at the aggregate and at the sectoral level (Tables 1, 2 and 3, respectively).

**Table 1** Pearson's pairwise correlation coefficients—aggregate indicators, World (1970–2017)

| % shares in GDP | Total exports | Total imports | Total trade |
|---|---|---|---|
| Inward FDI | 0.793* | 0.774* | 0.785* |
| | (0.000) | (0.000) | (0.000) |
| Outward FDI | 0.785* | 0.765* | 0.776* |
| | (0.000) | (0.000) | (0.000) |
| Total FDI | 0.794* | 0.774* | 0.785* |
| | (0.000) | (0.000) | (0.000) |

*Source* UNCTAD (FDI), WDI (Trade); Authors' calculations
*Note p*-values are reported in parentheses, *indicates significance at 1% level

**Table 2** Pearson's pairwise correlation coefficients—merchandise, services trade and FDI, World (1970–2017)

| % shares in GDP | Merchandise exports | Merchandise imports | Merchandise trade | Services exports | Services imports | Services trade |
|---|---|---|---|---|---|---|
| Inward FDI | 0.741* | 0.749* | 0.762* | 0.780* | 0.679* | 0.733* |
| | (0.000) | (0.000) | (0.000) | (0.000) | (0.000) | (0.000) |
| Outward FDI | 0.736* | 0.746* | 0.763* | 0.760* | 0.654* | 0.718* |
| | (0.000) | (0.000) | (0.000) | (0.000) | (0.000) | (0.000) |
| Total FDI | 0.743* | 0.752* | 0.767* | 0.776* | 0.672* | 0.731* |
| | (0.000) | (0.000) | (0.000) | (0.000) | (0.000) | (0.000) |

*Source* UNCTAD (FDI), WDI (Trade); Authors' calculations
*Note p*-values are reported in parentheses, *indicates significance at 1% level

**Table 3** Pearson's pairwise correlation coefficients—merchandise and services trade, World (1970–2017)

| % shares in GDP | Merchandise exports | Merchandise imports | Merchandise trade |
|---|---|---|---|
| Services exports | 0.940* | 0.939* | 0.945* |
| | (0.000) | (0.000) | (0.000) |
| Services imports | 0.943* | 0.938* | 0.937* |
| | (0.000) | (0.000) | (0.000) |
| Services trade | 0.937* | 0.932* | 0.940* |
| | (0.000) | (0.000) | (0.000) |

*Source* WDI; Authors' calculations
*Note p*-values are reported in parentheses, *indicates significance at 1% level

All the correlation coefficients are positive thereby suggesting a complementary relationship between goods trade, services trade and FDI, at least at the two levels of aggregation for the world economy as a whole. Even though these estimates only portray an indicative association (and do not establish any causal relation) between the three, however, their significance implies that an increase in FDI may lead to an increase in manufacturing/services trade and/or vice-a-versa. And, so is the case with manufacturing and services trade—a rise in one may propel another and/or vice-a-versa.

The bottom line is that any regulation that restricts any of these three forces of globalisation, will ultimately have a bearing on the other two. In fact, given their increasing inseparability over time (with greater fragmentation of production activities and servicification, servitization), it is not surprising that many of the issues that emerge with the trade-investment-services nexus have to do with policy coherence and thus, call for a common set of norms that guide their trade volumes at the national and at the multilateral level as well.

## 3 Trade Agreements and Investment Treaties—*Building or Stumbling Blocks to Multilateralism*?

Within the ambit of the WTO, GATT frames the guidelines for goods trade based on the principles of Most Favoured Nation and National Treatment, while the guidelines for investment related to trade in goods are detailed in TRIMs. Basically, the latter does not regulate investments but prohibits measures that violate the national treatment (Article III) and quantitative restrictions' requirements (on imports and exports, Article XI) of the General Agreement on Tariffs and Trade or the measures that create any type of restriction/distortion for trade in goods. The third is GATS, which is the only set of rules regulating international trade in services at the multilateral level. To the extent, this agreement regulates movement of natural persons and covers FDI in services (Modes 2 and 3, respectively), its provisions have a direct bearing on matters related to both investment protection and liberalisation (Sauve 1998). In fact, it could be construed as the only multilateral agreement, which from its very inception characterises FDI as a mode of international supply of services and hence, recognises the association between the two (if not with commodity trade). However, it is also worth noting that not all services covered by the GATS are opened to competition. The list varies from member to member as specified in their schedule of commitments (Article XVII(1)),[8] but the principle of MFN (Article II(1)) applies to all. Thus, despite the fact that the three forces are invariably linked to each other as established in Sect. 2, they are still regulated by different agreements and that to with different degrees of comprehensiveness.

[8]This is because, unlike GATT, GATS is based on the positive list approach.

The question then is how to harmonise the (goods/services) trade and (goods/services) investment related policies and formulate a comprehensive (unified) multilateral framework that acknowledges the association between them?

Efforts to integrate trade and investment related policies have a long-drawn history even at the multilateral level, and not just at the bilateral/plurilateral level. Even before the conclusion of the General Agreement on Tariffs and Trade, the interconnectivity between the two was first considered in the Havana Charter of 1948 that proposed the establishment of the International Trade Organisation (ITO), which was meant to be the third of the so-called Bretton Woods Institutions after WWII. The charter explicitly provided for issues related to FDI and foreign investors such as those related to obligations of the host economies to extend National Treatment and MFN status, etc. However, it never came into being due to opposition from the United States congress to other provisions under the charter related to regulation of anti-competitive policies of private businesses.

The next is OECD's attempt to formulate a Multilateral Agreement on Investment (or MAI) that was initiated during the 1960s (Henderson 1999). The objective was to further the FDI liberalisation process and to extend to foreign investment the same liberal treatment that already existed for international trade in commodities. As detailed in Henderson (*op. cit.*) and further noted in Nunnenkamp and Pant (2003), the MAI represented the most ambitious attempts taken thus far in this regard. However, even though the agreement was supposed to reduce the transaction costs of undertaking FDI to a large extent, especially for small foreign investors, and also had representatives from the World Bank, the WTO and the IMF, the attempt failed during the late 90s. Among the multiple factors that led to the breakdown of this agreement, while some related to the unwillingness of various countries (in particular, developing economies) to commit to broad definition of investment (as in the North American Free Trade Agreement or NAFTA), others related to clauses like cultural exceptions, dispute settlement and disagreement on inclusion of the clause related to labour and environmental standards, taxation, etc. (Dymond 1999; UNCTAD 1999).

The World Bank, in 1966, also took an initiative by setting up a multilateral specialised institution named as the International Centre for Settlement of Investment Disputes (ICSID). The aim was to encourage smooth international flow of investment and facilitate settlement of disputes between governments/governments and investors. In fact, 1970s also witnessed another important development in this context. United Nations Commission on Transnational Corporations and a centre on TNCs (UNCTC) was established in 1974 with an objective to devise a code of conduct on TNCs' operations and to limit corporate power through provision of guidelines to control their activities in the host countries. As with the previous attempts, contrasting views of the developing country members (who demanded a legally binding set of rules to govern the activities of the TNCs) with that of the developed country representatives (who were in favour of a voluntary code of principles), eventually led to the collapse of the system in early 1990s (Moran 2009).

The series of failed attempts, were, ultimately followed by the inclusion of TRIMs and GATS at the multilateral level. Even though these two agreements cover several investment related provisions and also acknowledged the differences in compliance' capacities between the developing and developed nations, however, as noted by Read (1999), they lack appropriate measures relating to expropriation, compensation and subrogation. Provisions for investor to state dispute settlement mechanism are also not covered in the two. Apart from these, two other WTO initiatives that at least provide minimal standards of protection for investment are Trade Related Intellectual Property Rights (TRIPS) and Dispute Settlement Undertaking (DSU). According to Article XXIII of GATS, all disputes related to the agreement are to be governed by the DSU. Even though the latter contains the usual provisions for negotiations, consultation, arbitration and compensation, it also lacks provision for investor-state dispute settlement mechanism (Sciarra 1998). On the other hand, TRIPs regulates the protection of intellectual property through the WTO.

Thus, there does not so far seem to exist any multilateral frame that guides both trade and investment and facilitate the association between the two. In fact, the history well establishes how difficult it has always been to attempt to contract a multilateral agreement even on only investment related issues. One of the theoretical reasons that dictate this failure could be the inability to attain an optimum outcome in the presence of imperfection in the economy, which actually forms the very basis of the presence of multinational corporations/firms.[9] Other reasons, as stated in the study by Nunnenkamp and Pant (*op. cit.*) that hinder the processing of a multilateral framework on investment are one, unlike commodity trade, it is always not possible to associate multi-national activity or FDI with a particular country(ies) and, two, multilateral attempts to constrain a country's sovereignty through redefinition of its jurisdiction (as in the case of investor to state dispute settlement) would be contested not only by developing but by their industrialised counterparts as well. This is because such a move guarantees those advantages to foreign firms that are not available to the locals, and hence, could lead to what can be called as 'reverse discrimination'.

The literature often argues that the absence of comprehensive norms guiding foreign investment, more importantly at the multilateral level, led to the proliferation of the so-called international investment agreements (or IIAs) by the trading countries at least in the pre-WTO period. As defined by UNCTAD, these IIAs can take two important forms—one is of a Bilateral Investment Treaty (BIT), which represents an agreement between two countries regarding promotion and protection of investments made by investors from respective countries in each other's territory. These agreements lay out various principles related to treatment of foreign investors, transfer of their funds, expropriation and mechanisms for dispute settlements. In fact, the great majority of the IIAs are BITs only—out of the 3766 treaties that have been signed so far, more than 3200 are bilateral treaties only. Even more, most of the countries are now signatory to at least one investment agreement, and some of them have contracted more than hundred such IIAS so far (Zhan 2016).

Considering the geographical distribution of these agreements, the upper panel of Fig. 3 suggests that most of these are contracted either between developing countries or between developed and developing countries. Moreover, since 2010, the largest

[9]See Footnote 3 for explanation.

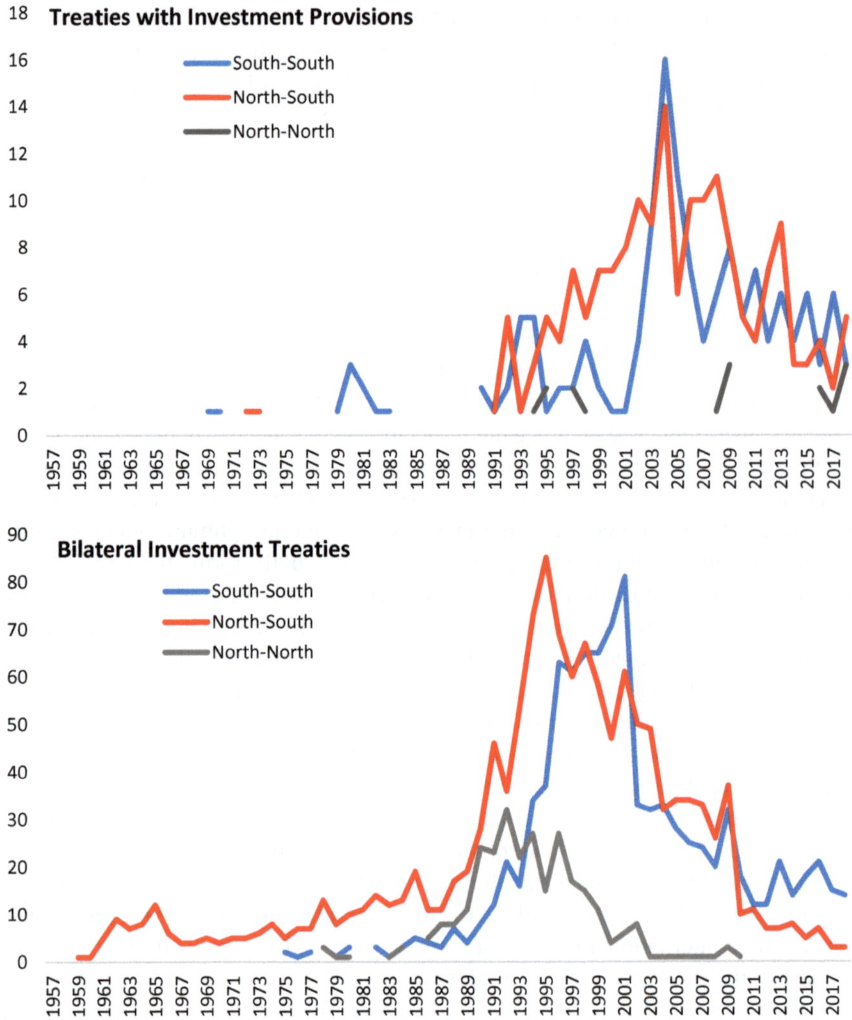


**Fig. 3** Number of international investment agreements signed per year. *Source* UNCTAD investment hub. *Note* The vertical axis, in each panel, represents the number of IIAs signed in a year

share of BITs has been an intra-developing country (or South–South) affair only. As a matter of fact, this clearly demonstrates the desire of their governments to facilitate protection and promotion of FDI, which is generally presumed to be associated with higher economic development and offers access to internationally available technologies and managerial know-how.

To the extent these treaties provide foreign investors with a clear legal framework so as to reduce uncertainty related to treatment of FDI (both pre and post entry) in potential host countries, they can very well be construed as (at least) reducing the transaction costs for them. However, this does not mean that a country should contract multiple such agreements, because that may even come at a cost by reducing transparency and making it rather difficult for the investors (particularly small firms engaging in FDI) to collect and evaluate essential information. Apart from this, some other major limitations of bilateral arrangements, as noted in the previous studies, are that they lack protection against violations of intellectual property rights (IPR), and in discretionary interventions by subnational authorities of the host countries that are not prevented by BITs.

The literature also seems to be inconclusive as regards the question of whether these treaties are a cause or a consequence of FDI (and higher trade as well) between different countries. Many of them seem to protect FDI once it has already been allowed, reserving admission to the discretion of the host country (Crawford and Kotschwar 2018).[10] While there exist some studies that portray the significance of these IIAs in attracting higher FDI flows (for instance, Neumayer and Spess 2005; Bhasin and Manocha 2016, etc.), there are others, which show that BITs do not necessarily represent a sufficient condition for inducing more of foreign investment, rather the amount of inward FDI is largely determined by factors other than these agreements (Hallward-Driemeier 2003; UNCTAD 1998a, b). More so, Blonigen and Davis, in their 2002 study, have even argued that in certain cases, formation of such treaties may actually lead to a reduction in international investment in case the agreements are meant to mitigate tax evasion rather than to fuel FDI flows.

Nevertheless, the countries around the world are still continuing to sign new BITs, though the rate has tapered off to a great extent over the past one decade and a half (upper panel of Fig. 3). UNCTAD's 2018 World Investment report (WIR 2018) also states that the number of such agreements concluded in 2017 was the lowest since the early 1980s. Moreover, for the first time in the history of these agreements, the world experienced higher number of terminations in comparison to the number of newly negotiated IIAs. One obvious reason for their declining attractiveness was the inclusion of TRIMs agreement within the WTO in the year 1995. Other than this, in a more recent study, Voon et al. (2014) have noted that several countries are terminating their BITs either due to unexpected outcomes in certain investor-state dispute settlement cases, or because these nations are now concluding wider economic partnership agreements. The latter actually represents the second category of International Investment Agreements, other than the BITs. Often referred to as *treaties with investment provisions* (or TIP), this category includes broad economic agreements such as a free trade or a regional trade agreement (RTA) that incorporate obligations commonly found in BITs, or treaties with limited investment related provisions, etc. The rise in the number of such agreements are also reflected in lower panel of Fig. 3.

In fact, in the absence of any comprehensive multilateral framework on trade and investment, it seems that the countries around the world are now trying to establish that by signing more and more of RTAs only (see Figs. 4 and 6). From the perspective of the WTO, RTAs allow its members to deviate from their MFN obligations with

[10]The BITs of the United States of America and Canada are exceptions to this category.

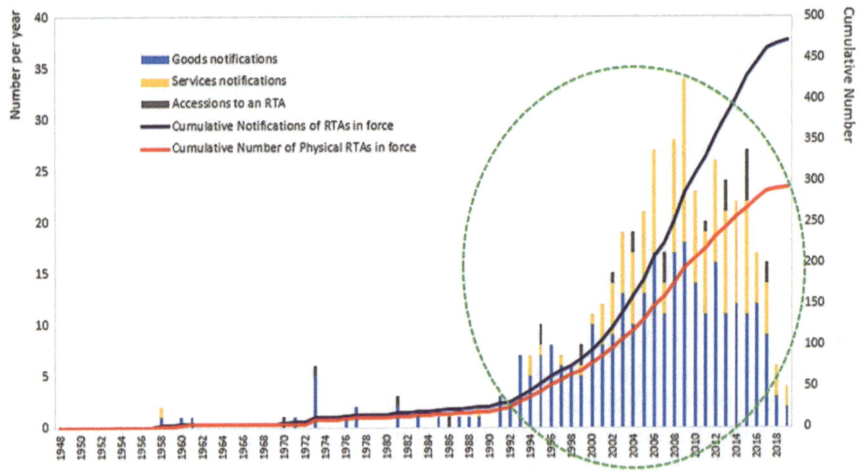


**Fig. 4** RTA in goods and services, 1948–2018. *Source* WTO Secretariat. *Note* Notifications of RTAs: goods, services and accessions to an RTA are counted separately. Physical RTAs: goods, services and accessions to an RTA are counted together

the objective of pursuing deeper liberalisation than at the multilateral level (Article XXIV of GATT, Article V of GATS). Even though, initially, majority of the RTAs were confined to goods and used to offer reciprocal (phased) reduction/elimination of tariff and non-tariff barriers on partners' imports, their definition, scope and coverage have broadened over time. In other words, through their participation in regional trade arrangements, the WTO members now also elaborate on some of the core disciplines of the multilateral trading system and develop regulatory provisions in areas beyond the WTO's mandate, of which investment is one. To this effect, these *deeper* trade agreements are now popularly referred to as the WTO-plus agreements.

Even though, it seems plausible to comment that BITs have been considered as a comparatively straightforward and simpler solution to define the rules guiding investment because contracting negotiations between two parties is always easier (or at least less complicated) than between multiple, diverse set of players, Fig. 6 shows that the preferential trade agreements have also started gaining attractiveness as an alternative platform to incorporate investment provisions along with trade related rules, at least since the early 2000s. More so, as noted by Crawford and Kotschwar (*op. cit.*), the average number of investment provisions in these preferential agreements has also increased since the formation of the WTO. While agreements entering into force in the initial four years from 1995, included (on an average) only 24 provisions, those that came into force during the period 2010–17, averaged 27.1. The study also notes that the negotiation of an investment chapter in NAFTA during the early 90s actually provided a template for extending the scope of a typical BIT from just investment protection to its liberalisation as well as regulation. Many agreements that incorporate measures related to services trade, also have a distinct chapter on investment that goes beyond the mode 3 provisions of the general agreement on trade in services and regulates a broader investment framework that applies to commodities/goods, IP and, (depending on the definition of investment), to portfolio investment as well. In fact, in the case of those RTAs that cover only goods and services without a distinct chapter on investment, some of them (for instance, GCC-Singapore, US-Bahrain, etc.) make reference to the existing BIT(s) between the contracting parties.

On the contrary, BITs are more likely to incorporate more comprehensive rules related to investment protection and tend to provide for investor-state dispute settlement mechanism more often than investment chapters of trade agreements.[11]

The other point to note is that even these regional trade agreements are not binding at the multilateral level. Also, like with BITs, RTAs are no less a controversial affair. One such controversy relates to the empirical reality that the world economy started experiencing an exponential growth in the number of such agreements at a time when world average tariffs were already low (i.e. post 1992, see Fig. 5). As is widely known now, there exists a plethora of both theoretical and empirical literature as well on the debate regarding whether RTAs are building or stumbling blocks to multilateralism. Empirically also, very few RTAs have shown to be beneficial for the member countries and the most successful ones are those where, before the conclusion of RTAs, countries were already trading largely among themselves.[12] Thus, it seems that not economics, but political economy is what is guiding the economic integration of the world market today. However, to the extent, RTAs, unlike BITs, provide a platform to place investment within a broader trade and investment framework, it seems plausible to conclude that these plurilateral investment treaties, when they include a comprehensive treatment of investment issues, could be considered to (at least by definition) complement a multilateral framework and the WTO as well (Fig. 6).

## 4 Concluding Remarks—*Recent Episodes of Trade Wars and the Future of Multilateralism*

The year 2018—or what can be referred to as the year of '*Trump-tariffs*'—witnessed a closer to a full-scale trade war involving the world's two largest trading economies viz. China and the US imposing multiple reciprocal rounds of tariffs on each other's imports—with threats of more of the same. While all this began with US's announcement of an increase in its import duties on steel and aluminium items on national security grounds, followed by subsequent tariffs on its imports from China worth USD 250 billion (based on section 301 of the Trade Act of 1974), the country's actions actually instigated a series of protectionist stance being adopted by various economies all around the world. China, of course, responded in kind, by raising the tariffs rates on American goods worth more than USD 110 Billion. As per the latest

[11] UNCTAD (2006).

[12] Here, a direct reference can be made to the so-called natural trading partner hypothesis as explained by Wonnacott and Lutz in their 1989 study.

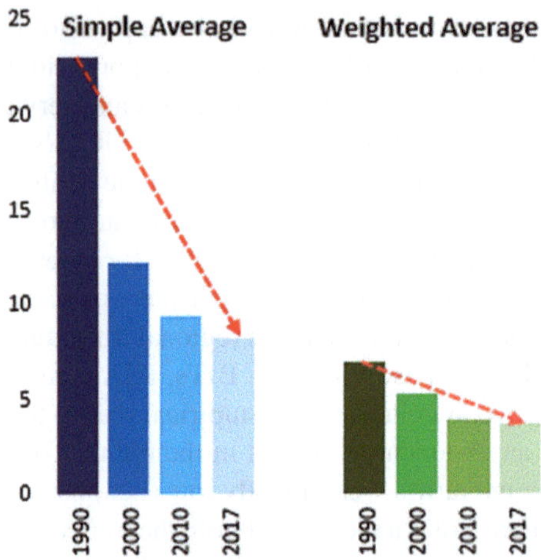


**Fig. 5** MFN tariffs (simple average and weighted average)—all products, World. *Source* UNCTAD's trade analysis information system's database. *Note* Average, here, has been taken across all the harmonised system of classification's 98 chapters and all the countries covered in the UNCTAD database

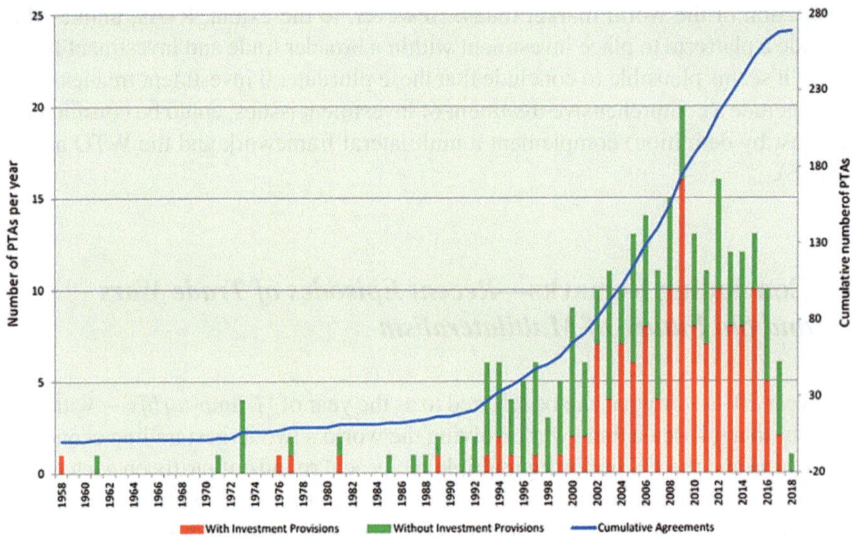


**Fig. 6** Preferential trade agreements with investment provisions. *Source* Adapted from Crawford and Kotschwar (*op. cit.*); *Primary source* WTO RTA database

WTO trade monitoring report (WTO OMCC 2018), the G20 economies (of which China and the US are a part) applied 39 new trade restrictive measures including stricter customs procedures, higher tariffs, taxes/export duties, etc. during the review period that ended in May of 2018. In fact, a year before, US even withdrew its partnership from the 12-nation Trans Pacific Partnership (TPP) agreement.

While it seems that all these events involve only a handful of economies, yet their effects appeared to have ruptured the entire world economic order in a short span of only one year. The concern goes even deeper, in that many now fear that the existing multilateral system (or the WTO) may become abraded by exceptions, discriminatory trading arrangements, and by exploitation of various trade measures and distortions that are not yet covered by its rules. One major reason as to why this is happening is because the economic activities of various countries are now highly integrated with each other. As is established in Sect. 2, fragmentation of production activities, rising trends of offshoring and outsourcing and rapid expansion in the activities of the MN firms have made economies so much interdependent on each other that a disturbance in one spill overs onto the others as well. Consequently, these measures and countermeasures resulting from steel and aluminium tariffs imposed by the US, may not only impact the retailers who sell goods from all over the globe, or say, manufacturers of automobiles who would be forced to raise their prices to deal with the higher cost of intermediate inputs of steel/aluminium, consumers—who are always the ultimate losers from trade wars, but would also affect the markets of other products in this integrated setup. In essence, this means that even though adopting a beggar-thy-neighbour policy stance, may lead to some short-term gains for the participating economies, but would ultimately generate longer-term world-wide inefficiencies, an effect of which may fall on to those who initiated the crises as well. Not only trade but jobs/employment, GDP, purchasing power, productive-efficiency, etc.—all that were created as a by-product of higher trade, may also get disrupted.

In such a case, for global commerce to thrive with certainty, it is essentially very important to have a system, a mandate that prevents economies from adopting such policies by framing enforceable obligations. At a time, when the world already fears the loss of credibility of such a system, it seems plausible to emphasise the role of bilateral/plurilateral or regional agreements as insurance against much greater loss of trade and harmony in the world market. In fact, these so-called sub-multilateral arrangements, which of course have the WTO rules as their foundations, can provide a patchwork of guidelines and mechanisms and at least pave a way towards multilateral trading/investment system.

## References

Batra, R. N. (1973). *Studies in the pure theory of international trade*. Berlin: Springer.

Batra, R. N., & Casas, F. R. (1973). Intermediate products and the pure theory of international trade: A Neo-Hecksher-Ohlin framework. *The American Economic Review, 63*(3), 297–311.

Batra, R. N., & Naqvi, N. (1989). Non-traded and intermediate goods and the theory of protection. *European Economic Review, 33*(4), 721–735.

Bhagwati, J. N., Panagariya, A., & Srinivasan, T. N. (1998). *Lectures on international trade*. Cambridge: MIT press.

Bhasin, N., & Manocha, R. (2016). Do bilateral investment treaties promote FDI inflows? Evidence from India. *Vikalpa, 41*(4), 275–287.

Blonigen, B. A., & Davies, R. B. (2002). *Do bilateral tax treaties promote foreign direct investment?* No. w8834. National Bureau of Economic Research.

Casas, F. R. (1972). The theory of intermediate products, technical change and growth. *Journal of International Economics, 2*(2), 189–200.

Crawford, J. A., & Kotschwar, B. (2018). *Investment provisions in preferential trade agreements: Evolution and current trends*. WTO Staff Working Paper No. ERSD-2018-14.

Cusmano, L., Mancusi, M. L., & Morrison, A. (2010). Globalization of production and innovation: How outsourcing is reshaping an advanced manufacturing area. *Regional Studies, 44*(3), 235–252.

Dadush, U. (2015). *WTO accessions and trade multilateralism*. Cambridge: Cambridge University Press.

Dymond, W. A. (1999). The MAI: A sad and melancholy tale. In F. O. Hampson, M. Hart, & M. Rudner (Eds.), *Canada among nations*. Oxford: Oxford University Press.

Gereffi, G., & Lee, J. (2012). Why the world suddenly cares about global supply chains. *Journal of supply chain management, 48*(3), 24–32.

Goldar, B., Banga, R., & Banga, K. (2017). India policy forum. http://www.ncaer.org/Events/IPF-2017/IPF-2017-Goldar-Banga-Banga-Conf-version.pdf.

Hallward-Driemeier, M. (2003). *Do bilateral investment treaties attract FDI?: Only a bit… and they could bite*. Washington, DC: World Bank, Development Research Group, Investment Climate.

Heckscher, E. F. (1919). *The effect of foreign trade on the distribution of income*.

Henderson, D. (1999). *The multilateral agreement on investment: A story and its lessons*. Wellington: New Zealand Business Roundtable.

Hoekman, B., & Shepherd, B. (2017). Services productivity, trade policy and manufacturing exports. *The World Economy, 40*(3), 499–516.

IMF BOPs.

Lanz, R., & Maurer, A. (2015). *Services and global value chains: Some evidence on servicification of manufacturing and services networks*. WTO Staff Working Paper No. ERSD-2015-03.

Mill, J. S. (1848). *Principles of political economy with some of their applications to social philosophy, 1857* (pp. 467–474). Manchester: George Routledge and Sons.

Miroudot, S., & Cadestin, C. (2017). *Services in global value chains: From inputs to value-creating activities*. OECD Trade Policy Papers, No. 197. Paris: OECD Publishing. http://dx.doi.org/10.1787/465f0d8b-en.

Moran, T. H. (2009). The United Nations and transnational corporations: A review and a perspective. *Transnational Corporations, 18*(2), 91–113.

National Board of Trade. (2013). *Global value chains and developing countries an introduction*. Sweden: Kommerskollegium.

Neumayer, E., & Spess, L. (2005). Do bilateral investment treaties increase foreign direct investment to developing countries? *World Development, 33*(10), 1567–1585.

Nunnenkamp, P., & Pant, M. (2003). *Why the case for a multilateral agreement on investment is weak*. Kiel Discussion Papers 400. Kiel: Institute for World Economics.

OECD. Stat. Organisation of Economic Cooperation and Development. Retrieved February 17, 2019, from https://stats.oecd.org/.

Ohlin, B. (1933). *International and interregional trade*. Cambridge, MA: Harvard Economic Studies.

Pant, M., & Srivastava, D. (2015). *FDI in India: History, policy and the Asian perspective*. New Delhi: Orient BlackSwan.

Read, P. (1999). International investment in the WTO: Prospects and challenges in the shadow of the MAI. www.bond.edu.au/law/blr/vol11-2/Read.doc.

Ricardo, D. (1921). *The first six chapters of the principles of political economy and taxation of David Ricardo, 1817*. New York: Macmillan.
Samuelson, P. A. (1948). International trade and the equalisation of factor prices. *The Economic Journal, 58*(230), 163–184.
Sauve, P. (1998). *Multilateral attempts at investment rule making: Why so difficult?*. Mimeo: Harvard University.
Sciarra, V. P. (1998). The world trade organisation: Services, investment and dispute resolution. *International Lawyer, 32*(3), 9–23.
Smith, A. (1776). *An inquiry into the wealth of nations* (pp. 1–11). London: Strahan and Cadell.
Taglioni, D., & Winkler, D. (2016). *Making global value chains work for development*. Washington, DC: The World Bank.
Taussig, F. (1931). *The tariff history of the United States*. New York: GP Putnam's Sons.
Trade in Value Added (TiVA) database. Organisation of Economic Cooperation and Development. Retrieved November 7, 2017, from https://stats.oecd.org/index.aspx?queryid=75537.
UNCTAD. Investment policy hub. Retrieved February 16, 2019, from https://investmentpolicyhub.unctad.org/.
UNCTAD. Trade Analysis Information System (TRAINS). Retrieved February 16, 2019, from https://unctad.org/en/pages/ditc/trade-analysis/non-tariff-measures/ntms-trains.aspx.
UNCTAD. (1998a). *Bilateral investment treaties in the mid-1990s*. New York: United Nations.
UNCTAD. (1998b). *World investment report: Trends and determinants*. New York: United Nations.
UNCTAD. (1999). *Lessons from the MAI*. New York: United Nations.
UNCTAD. (2006). *Investment provisions in economic integration agreements*. New York and Geneva: United Nations.
UNCTAD. (2018). *World investment report: Investment and new industrial policies*. Geneva: United Nations.
Vanek, J. (1968). The factor proportions theory: The n—factor case. *Kyklos, 21*(4), 749–756.
Voon, T., Mitchell, A., & Munro, J. (2014). Parting ways: the impact of mutual termination of investment treaties on investor rights. *ICSID Review, 29*(2), 451–473.
Wonnacott, P., & Lutz, M. (1989). Is there a case for free trade areas? *Free Trade Areas and US Trade Policy, 59*, 84.
World development indicators. The World Bank. Retrieved February 15, 2019, from https://data.worldbank.org/data-catalog/world-development-indicators.
World Economic Forum. (2013). *Foreign direct investment as a key driver for trade, growth and prosperity: The case for multilateral agreement on investment*. Geneva: World Economic Forum.
WTO OMC (2018). *Report on G20 trade measures*. Geneva.
WTO RTA database. WTO. Retrieved November 9, 2017, from https://rtais.wto.org/UI/PublicMaintainRTAHome.aspx.
WTO. WTO-UNCTAD-ITC annual trade in services dataset. Retrieved February 16, 2019, from https://www.wto.org/english/res_e/statis_e/trade_datasets_e.htm.
Zhan, J. X. (2016). International investment rule-making: Trends, challenges and way forward. In K. Singh, & B. Ilge (Eds.), *Rethinking bilateral investment treaties: Critical issues and policy choices* (pp. 17–27). New Delhi: Both Ends, Madhyam, Centre for Research on Multinational Corporations.

# Part III
# Future of Work

# Chapter 6
# Technological Change and the Future of Work—Some Issues from a Developing Country Perspective

**Kim Jurgensen and Imraan Valodia**

**Abstract** The paper examines the challenges and opportunities for developing countries that may emanate from the fourth industrial revolution. The paper argues that there is very little concrete evidence to suggest that the new artificial intelligence and machine learning based technologies will necessarily destroy large number of jobs. In fact, the evidence that does exist suggests that the impact on total employment will not be nearly as extensive as has been suggested. In some economies and some sectors, we can expect employment to grow. In most developing countries, a large proportion, if not the majority, of workers are employed in the informal economy. There has been no assessment of the likely impacts of the fourth industrial revolution on the informal economy. It is also important to consider the potential of new technology to advance gender equality—for example by improving working conditions in areas such as the care economy, where most women are employed. The potential of the fourth industrial revolution to place a higher value of care work, and to reshape the distribution of unpaid work are important issues that need to be considered.

## 1 Introduction

Technological change is a continuous process that affects all aspects of economic and social life. A collection of technological change processes which effect deep-seated and fundamental changes in social and economic life is sometimes referred to as a technological revolution. The industrial revolution was one such set of events. In recent times, the concept of the 4th industrial revolution (4IR) has gained prominence and is now the focus of much debate. In this article, we discuss this concept, and raise a number of issues which need to be addressed from a developing country perspective. Given that the debate and literature on these issues has been dominated

The original version of this book was revised: Missing abstracts of chapters 3, 6, 8, 9 and 11 have now been included. The correction to this book can be found at https://doi.org/10.1007/978-981-13-8106-5_12

K. Jurgensen · I. Valodia (✉)
Faculty of Commerce, Law and Management, University of Witwatersrand, Johannesburg, South Africa
e-mail: imraan.valodia@wits.ac.za



R. Kathuria and P. Kukreja (eds.), *20 Years of G20*,
https://doi.org/10.1007/978-981-13-8106-5_6

by considerations in the developed world, there is an urgent need carefully to consider its impacts on developing economies: because the structure of these economies, especially the nature of the labour market, is so different, the likely impact of the 4IR may also be quite different. We specifically focus on the possible implications on inequality and labour markets in developing countries.

The third industrial revolution saw information technology and electronics being used to automate production and while the 4th industrial revolution (4th IR) builds on this it is differentiated by the speed of development and scope of its impact. Developments in artificial intelligence, the Internet Of Things, Artificial Intelligence, robotics, automated vehicles, 3-D printing, nanotechnology, biotechnology, quantum computing, materials science and energy storage, coupled with how many people have access to some form of technology, means there are few aspects of our lives which will not be touched by the 4th IR.

## 2 Inequality

There is now some consensus in the economic development literature that while globalisation has for the most part generated lower levels of poverty, levels of inequality have grown substantially since the early 1970s (Piketty 2017). In many developing countries, levels of inequality are extremely high and have been increasing (Kanbur 2008). In China, despite spectacular rates of economic growth over the last two decades, a number of protests in the hinterland and coastal cities have highlighted the concerns about growing levels of inequality. Similarly, in India, while in the aggregate poverty levels have declined, the economic benefits of globalization have accrued disproportionately to high-income groups and increased levels of inequality. In South Africa, levels of inequality are among the highest in the world—the statistics are quite telling: the top 10% of the population earn about 60% of all income and own 95% of all assets. According to recent statistics, the Gini coefficient of income in South Africa has remained unchanged, at 0.66, since the early 1990s. The labour market in South Africa continues to generate some of the highest levels of inequality in the world. While executive salaries are some of the highest in the world, low pay is widespread, with over half of all full-time, formal sector, workers earning less than USD250 per month in 2016 (Valodia et al. 2016). The post-Apartheid period has seen significant growth in wage inequality, in spite of a profusion of redistributive policies enacted by the state, and the policies in place to address vulnerable work. We are particularly interested in how technology will impact the lives of poor and vulnerable people, and what effect it will have on inequality.

Technological change has different impacts on different groups—different income groups, men and women, the employed and the unemployed, and so on. At the aggregate level, if the pattern of growth generated by the 4IR reduces the level of inequality (in a similar fashion to the patterns of growth generated by the so-called east Asian miracle), the benefits of the 4IR will accrue disproportionately to low-income earners. Conversely, if the pattern of growth generates increases in levels of inequality (similar to what has happened in most developing countries over the last two decades), then the benefits of the 4IR would have accrued disproportionately to high income groups. The aggregate pattern will be driven very much by how particular countries (developed vs. developing), income groups, classes, genders and other social groups, benefit or lose as a result of the 4IR. A comprehensive analysis of the likely impact of the 4IR on inequality should seek to understand both how these new technological changes will impact on our already high levels of inequality and what policies and mechanisms can ameliorate the cost to the most vulnerable sections of our population (who are unable to absorb these 'shocks'), and how technology can lead to greater levels of equality.

Technological change is not a process that is independent of social norms and regulations. Instead, these social norms and regulations fundamentally shape the both the process of technological change and its outcomes. The worst response would be to assume a one-size-fits-all approach that is based on how wealthy countries and high-skill, high income workers will adjust to this new world of working.

The editor of MIT Technology Review, Rotman (2013), points out that for much for the post Second World War period, technological progress and its associated increase in productivity went hand-in-hand with increases in the level of employment. Thus, over the past half century, many have viewed technological progress as being inevitably linked with a reduction in inequality. Rotman argues that there current process of technological change may however see a break in the relationship between productivity growth, employment growth and the growth in mean incomes. Piketty (2017) argued that it is unlikely that developments in technology will see "the triumph of human capital over financial capital and real estate, capable managers over fat cat stockholders, and skill over nepotism" (2017, 29). Erik Brynjolfsson of MIT's Sloan School and co-author of The Second Machine Age, told Rotman that "my reading of the data is that technology is the main driver of the recent increases in inequality. It's the biggest factor". This sentiment has been shared by Bart Selman of Cornell University and IMB researchers Banavar and Francesca Rossi, as well as Venture Capital founder John Frankel who told TechCrunch in 2014 that:

> Technological disruption seems to be accelerating and we think it is due to a secular confluence of advances in technology and development of platforms, which leads to more unemployment in the short term. … I am concerned that if robotic technology gets cheap enough we reach a tipping point where too many industries are disrupted at the same time, leading to massive unemployment and too long to retrain people.

From a consumer point of view, recent new technologies have largely served to benefit the wealthy who can afford the products and services they offer—for example, smartphones, streaming of music and entertainment, advances in transportation systems, and so on. On the other hand, these new technologies have also significantly benefitted low income groups. Mobile telecommunication has fundamentally improved access to telephony and communications to low-income groups. Some benefits in health research, drone technology as a means to deliver medicine in rural areas, and banking the unbanked through cashless money systems, have also disrupted markets to the benefit of those who have previously been excluded. However, on balance, the consensus appears to be that technology has in recent times exacerbated inequality.

In an answer to a question on Reddit on how humanity would deal with technological developments, the late Stephen Hawkings warned that:

> If machines produce everything we need, the outcome will depend on how things are distributed. Everyone can enjoy a life of luxurious leisure if the machine-produced wealth is shared, or most people can end up miserably poor if the machine-owners successfully lobby against wealth redistribution. So far, the trend seems to be toward the second option, with technology driving ever-increasing inequality. (Newsweek; 14 March 2018)

Notwithstanding the dire warnings of a number of very prominent commentators, we believe that it is important to recognise that technological change in not an exogenous force that policymakers have no control over. On the contrary, much of the investment in research on new technologies is funded from public resources which can be channelled in a manner that serves the public interest. As so eloquently put by Tony Atkinson (2015), the doyen of inequality studies:

> The direction of technological change should be an explicit concern for policymakers, encouraging innovation in a form that increases the employability of workers and emphasises the human dimension of service provision.

Thus, besides being able to address access to services for previously marginalized communities, new technology development need not be seen as a teleological process that will necessarily lead to higher levels of inequality. Even if the employment impacts (we discuss this fully below) do turn out to be as dire as some are predicting, new forms of ownership will need to be explored to ensure that not only a small group of society benefits from the 4IR. Furthermore, the distribution of the gains from technological development is likely to be shaped by a number of forces—inter alia, the power of the developing world to shape the trajectory of technological change; the power of policymakers to influence the process; the power of the owners of capital and workers to govern and shape the outcomes; and the power of other social actors, such as civil society, to impact on and shape these processes. At things stand, we have very little, if any, empirical evidence in the developing world of how these processes are being influenced and what the outcomes may be.

## 3 Technology and Jobs—The Predictions

The impact of the 4IR on work is likely to be the most significant factor shaping its overall impact on society. We should start with an understanding of what we mean by 'work'. Most commentators tend to focus on paid work and completely ignore unpaid work, and the interactions between paid and unpaid work. The reality is that we spend most of our time doing unpaid work (Folbre 2012) and there is a gendered distribution of unpaid work, with a large number of women in our society having to deal with the burdens of low-paid work and an unequal burden of unpaid care work. Technological change has the possibility of significantly altering the nature of both paid and unpaid work. In most developing countries, most jobs—especially for women—have over the last three decades been created in the informal economy. The conversation around technological advances must also look at work in the informal economy.

There has been a lot written on the employment threats of the 4th IR, much of it from wealthy nations. Writing in the *Philippine Star* in 2017, Elfren Cruz reported that the job losses technology had generated in the manufacturing sector were now being felt in the services sector, citing the increase of Amazon's automated picking and packing system from 30,000 robots in 2015 to 45,000 robots in 2016—jobs previously done by humans. The popular press regularly reports on technology replacing workers, especially in services such as banking and finance. More affordable computing services and better storage capacity are also making clerical jobs in the services industry obsolete as computers are more efficiently able to perform routine tasks. In an interview in the MIT Technology Review Brian Arthur described the subtly of the autonomous economy where different digital processes are able to interface to produce new solutions that makes them even more efficient (12 June 2013).

Erik Brynjolfsson and Andrew McAfee have written about "the great decoupling". They note that despite record levels of both wealth creation and productivity levels in the US, employment rates and median incomes have not kept up. They also argue that technology not only eliminates certain jobs, but additionally leaves the average worker worse off (Interview with McKinsey 2014).

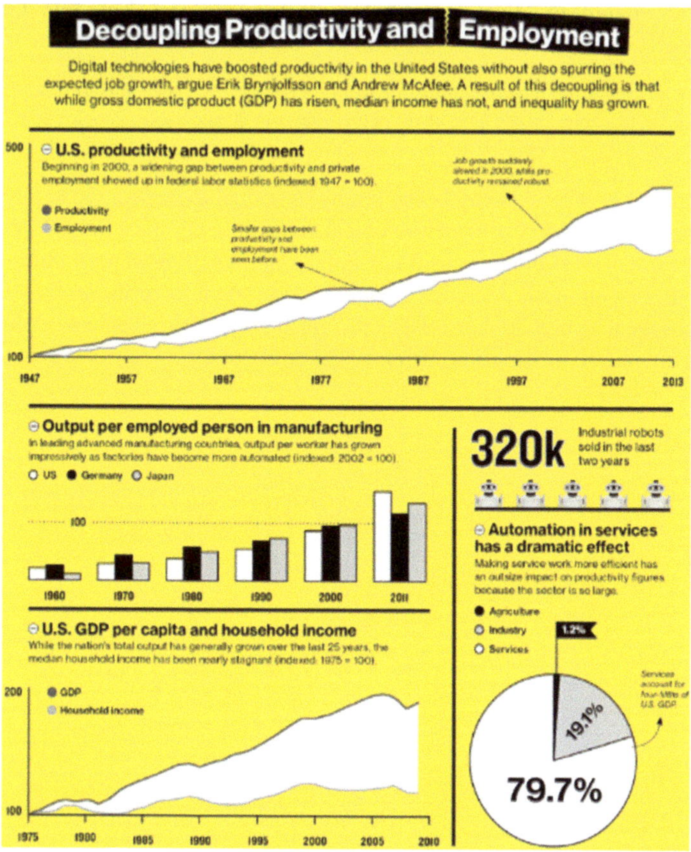

Just a year before their report, Paul Krugman had written that the benefits of increasing productivity were not being shared by the majority of workers but were rather increasingly inequality. He argued that the growing wealth of the 1% could not be explained by educational returns because their wealth growth was far higher than the average of degreed workers. (Krugman 2013). The ILO's Global Wage Report in 2013 clearly stated that "Between 1999 and 2011 average labour productivity in developed economies increased more than twice as much as average wages" (2012/13, xiv).

However, Harvard economist Richard Freeman argues that the threat to jobs is largely hype, and points out that throughout the decades human beings have adjusted to new technologies (Freeman 2015). He noted that in the 1940s the Second World War created a labour deficit; in the 1960s the American labour market survived the automation scare, and the dot-com boom of the 1990s created an all-time high of employed adult Americans. He also argued that technology has allowed for more qualitative jobs where machines do the largely manual work, or that hours of work will be reduced and people will spend more of their time on leisure activities. These scenarios of course applies far more to developed than developing countries.

Fellow Harvard economist Lawrence Katz agrees that history demonstrates the ability of humanity to adjust to technological developments. Katz told *Technology Review* that:

> There is no long-term trend of eliminating work for people. Over the long term, employment rates are fairly stable. People have always been able to create new jobs. People come up with new things to do. (12 June 2013)

This argument is at least partly borne out by historical evidence: the nature of work has consistently changed with technological developments since the 1700s. Over the 100 years since 1900 the proportion of Americans working in agriculture dropped from 41 to 2%; similarly increased automation in manufacturing in the 1980s saw US employment figures in that sector drop from 30 to 10% (Rotman 2013). Yet the unemployment rate in America currently sits at about 4%.

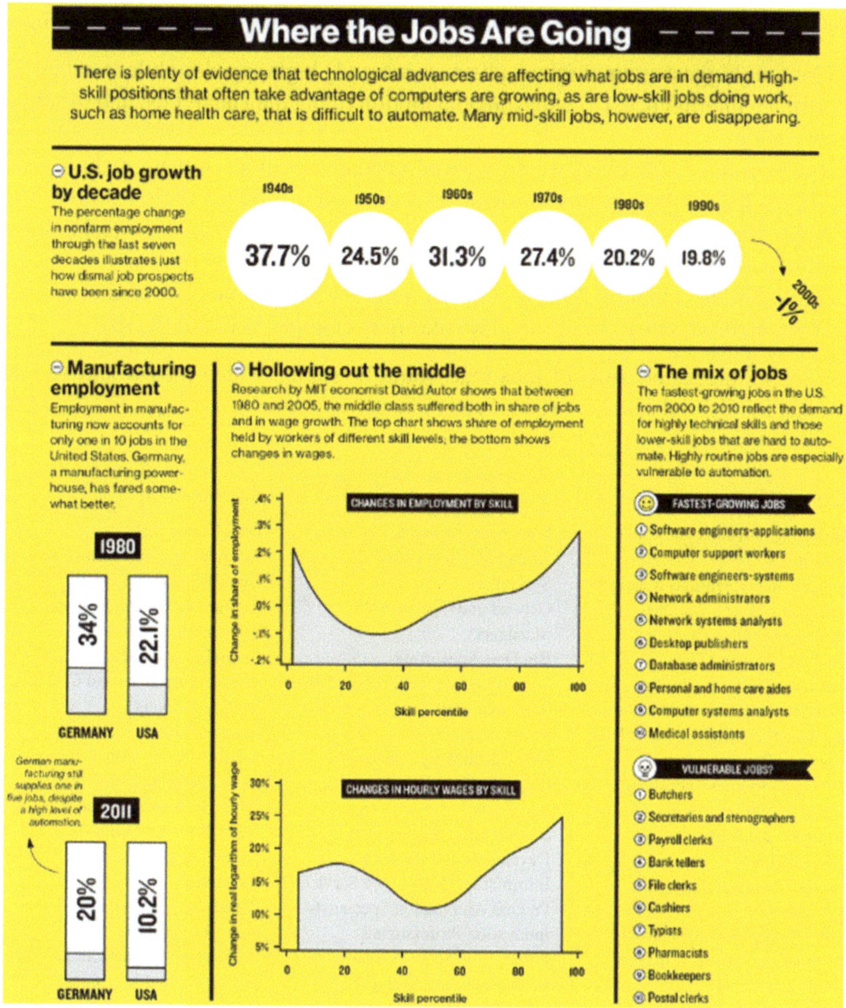


Katz does acknowledge that the range of influence of current technology is greater than any seen before. In fact a report by Deloitte in 2016 suggested that 39% of the jobs (114,000) in the legal sector were at risk over the next ten years due to automation in South Africa (Deloitte 2016). The report predicted that technological developments would see a decline in the need for traditional lawyers while other skills such as technology ability would become increasingly important.

The World Economic Forum's (WEF) 2016 Future of Jobs report predicted up to 7.1 million people could lose their jobs as a result of technology—mostly in white-collar and administrative jobs. At the same time the report predicted the creation of just over two million jobs in areas such as computers, maths, architecture and engineering.

The 2018 WEF report had a more positive outlook with the following key findings

- The four biggest technological advances were (1) high-speed mobile internet; (2) artificial intelligence; (3) widespread adoption of big data analytics; and (4) cloud technology
- By 2022 most companies would have adopted one or more of these technologies
- Almost half of companies surveyed expect to have reduced their workforce by 2022, although 38% anticipate an increase in jobs based on new technology-influenced roles
- One estimate is that by 2022 around 75 million jobs may be displaced as a result of automation, but 133 million new roles may emerge (WEF 2018, 10)

The report suggested a list of jobs that would be stable, which jobs would be new roles and which jobs were at risk of redundancy.

| Stable roles | New roles | Redundant roles |
|---|---|---|
| Managing Directors and Chief Executives | Data Analysts and Scientists[a] | Data Entry Clerks |
| General and Operations Managers[a] | AI and Machine Learning Specialists | Accounting, Bookkeeping and Payroll Clerks |
| Software and Applications Developers and Analysts[a] | General and Operations Managers[a] | Administrative and Executive Secretaries |
| Data Analysts and Scientists[a] | Big Data Specialists | Assembly and Factory Workers |
| Sales and Marketing Professionals[a] | Digital Transformation Specialists | Client Information and Customer Service Workers[a] |
| Sales Representatives, Wholesale and Manufacturing, Technical and Scientific Products | Sales and Marketing Professionals[a] | Business Services and Administration Managers |
| Human Resources Specialists | New Technology Specialists | Accountants and Auditors |
| Financial and Investment Advisers | Organizational Development Specialists[a] | Material-Recording and Stock-Keeping Clerks |
| Database and Network Professionals | Software and Applications Developers and Analysts[a] | General and Operations Managers[a] |
| Supply Chain and Logistics Specialists | Information Technology Services | Postal Service Clerks |
| Risk Management Specialists | Process Automation Specialists | Financial Analysts |
| Information Security Analysts[a] | Innovation Professionals | Cashiers and Ticket Clerks |
| Management and Organization Analysts | Information Security Analysts[a] | Mechanics and Machinery Repairers |
| Electrotechnology Engineers | Ecommerce and Social Media Specialists | Telemarketers |
| Organizational Development Specialists[a] | User Experience and Human-Machine Interaction Designers | Electronics and Telecommunications Installers and Repairers |
| Chemical Processing Plant Operators | Training and Development Specialists | Bank Tellers and Related Clerks |
| University and Higher Education Teachers | Robotics Specialists and Engineers | Car, Van and Motorcycle Drivers |
| Compliance Officers | People and Culture Specialists | Sales and Purchasing Agents and Brokers |
| Energy and Petroleum Engineers | Client Information and Customer Service Workers[a] | Door-To-Door Sales Workers, News and Street Vendors, and Related Workers Statistical, Finance and Insurance Clerks |
| Robotics Specialists and Engineers | Service and Solutions Designers | Lawyers |
| Petroleum and Natural Gas Refining Plant Operators | Digital Marketing and Strategy Specialists | |

*Source* Future of Jobs Survey 2018, World Economic Forum
*Note* Roles marked with [a]appear across multiple columns. This reflects the fact that they might be seeing stable or declining demand across one industry but be in demand in another

In line with David Autor's argument that "Most work processes draw upon a multifaceted set of inputs" (2015, 6), management consulting firm McKinsey has been analysing the labour market to understand how jobs actually function. McKinsey's James Manyika argued that rather than massive job losses, skill demands will change as components of, rather than entire, jobs are automated. Furthermore, the process of technological change will create new jobs too. The McKinsey research shows that at least 30% of activities can be automated in 60% of all occupations. This number could increase to half of all work activities by 2055. This information is important because it moves away from the threat of entire jobs being lost, and starts to look at components of jobs that can be automated instead. Manyika estimates that less than 5% of all jobs can be completely automated. But even at these levels adoption will depend on technical capability, feasibility, human versus machine costs, possible benefits such as productivity and quality, and social acceptance. Most interesting is McKinsey's estimates of the likely impact of 4IR technologies on employment between developed and developing countries. Using the framework above, their best current estimates suggest that for the USA over the period 2016–2030, 39 million jobs will be lost, while 55 million new jobs will be created—thus, a net increase in job by 15 million. For Germany, they estimate that the net result will be 3 million jobs lost. For India, by contract, McKinsey estimate that the net growth in employment will be 138 million, with 57 million jobs lost and a total of 195 million new jobs created. Thus, the churning process arising out of the 4IR will, at least according to McKinsey, result in significant net job creation in India.

Another aspect of the debate is how this will affect population demographics. Manyika argues that aging trends across the world make it much more likely that there will be a human labour deficit than surplus. This view is shared by the International Labour Organisation which stated in its 2018 World Employment and Social Outlooks Trends report that the combination of an aging (and early retiring) population and declining birth rates mean that the workforce will be under enormous pressure to support the retired population. The report noted that in 2017, developed countries had 3.5 retired people for every 10 working people, and that this number is likely to increase to five retired people for every 10 working people by 2030.

The McKinsey research looked particularly at tasks performed by machines. Although currently most tasks are dominated by humans, their prediction was that by 2022 machines would contribute to 57% of tasks. This is in line with the WEF prediction that the ratio of human:machine performance on tasks across 12 industries would change from 71:29% in 2018 to 58:42% in 2022.

But there is no consensus on who is most vulnerable to job losses—across countries, regions or developing versus developed economies. The WEF 2016 research suggested that the highest ratio of jobs created per jobs lost are expect to be in ASEAN (3.72 jobs gained per job lost), Mexico (3.06), United Kingdom (2.91), United States (1.37) and Turkey (1.14) (WEF 2016).

As it evident from this high-level review of the state of the research on the 4IR and employment, we only have a handful of serious empirical studies that have tried to estimate the job impacts of the 4IR. Those that have been done focus almost exclusively on the developing world. As things stand, there is no serious empirical work on the likely impact of the 4IR in the developing countries. Moreover, serious questions remain to be answered: what is the likely impact on wages?; how will the 4IR impact on employment and incomes in the informal economy, which makes up a significant proportion of employment in all developing countries? what might the impact be on rural-urban migration?; what are the likely impacts on women's income relative to men? These and related questions are fundamental to a comprehensive understanding of the possible impacts in developing countries. As things stand, there is an almost complete lack of any reliable data on any of these issues in the developing countries.

## 4 The Developing Country Reality—Employment and the Care Economy

In developing countries, and countries with high levels of inequality, planning for the likely impacts of the 4IR is crucial. As we have argued, technological change is a process that can be shaped and influenced. As more jobs in manufacturing become automated, countries will look to other industries to absorb the workforce. But this approach should be cognisant of how jobs are broken into components, and where to build on the human capital and where to invest in technology. Furthermore, it requires a careful examination of the likely churning effects of the 4IR, rather than on making policy on the hype about job losses. The services sector is an example where technology may make it easier for consumers to do certain tasks without the support of an agent, but where human interaction is still crucial in areas such as hotels, restaurants, real estate, communications and PR.

Depending how we respond to ongoing technological developments we may be able to harness these for good. An understanding of the labour market as composed of multiple tasks rather than complete jobs means that there are new possibilities of maintaining and creating jobs. This might involve companies breaking up tasks into those that can be automated and those that require human beings. This can further be supported by technology that allows for remote work and flexible times which are issues likely to attract more women particularly into the labour market.

One of the very important transformational potentials of the 4IR is to significantly change the current patterns of gender inequality in work. Some of the statistics we know from the ILO include (ILO 2016):

- A global gender wage gap of 23% which at current rates will take 70 years to close
- Across countries women do paid work for fewer hours and do around two and a half times more unpaid work in the home than men, although it is worth noting this changes in developing countries where women do 4:11 h of unpaid and 5:09 h of paid work a day, compared to men who do 1:31 h of unpaid and 6:36 h of paid work in a day which shows that not only do women spend far more time on unpaid work but they spend more time on work in total than men.

- Women are more likely to work in part-time jobs—while they make up 40% of global workforce they represent 57% of part-time workers and most importantly are far more likely than man to be in time-related underemployment work.
- 16.4 billion hours per day are spent in unpaid care work—the equivalent to 2 billion people working eight hours per day with no remuneration

What we know also is that there are structural, economic and social barriers across the globe that prohibit women from breaking out of generational poverty patterns.

It is important to recognise that care work has very special characteristics which make it more difficult to outsource work to machines—care requires a human touch, and there is a high degree of personal involvement which impacts significantly on the quality of care provided. The result is that care work could well be priced at its true economic value and this may well foster a change in the unequal incidence of care work in our societies.

If we use the care sector as a case study of gender inequality in the labour market, we have the opportunity through 4IR to both change the political approach to care work and at the same time to change these gendered power dynamics. Care work is generally under or unpaid work, largely because it is women who make up the majority of workers in this sector. It is not an area of work that lends itself to mechanisation, but generally because of its gendered nature remains undervalued and underpaid.

So there is a strong argument to be made about mainstreaming care work and bringing it into the decent work context that ensures workers in this industry pays a living wage, guarantees secure employment and recognises the value that women contribute. Stephen Hawking noted that "The automation of factories has already decimated jobs in traditional manufacturing and the rise of artificial intelligence is likely to extend this job destruction deep into middle classes, with only the most caring, creative or supervisory roles remaining" (The Guardian 2016). The 4th IR therefore provides us with an excellent opportunity to rethink both the labour market and the broader societal priorities. Aging populations, continuous challenges to address inequality including in areas of health and education, a highly skewed ownership of economic assets, and a gender-skewed labour market could open the policy space for better paid, more secure and more valued jobs in the care sector, and across the entire economy. This will serve society, address technological threats in at least one sector and profoundly affect the gendered inequality in the labour market.

Our approach to the 4th IR must be about securing jobs where possible; building jobs out of tasks that will not be automated; researching industries that are least likely to be affected by technology; harnessing technology to bring more people into the labour market; and using new technological processes to build a more equitable society. Stephen Hawking was right that we cannot continue to ignore inequality, but the important message is that if the choices we make are driven by a desire to eliminate that, we may be able to work through the disruptions that have already arrived.

## References

Atkinson, A. (2015). *Inequality: What can be done?* Cambridge: Harvard University Press.

Autor, D. H. (2015). Why are there still so many jobs? The history and future of workplace automation. *Journal of Economic Perspectives, 29*(3) (Summer).

Deloitte. (2016). *Developing legal talent—Stepping into the future law firm*. https://www2.deloitte.com/uk/en/pages/audit/articles/developing-legal-talent.html.

Elfren, S. C. (2017). Technology increases income inequality. *The Philippine Star*, February 5, 2017. https://www.philstar.com/opinion/2017/02/05/1669253/technology-increases-income-inequality.

Evans, J. (2014). VCs on inequality, unemployment and our uncertain future. *Techcrunch*, February 15, 2014. https://techcrunch.com/2014/02/15/vcs-on-inequality-unemployment-and-our-uncertain-future/.

Folbre, N. (2012). *For love and money: Care provision in the United States*. New York: Russell Sage.

Freeman, R. (2015). Who owns the robots rules the world. *IZA World of Labor*, May 2015. https://wol.iza.org/about.

Goodkind, N. (2018). Stephen Hawking advocated for wealth redistribution to prevent mass poverty in his final Reddit posts. *Newsweek*, March 14, 2018. https://www.newsweek.com/stephen-hawking-wealth-redistribution-reddit-845497.

Hawking, S. (2016). This is the most dangerous time for our planet. *The Guardian*, December 1, 2016. https://www.theguardian.com/commentisfree/2016/dec/01/stephen-hawking-dangerous-time-planet-inequality.

http://www.digitaljournal.com/business/digital-transformation-will-impact-on-employment/article/528823.

https://www.technologyreview.com/s/531726/technology-and-inequality/.

International Labour Organisation. (2012/13). *Global wage report—Wage and equitable growth*. https://www.ilo.org/wcmsp5/groups/public/—dgreports/—dcomm/—publ/documents/publication/wcms_194843.pdf.

International Labour Organisation. (2016). *Women at work trends 2016*. https://www.ilo.org/wcmsp5/groups/public/—dgreports/—dcomm/—publ/documents/publication/wcms_457317.pdf.

Kanbur, R. (2008). Globalization, growth and distribution: Framing the questions. Working Paper #5, Commission on Growth and Development, Washington: World Bank.

Krugman, P. (2013). Sympathy for the Luddites. *New York Times*, June 13, 2013. https://www.nytimes.com/2013/06/14/opinion/krugman-sympathy-for-the-luddites.html.

Piketty, T. (2017). *Capital in the 21st century*. Cambridge: Massachusetts.

Rotman, D. (2013). How technology is destroying jobs. In *MIT Technology Review*, June 12, 2013. https://www.technologyreview.com/s/515926/how-technology-is-destroying-jobs/.

Valodia, I., Collier, D., Cawe, A., Lijane, M., Koyana, S., Leibbrandt, M., et al. (2016). *A national minimum wage for South Africa*. Johannesburg: NEDLAC. Retrieved from http://new.nedlac.org.za/wp-content/uploads/2016/11/NMW-Report-Draft-CoP-FINAL1.pdf.

World Economic Forum. (2016). *The future of jobs employment, skills and workforce strategy for the fourth industrial revolution*. Global Challenge Insight Report 2016. http://www3.weforum.org/docs/WEF_Future_of_Jobs.pdf.

World Economic Forum. (2018). *The future of jobs report*. Insight Report 2018. http://www3.weforum.org/docs/WEF_Future_of_Jobs_2018.pdf.

# Chapter 7
# The Changing World of Work in Developing and Emerging Economies

**Radhicka Kapoor**

**Abstract** The world of work is changing at a magnitude that we have yet to fully grasp, let alone respond to. Over the past several decades, the workplace has been transformed by globalization, changing power dynamics, and new and emerging technologies—including artificial intelligence, robotics, and big data. These changes are playing an increasingly important role in shaping the jobs of the future, by shifting jobs between sectors, transforming the kinds of tasks that are done in existing jobs, and changing how people connect to work. However, these changes are not impacting people equally, with some workers bearing the brunt of these challenges disproportionately, thereby exacerbating overall inequality. Not only are the implications different across individuals but also across countries. The way the future of work is going to pan out across countries depends on their history, culture, demography, politics and social and economic development. The existing discourse on the future of work largely seems to focus on the advanced world. Out of the 3.4 billion global labour force that we have in the world today just about 20% is accounted for in the developed world. A large part of it is in developing and emerging economies where informality and precariousness is the norm and not impact the exception. Large masses of the workforce here are trapped in low productivity jobs, low paying jobs with very low initial conditions. The magnitude of the challenge of future of work in these economies is of completely different order. This essay attempts to widen the ambit of the discussion on the future of work by examining the issue from the lens of developing and emerging economies.

## 1 Introduction

The world has gone through three 'industrial revolutions' since the eighteenth century. Each of these has fundamentally changed the world around us. The technological advancements, underlying these three revolutions, have been the the principal source of economic growth and development of nations. It is now widely believed that we

R. Kapoor (✉)
Indian Council for Research on International Economic Relations, New Delhi, India
e-mail: rkapoor@icrier.res.in



R. Kathuria and P. Kukreja (eds.), *20 Years of G20*,
https://doi.org/10.1007/978-981-13-8106-5_7

are standing at the brink of what has been described as the fourth industrial revolution (commonly referred to as Industry 4.0). Although Industry 4.0 is conceptualized as an upgrade on the third industrial revolution, it has been argued by many that the speed, scope and sheer pervasiveness of it distinguishes it from the earlier phases placing the world of work in a state of flux (Schwab 2016). The technologies that define Industry 4.0, unlike the technologies of the three Industrial Revolutions that preceded it are expected to challenge our ideas about what it means to be human. Artificial intelligence, quantum computers, biotechnology, blockchain technology, three-dimensional printing and lightweight robots are all posited to disrupt the world of work.

The 19th International Conference of Labour Statisticians (ILO 2013) defined work as follows: "*Work comprises any activity performed by persons of any sex and age to produce goods or to provide services for use by others or for own use*". Further, the world of work comprises of multiple actors. In fact, our idea of work today is made up of several dimensions—"*a factor of production, the essence of humanity, and the pivot of the system of distribution of wealth, benefits and protection, dimensions that collide and are the reason why so many interpretations affect the concept of work today*" (ILO 2016c).

Drawing on the above notion, we envisage the world of work to comprise of interactions between four key actors—individuals, firms, governments and society. Individuals as workers form an important part of the production process; hence, work defines an individual's place in society, through the existing occupations and domains. For individuals as consumers, work defines aspects of life outside of it, including a person's standard of living, their social status, self-esteem, and levels of satisfaction and contentment. Beyond the individual, work is influenced by the production processes and technologies that characterize firms in an economy, at a point in time. The nature and constitution of work determine the character of a civilisation and consequently a society's economic, political and cultural attributes. These in turn shape the form and nature of work processes as well as the role and status of the workers within society. Moreover, society, organisations and institutions define the socio-economic contexts in which work exists, with implications for the social contract and nature of relationships between employees and employers. In this regard, governments and society are important agents that both shape work and are influenced by it.

While there is considerable anxiety about the impact of technological advances on the world of work, it is imperative to recognise that although technology is a powerful force shaping the world of work, it does not evolve in isolation (Rose 2016). Simply because something is technologically possible doesn't mean that humans will embrace it. In fact, the history of technology is replete with examples of innovations which never really took off or had a very short life span. The pace and direction of technological advances will depend not just on technological feasibility, but a multitude of factors. Rose (2016) notes that the future world of work will depend not just on the technological environment but also economic, social, legal, cultural, political and historical factors. This suggests that the changes in the world of work are unlikely to evolve and play out in the same way across countries. In fact, ILO (2017b) posits that 'there is no one single Future of Work'. The World Development Report (WDR 2016) also notes that the magnitude and speed of technological forces are likely to vary across countries depending on the economic and employment structure of the labour market. The report anticipates that advanced economies using more technology at work are likely to witness more disruptions compared to developing and emerging economies. Although a smaller share of workforce is in routine occupations, higher wages make them more prone to automation. In developing countries, where wages are low and technology adoption is slower, disruptions are expected to arrive with a time lag.

The heterogeneities in the way the world of work will evolve across countries highlight the need to adapt the global narrative on the subject to local conditions and bring in the perspective of developing and emerging economies such as India. Much of the current narrative and literature on the impact of technological progress on the world of work has focused on the developed world. This is rather surprising given that of the global labour force of 3464.9 million, the developed world accounted for a mere 17.3% of this figure. These statistics reflect the need to expand the ambit of discussion on future of work to capture the concerns and anxieties of developing and emerging economies which account for more than four-fifth of the global workforce. With large masses of their workforce trapped in precarious and informal employment, the magnitude and nature of the challenges arising in the future world of work in these economies are of a completely different order. ILO estimates suggest that in 2018, developing and emerging countries collectively accounted for about 95% of the 1.4 billion workers engaged in vulnerable forms of employment worldwide. ILO projections also indicate that about 72% of the total employed in both South Asia and Sub-Saharan Africa will continue to remain in vulnerable employment till 2020. In sharp contrast, the projections of vulnerable employment in developed economies are expected to remain significantly lower at 9.9% over the same time horizon. These statistics highlight the stark difference in the labour market realities of emerging/developing economies and developed economies. It is also worth noting that even the concept of work in developed and developing countries is not entirely the same. The issue of a "trade-off between work and leisure" which is a problem in the developed world, does not depict the reality in developing and emerging countries where under employment and disguised employment are the norm.

This essay sets the stage for a discussion on the future of work in developing and emerging economies by analyzing the effects of the full range of forces shaping Industry 4.0 on each of the above-mentioned four agents—individuals, firms, governments and societies. The decisions made by the four key actors in the world of work are crucial in determining the trajectory of technological advances. A discussion on the future of work in the context of the emerging technological changes would be incomplete without understanding the drivers and determinants of technological change. This is important so that we do not give these technological changes an anonymity and exogeneity in the course of our discussion but attempt to unpack what drives it. While, this is indeed a challenging exercise, our framework enables us to discuss the future of work, in all its breadth and diversity and expand the horizon of the debate from the narrow lens of jobs to a broader set of distributional and macroeconomic issues.

## 2 Technological Changes and Jobs: Risk or Opportunity?

Economists have long endeavored to understand the impact of technological change on labour markets. There have been recurring warnings over the last two decades that technology will replace human labour and spell the end of human work. Concomitantly, others have argued that a doomsday prediction of jobs is unwarranted as the past two centuries of technological change have not made human labour redundant and have in fact increased demand for labour and wages. In a recent study, Acemoglu and Restrepo (2018) attempt to outline and deconstruct the various channels through which technology impacts jobs. At the core of their framework is the powerful displacement effect. This corresponds to the notion that automation and thus, AI and robotics replace workers in tasks that they previously performed, thereby reducing the demand for labour and lowering wages. The authors outline multiple forces which counteract the displacement effect. Significant amongst these is the reinstatement effect. This effect refers to the creation of new tasks which generate additional labour demand and consequently an increase in the share of labour in national income. The creation of new tasks could create new occupations which have not existed thus far. For instance, jobs such as data scientist did not exist before, but because computers have made enormous data sets analysable, such new jobs have emerged for people to interpret huge pools of information.

A plethora of studies have attempted to quantify the impact of Industry 4.0 on jobs and estimate the number jobs at risk of displacement. Frey and Osborne (2013) (henceforth, FO) estimated that 47% of total jobs in the United States were at risk of automation, owing to advances in Machine Learning (ML) and Mobile Robotics (MR). A number of studies have estimated the share of jobs that are at risk of automation in advanced and emerging economies using FO's (2013) methodology. These estimates range from 59% in Germany (Brzeski and Burk 2015) to 77% in China and 69% in India (WDR 2016). Bessen (2015) has argued that automating a task does not mean that the entire occupation would be automated. Given the distinction between occupations and tasks, Arntz et al. (2016) adopt a task-based approach to calculate the share of jobs at high risk of automation. They find this approach to significantly reduce the estimate of job loss due to automation. Their results suggest that 9% of jobs in the U.S. are at high risk of automation, whereas for the OECD countries, their estimates range from 6% in Korea to 12% in Germany and Austria.

While, the above-mentioned studies provide important insights into the extent of jobs at risk of automation, one needs to be cautious in interpreting and analyzing these numbers in the context of developing countries. First, these studies directly map the U.S. occupational structure and assume that a job which is automatable in the US will also be automatable in India. This presumes that the task content, knowledge, skills and abilities required to perform the various activities an occupation entails are identical. Such assumptions would lead to an overestimation of jobs at risk of displacement on account of technologies.

Second, the above-mentioned approaches to derive estimates of the number of jobs at risk of automation do not factor the economic viability of technologies driving Industry 4.0 relative to labour costs. As noted by the ILO (2017b) these studies examine "the probability that a job could be automated, not the probability that it (or the tasks therein) will be "automated" (ILO 2017b, p. 32). Given the significant financial cost associated with adopting and implementing new technologies, the difference between the two probabilities would be quite large in developing countries like India. For instance, ILO (2016b) observes that ASEAN countries (including Cambodia, Indonesia, the Philippines, Thailand and Vietnam) witness a higher share of jobs at risk of displacement (56%) compared to the U.S. (47%).[1] However, the lower labour costs as well as slower introduction of technologies in the ASEAN region result in a lower propensity of automation, in practice. Thus, in addition to technical feasibility, economic feasibility will be an important determinant of whether a job will be automated.

While, it is difficult to quantify the impact of automation on employment, what is certain is a change in the form of employment. Globally, there has been a rise in non-standard forms of employment (NSFE) including increases in temporary work, part-time work, temporary agency work and subcontracting, dependent self-employment and disguised employment relationships. The gig or platform economy has emerged as an important alternative work arrangement, largely sourced through 'Crowdwork' and 'Work-on-demand via apps'. NSFE have the potential to bring benefits to employers and individuals, create new opportunities and diverse choices and offer increased flexibility. This is particularly important for women as it enables them to balance work and family responsibilities. On the downside though, these forms of employment are often associated with job insecurity, earnings volatility, limited access to social protection schemes, health and pension benefits, training and career advancement and job dissatisfaction. For instance, workers in NSFE often earn less than workers in "standard jobs", even if they have similar attributes and perform the same work (ILO 2017c). Labour market studies show that being employed as a temporary or temporary agency worker entails a penalty which can reach as high as 30%. These penalties associated with part time employment are in the form of wage penalties in Europe and US. Additionally, given that these forms of employment create income security and pay is uncertain, workers are often compelled to taken on a second job and this has implications for work-life balance.

Another key concern with respect to NSFE is that this work occurs outside the framework of labour and social security laws, without the protection of laws and regulations covering minimum wages, social protection and other benefits. This has negative implications in terms of workers' rights and representation for they may lack access to freedom of association and collective bargaining rights. This could either stem from legal reasons or may be a manifestation of their tenuous attachment to workplace. This could also lead to discrimination and violation of fundamental rights at work (ILO 2017c). Importantly, the emergence of the gig economy has created new forms of invisible work, such as "virtual labour" or "digital labour"

---

[1] These estimates are based on Frey and Osborne's approach.

(ILO 2017b). ILO (2017b) cites the example of micro-taskers or virtual assistants who are performing a variety of tasks that underlie social media activities. Despite the fact that they are the human labour behind the technology, these workers are "invisible" as it is widely perceived that algorithms and new technologies do the work supplied through information and communication technology (ICT) channels. The emergence of such "invisible workers" throws up challenges for the world of work as not only does their work have no dedicated location but also because their employment relationship is not recognized within the existing regulatory framework (ILO 2017b).

Whilst, we recognise the pitfalls of NSFE, it is also important to acknowledge that NSFE may not always be a matter of concern. It may also be a matter of choice. For some the shift from formal employment to NSFE could be voluntary, whilst for several others it may simply be driven by unavailability of alternative secure and gainful work opportunities. In developing countries such as India which lack well-regulated labour institutions, the increase in temporary or part-time work, generates significant concern as it compounds the existing challenge of informal employment. Gig economy is not new in India with most workers already working for multiple employers on a piece rate basis. In India, the proportion of regular employees who had no job contract was close to 60% in 2004–05. For casual labour, it was over 95%. The high share of employees with no job contracts has been a persistent phenomenon in India and the new platform economy is only accentuating this trend. The existing high incidence and persistence of informality in developing and emerging economies, coupled with the proliferation of NSEs in Industry 4.0, suggests that we need to examine how best workers can be protected.

## 3 Changing Nature of Firms

Globally, traditional industry is in the midst of a transformation that is driven by technologies such as robots, 3D printers, and different kinds of data-driven innovation. Digital technologies underlying Industry 4.0 have given rise to a number of new business models which are fundamentally altering the nature of firms. These include varieties of e-commerce, app stores, online advertising, cloud computing, high speed trading, and online payment services. Advances in ICT have enabled firms to scale up faster at a substantially greater scale and over significantly longer distances than was ever envisaged before. Online retailers have transformed the business model of brick-and-mortar stores by selling traditional physical goods (such as books) digitally. This has led to blurring of firm boundaries (WDR 2019). Platform based businesses have yielded significant gains by allowing technology to reach a larger number of people faster than ever before. They generate value by creating a network effect, connecting customers, producers and providers, and facilitating interactions and transactions in a multi-sided model (WDR 2019). Interestingly, these new and innovative companies have the luxury of operating globally without being big as their operations are no longer subject to barriers such as capital or assets to the extent they were in the past.

The speedy ascent of platform firms also raises a complex set of challenges. The first pertains to the issue of firms growing rapidly from local startups to global giants without generating significant employment. With firms becoming more 'virtual' in nature and their profits originating from technology, algorithms and data, they are able to expand without many employees. The second set of challenges relates to issues of competition, privacy and taxation. Emergence of new platforms and network effects leads to concentration of market power in the hands of selected few, making the task of competition authorities rather difficult. Safeguarding the privacy and security of individuals is also becoming increasingly challenging as tracking consumer behavior is becoming very profitable. Additionally, digitalization has also raised concerns about the structure of international taxation with rapid expansion of new business models and changes in the structure of value chain.

Whilst, there is considerable discussion about the 'superstar firms', which have embraced new technologies, thereby reaping significant technological dividends, there are several laggard firms which have failed to do so. Global evidence points to the fact that although technologies are diffusing at a much faster rate than ever before, adoption of technology across firms within a country is also skewed (OECD 2018). This differential pace of technological adoption in turn has significant productivity effects. Using a micro-level dataset of firms in OECD member countries, Andrews et al. (2016) find that while 'frontier firms' in manufacturing witnessed average productivity growth of 2.8% per year between 2001 and 2013, the laggards saw increases of just 0.6 percent per year. This not only led to growing productivity differentials between the laggard and frontier firms, but also weighed on aggregate productivity growth.

However, it needs to be pointed out that the challenge is not simply one of closing the divide between frontier and lagging firms, but also between firms in developing and developed countries. The slow pace at which innovations spread from early adopters in advanced economies to firms in developing countries poses a significant challenge and is likely to exacerbate the growing divergence between firms that are global leaders and the rest. Firms in developing countries stand far away from the technology frontier and are likely to have substantial difficulty in not only using modern technology but also accessing the necessary complementary assets such as skilled workers, intangible capital and digital infrastructure. Additionally, technologies developed might need to adapt to local conditions (such as limited telecommunications infrastructure or unreliable power supply) to adjust to local demand in these countries.

Exploiting the potential of new technologies which can accelerate productivity growth requires closing the divide between frontier and lagging firms, in particular small firms. This requires a coordinated effort on multiple fronts. First, enterprises need to invest in complementary assets, in particular intangible capital. New technologies are partly embodied in physical assets and partly in intangible assets, and require practical investigation and tacit knowledge to implement. This requires investments in knowledge-based capital. For instance, local R&D is key to incorporate and adapt foreign technologies to local conditions. Second, realizing the gains from technologies entails workers acquiring new skills. It also typically involves restructuring organizational forms and amending business models. This in turn requires skilled workers and managers. The paucity of these is likely to be a significant bottleneck in emerging markets. Third, fully benefitting from digital technologies requires investment in digital infrastructure and comprehensive, reliable and secure telecommunications infrastructure, including high bandwidth broadband, wireless networks and mobile and landline telecommunications networks. Providing coverage to remote rural areas, particularly in large countries, will facilitate the development of integrated domestic markets (OECD 2017). Technologies that work well in the developed world may fail to have any tangible impact in the developing world.

An additional challenge for developing economies is the existence of a large number of informal firms. Characterized by inadequate access to finance and low managerial skills, informal firms are constrained in their ability to invest in physical and intangible capital as well as training of their workers (La Porta and Shleifer 2014). They are likely to face significant hurdles in harnessing the potential of new technologies. This exacerbates the productivity differential between laggard firms, most of who are in the informal sector, and the 'superstar firms' in the formal sector. Furthermore, informal firms may also face an existential crisis as technological advances enable high-quality goods to be produced at lower cost, displacing the lower-quality and lower-price model many informal enterprises rely on (Hallward-Driemeier and Nayyar 2017). On the flip side though, some aspects of the digital transformation, for instance e-payments and mobile payments, may present new opportunities to informal firms and even encourage informal businesses to formalize (McKinsey Global Institute 2016). The impact of Industry 4.0 on firms in informal sector has attracted relatively scant attention in the existing literature.

The above mentioned issues create a larger macroeconomic challenge for developing and emerging economies. Over the decades, GSCs have come to dominate international trade and the production and distribution of goods (and services) across many sectors of the economy. GSCs have had a positive impact on job creation, with the ILO estimating that they account for 453 million jobs worldwide in 2013. Participation in GSCs has enabled workers in developing countries to get a foothold in the world of formal work and boosted entrepreneurship and economic growth via technological transfers and the adoption of new production practices. The abundance of cheap labour was one of the factors responsible for the integration of developing countries in GSCs. However, recent technological advances and the adoption of labour saving techniques of production have reduced the relative importance of labour costs vis-a-vis other factors of production in determining competitiveness and hence location decisions. This has generated concerns about the possibility of 'reshoring' i.e. the process of transferring business operations that were moved to low income or emerging countries back to the high income countries from where they were originally relocated. This has raised two pressing questions. One, will reconfiguration of GVCs reverse the importance and length of GVCs and reorient global trade and production back towards advanced countries. And, two, whether a structural transformation driven by technology and automation will render the path of low-skill and labour-intensive manufacturing, adopted by East Asian economies like China, Japan, and the Republic of Korea, a less accessible path of growth, development and job creation for economies like India. The adoption of 3D printing technologies by shoe manufacturer, Adidas, and the establishment of a fully automated shoe factory referred to as 'Speedfactory' in Germany which eliminated 1000 jobs in Vietnam underlies such concerns.

## 4 Rising Inequality

Since the 1950s discussions on inequality have been dominated by Simon Kuznet's idea that as per capita national income of a country increases, initially inequality in income distribution rises. Thereafter, after reaching a peak corresponding to intermediate levels of income, income inequality falls. The idea behind this was that as countries become more technologically developed and more people are able to take advantage of the resulting opportunities, their talents, skills, training, and acumen, in other words their human capital will allow us to prosper (Rotman 2014). However, with increasing automation, robotic usage, AI and 3D printing, these effects might not actually play out. Automation and robotics, for instance, transfer income from labour to owners of capital and robots. This in turn causes the transfer of large amounts of national income from labour (in wages) to capital (in profits), as income from tech-generated growth flows primarily to owners of capital. The decline in labour share of national income worldwide over the past few decades is well established in the literature. The IMF's World Economic Outlook (2017) observes that the share of national income accruing to workers has been declining since 1980s. It notes that in advanced economies, labour income shares reached their lowest level of the past half century just prior to the global financial crisis of 2008. Importantly, it has not recovered since. For emerging and developing markets, too, the IMF notes that labour shares have been declining since the early 1990s. Importantly, the report argues that in advanced economies, about half of the decline in labour shares can be traced to the impact of technology. Advances in technology which enable machines to replace human labour, particularly in tasks that can be easily automated, have meant that owners of capital have benefitted at the expense of workers squeezing their share in national income. Global trends outlined in WDR (2016) reinforce the declining trend share of national income accruing to labour, especially routine labour.[2]

While technological advances have benefitted owners of capital vis-à-vis labour, it is important to note that not all workers have been impacted uniformly. From the literature on job polarization we know that middle skill workers have borne a disproportionately large share of the displacement effect in labour markets relative to low skilled and high skilled workers. The phenomenon of job polarization and hollowing of the middle skill jobs have together increased the wage premium between low and high paying ones, thereby increasing wage inequality between skilled and unskilled workers. Importantly, since high-skill occupations require higher educational attainments, many advanced economies have witnessed an increase in the education wage

---

[2]Brazil and Ukraine are notable exceptions.

premium over the past three decades (IMF 2018). On the other hand, those employed in routine and manual jobs face significant risk of job loss. In the absence of adequate opportunities to acquire new relevant skills, many of those who are at risk of job loss are often compelled to resort to lower skilled and lower paying jobs. This could potentially lead to precarious forms of employment increasing alongside long-term unemployment (ILO 2017b). Additionally, it should be noted that the declining labour share of national income is also attributable to the declining bargaining power of labour. The generation of a pool of surplus labour from automation, the proliferation of temporary and part-time work arrangements have created a constant threat of unemployment and 'take it or leave it' type offers for workers. Owing to their reduced bargaining power relative to firms, workers face significant insecurity, vulnerability and downward pressure on wages Guellec and Paunov (2017).

While the phenomenon of jobs and skills polarization are central to the argument of rising inequality, there is another critical source of inequality in today's technology driven economy, namely the power of ideas. Industry 4.0 will disproportionately favour a small group of individuals, in particular high-tech entrepreneurs, whose ideas and products can be disseminated widely and produced easily by software and other technologies. Drawing on Rosen's (1981) paper, "Economics of Superstars", Brynjolsson et al. (2014) argue that such innovative individuals are benefitting from a winner-take-all effect and the economy may end up being dominated by a niche group which "innovates and creates". The authors observe that the "distribution of income for this creative class will typically take the form of a power law, with a small number of winners capturing most of the rewards and a long tail consisting of the rest of the participants." In this context, Brynjolsson et al. (2014) cite the example of founders of start-ups such as Instagram, who are growing rich at a staggering rate. In 2017, the founder and CEO of Snapchat—a photo sharing app launched in 2011—at 26 was the youngest billionaire in the world. In fact, it has been observed in the United States that the income share of the top 1% has soared, rising from earning on average 27 times more than the bottom 1% in 1980s to 81 times more in 2014. Guellec and Paunov (2017) have argued that the increasing income share of the top income groups can be attributed to the increasing importance of digital innovation-new products and processes based on software code and data. Digital innovation has magnified innovation-based rents, leading to greater revenue accumulation at the top of the income distribution, while only yielding marginal gains for the average worker.

That digitalisation increases the innovation-based rents holds true not just at the level of the individual, but also firms. Guellec and Paunov (2017) track the growth of firm profits and find evidence of increasing winner-take-all dynamics. They note that the top percentile of firms ranked by the return on invested capital (ROIC) have grown most significantly, from less than 30% in the early 1990s to 100% in 2014. On the other hand, the lowest percentiles (25th) had a constant ROIC and the median increased slightly. They also cite evidence of a rise in the share of nominal GDP of the Fortune 100 biggest American companies from 33% in 1994 to 46% in 2013 Guellec and Paunov (2017). Typically, players closely associated with the digital economy have gained in importance in this ranking. While tangible assets such as hardware and computers yield fixed returns, the knowledge developed helps capture increasing returns to scale in the market. Globalisation has further enabled firms to capture returns not only domestically, but also in the international market, thus exacerbating inequality within and across countries.

The distributional challenges outlined above in turn pose significant macroeconomic problems of a shortfall in aggregate demand and weak economic growth. With the concentration of income in the hands of those who have a higher propensity to save rather than spend, aggregate demand is likely to weaken. For instance, automation, robotization and other technological advances are likely to transfer income from workers to owners of machines and capital. Similarly, the emergence of high-tech entrepreneurs has led to concentration of income among top income earners, who have a lower propensity to consume compared to those in lower deciles of income distribution. The phenomenon of decoupling of wages from productivity (wherein wage growth lags behind productivity growth) observed in several advanced economies over the last few decades poses a further risk to growth through inadequate demand and consumption. As wages lag behind productivity, not only do workers not get a fair share of the income produced, but their consumption which constitutes a significant portion of aggregate demand also does not grow. This decline in aggregate demand could potentially depress investment too, acting as a drag on growth.

The failure to share technological dividends across society is likely to create a large group of unhappy losers globally and have a political and social backlash. This can pose a significant threat to economic development. That innovation and technological change are drivers of economic growth is unambiguously accepted. But if the process of economic transformation has an adverse effect on income distributions as discussed above, it can potentially undermine the sustainability of the growth process itself. Governments worldwide cannot afford to escape the distributional issue arising in the changing world of work.

## 5 Conclusion

Much of the public debate on the impact of Industry 4.0 on the future of work focuses on the impact of automation on labour markets. We attempt to look at the future world of work, in a comprehensive and holistic manner by analyzing the implications of the ongoing technological revolution on all the actors in the world of work. Finding solutions which enable us to cope with a world of work marked by greater diversity, discontinuity and uncertainty—requires partnership and co-ordination amongst all actors in the world of work. Governments, in particular, have an important part to play in enabling their citizens weather technological change with the least amount of disruption. Four key policy responses include investing in skills and educations, adapting social protection systems and labour market institutions, enhancing digital infrastructure and reforming tax and expenditure policy. While these four themes form the core of the development agenda to address the challenges posed by the world of work, the framework needs to be adapted to different country contexts. The magnitude and speed with which technological forces will impact the world of work will vary across countries. The nature and extent of disruptions will depend on economic, social, cultural and a host of country specific factors. This in turn suggests that different countries would need to prioritise and structure their policy responses differently depending on their specific characteristics. A 'one-size-fits-all' approach will not work.

Despite posing several challenges, the current wave of technological advances offer unparalleled opportunities. They have the potential to bring in significant productivity gains, enhance growth and raise standards of living. Maximizing these potential benefits requires that policy makers strengthen the resilience and adaptability of their economies so that they can harness these challenges to achieve inclusive and sustained growth. The G20 which brings together both developed and developing/emerging economies provides an important platform for facilitating dialogue and cooperation to build a world of work where no one is left behind. There is a need to turn the challenges associated with industry 4.0 into opportunities that countries across the world can grasp. This requires appropriate policy deliberations at the G20 level. For these deliberations to be meaningful and constructive, the global narrative on the subject needs to be adapted to country specific conditions. As mentioned before, workers in developing and emerging economies account for a disproportionately large share of global workforce. Yet, the discourse around the future of work continues to revolve around the developed world. The role of the G20 assumes greater significance in ensuring that the perspective and unique challenges of economies like India informs the global debate on the future of work.

## References

Acemoglu, D., & Restrepo, P. (2018). *Artificial intelligence, automation and work.* NBER Working Paper 24196.

Andrews, D., Criscuolo, C., & Gal, P. N. (2016). *The best versus the rest: The global productivity slowdown, divergence across firms and the role of public policy.* OECD Productivity Working Paper No. 5.

Arntz, M., Gregory, T., & Zierahn, U. (2016). *The risk of automation for jobs in OECD countries—A comparative analysis.* OECD Social, Employment and Migration Working Papers.

Bessen, J. (2015). *Learning by doing: The real connection between innovation, wages, and wealth.* New Haven: Yale University Press.

Brynjolfsson, E., McAfee, A., & Spence, M. (2014). New world order: Labor, capital and ideas in the power law economy. *Foreign Affairs, 93,* 44.

Brzeski, C., & Burk, I. (2015). Die Roboterkommen. Folgen der Automatisierungfür den deutschenArbeitsmarkt ["The Robots Come. Consequences of Automation for the German Labour Market"]. *ING DiBa Economic Research.*

Frey, C. B., & Osborne, M. (2013). *The future of employment: How susceptible are jobs to computerization?* Oxford Martin School Working Paper.

Guellec, D., & Paunov, C. (2017). *Digital innovation and the distribution of income.* NBER Working Paper No. 23987.

Hallward-Driemeier, M. C., & Nayyar, G. (2017). *Trouble in the making? The future of manufacturing-led development.* World Bank Group.

International Labour Organisation. (2013). *Statistics of work, employment and labour underutilization*. Report II, 19th International Conference of Labour Statisticians.
International Labour Organization. (2016a). Non-standard employment around the world: Understanding challenges, shaping prospects.
International Labour Organization. (2016b). ASEAN in transformation: How technology is changing jobs and enterprises.
International Labour Organisation. (2016c). *The future of work: The meaning and value of work in Europe*. ILO Research Paper No. 18.
International Labour Organization. (2017a). New automation technologies and job creation and destruction dynamics. *Employment Policy Brief.*
International Labour Organization. (2017b). Inception report for the global commission on the future of work.
International Labour Organization. (2017c). *Strengthening social protection for the future of work.* Paper presented at the 2nd meeting of the G20 Employment Working Group.
International Labour Organization. (2017d). The future of work we want: A global dialogue.
International Monetary Fund. (2018). *Technology and the future of work*. IMF Staff Note to The Group of 20.
McKinsey Global Institute. (2016). Digital finance for all: powering inclusive growth in emerging economies.
OECD. (2017). *The future of global value chains—Business as usual or "a new normal"?*. OECD Science, Technology and Innovation Policy Papers No. 41.
OECD. (2018). *Achieving inclusive growth in the face of digital transformation and the future of work*. OECD Report to G-20 Finance Ministers.
Porta, R. L., & Shleifer, A. (2014). *Informality and Development*. NBER WP20205.
Rose, M. (2016). Vocational education and the new world of work. *The Hedgehog Review: Critical Reflections on Contemporary Culture.*
Rotman, D. (2014). Technology and inequality. *MIT Technology Review*.
Schwab, K. (2016). The fourth industrial revolution. *World Economic Forum*.
World Development Report. (2016). The race between skills and technology. *World Bank.*
World Development Report. (2019). World development report 2019: The changing nature of work. *World Bank.*

# Part IV
# Role of Technology for Adaptation and Mitigation of Climate Change

# Chapter 8
# Rethinking Technology for a 1.5 °C World

**Ulka Kelkar and Apurba Mitra**

**Abstract** The Paris Agreement to the United Nations Framework Convention on Climate Change (UNFCCC) calls on all countries to take action to limit global warming to 2 °C above pre-Industrial Revolution levels, and ideally to 1.5 °C. The new special report of the Intergovernmental Panel on Climate Change (IPCC) warns of the dangers of every additional degree of warming and identifies technological pathways to reduce greenhouse gas (GHG) emissions in a way that we return to a 1.5 °C world by the end of this century. The voluntary commitments currently offered by countries, however, are expected to result in global warming of 2.7 °C to 3.7 °C. This paper examines the role of technology and supporting policies in the transition to a decarbonized or climate-neutral world by mid-century. With the case of India, we discuss the types of technologies and policies that are required to be implemented during 2020–2050 to stay on track for 1.5 °C warming. We highlight the transformative low carbon technologies needed in three major sectors—transport, cooling, and data centres—and discuss the social and economic policies that are needed to support the low carbon transition.

## 1 Introduction

The Paris Agreement to the United Nations Framework Convention on Climate Change (UNFCCC) calls on all countries to take action to limit global warming to 2 °C above pre-Industrial Revolution levels, and ideally to 1.5 °C. The new special report of the Intergovernmental Panel on Climate Change (IPCC) on Global

The original version of this book was revised: Missing abstracts of chapters 3, 6, 8, 9 and 11 have now been included. The correction to this book can be found at https://doi.org/10.1007/978-981-13-8106-5_12

U. Kelkar (✉)
World Resources Institute (WRI) India, Bengaluru, India
e-mail: ulka.kelkar@wri.org

A. Mitra
World Resources Institute (WRI) India, Delhi, India

 
R. Kathuria and P. Kukreja (eds.), *20 Years of G20*,
https://doi.org/10.1007/978-981-13-8106-5_8

Warming of 1.5 °C warns of the dangers of every additional degree of warming and identifies technological pathways to reduce greenhouse gas (GHG) emissions in a way that we return to a 1.5 °C world by the end of this century (IPCC 2018). However, the voluntary commitments currently offered by countries as Nationally Determined Contributions (NDCs) under the Paris Agreement are expected to result in global warming of 2.7–3.7 °C.

The G20, which accounts for 85% of global GDP and 75% of global GHG emissions (WRI and UNDP 2018) can play a leadership role in the transition to a decarbonized world by mid-century to stay within 1.5 °C warming. This requires the adoption of a range of low carbon technologies as well as enabling policies. Some technologies may not be major contributors to mitigation at present but may have high scalability potential. For instance, the costs of solar panels have fallen sharply over time due to economies of scale in their production. As another example, purchases of electric vehicles today can create a network externality, whereby the charging stations that are set up today will lower the effective cost for future purchasers of electric vehicles (Gillingham and Stock 2018). Furthermore, some technologies and policies may have significant interaction effects such that the combined effect is more than the sum of its parts. For example, in India, higher grid penetration of renewables brought about by the National Solar Mission presents a less GHG intensive baseline for the Perform-Achieve-Trade (PAT) scheme for energy savings.

This paper examines the role of technology and supporting policies in the transition to a decarbonized world by mid-century. With the case of India, the next section discusses the types of technologies and policies that are required to be implemented during 2020–2050 to stay on track for 1.5 °C warming. The next three sections highlight the transformative low carbon technologies needed in three major sectors—transport, cooling, and data centres. The final three sections discuss the social and economic policies that are needed to support the low carbon transition.

## 2 Technologies and Policies for a Low Carbon Transition by Mid-Century: The Case of India

India's NDC commits to reducing the GHG emission intensity of its gross domestic product (GDP) by 33–35% from 2005 levels by 2030. Since 1990, India's emissions intensity (GHG emissions per unit gross domestic product, or GDP) has fallen by more than 50% (Fig. 1).

However, the continuation of currently-enacted policies and technologies is not sufficient to bend the trajectory of India's total GHG emissions. Instead there is a need to adopt new technologies and stronger policies across all key sectors to moderate the growth of GHG emissions with economic growth and demographic growth. For example, using the Energy Policy Simulator, a systems dynamics model for India (Mangan et al. 2018), Fig. 2 illustrates how the business-as-usual growth scenario of total GHG emissions in India might be reduced by almost 60% by adopting the following technologies and policies by 2050:

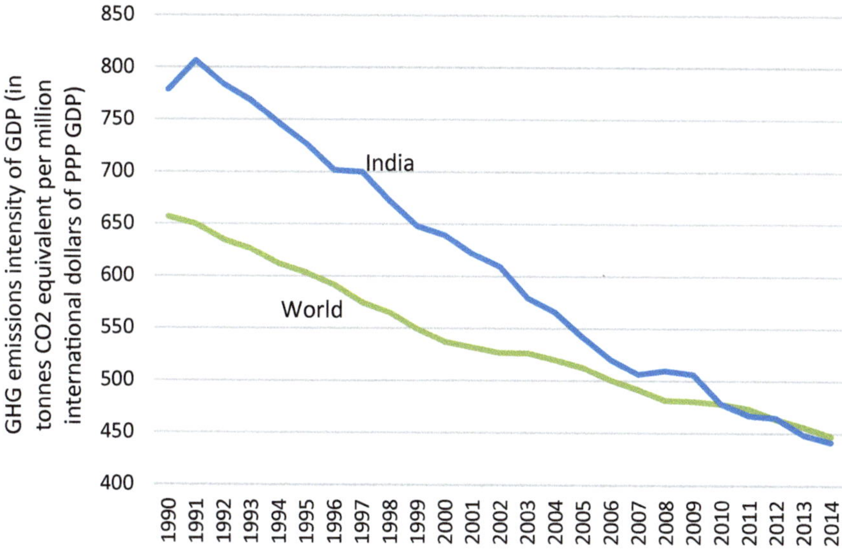


**Fig. 1** GHG emissions intensity of GDP in India. *Source* CAIT Climate Data Explorer (2017)

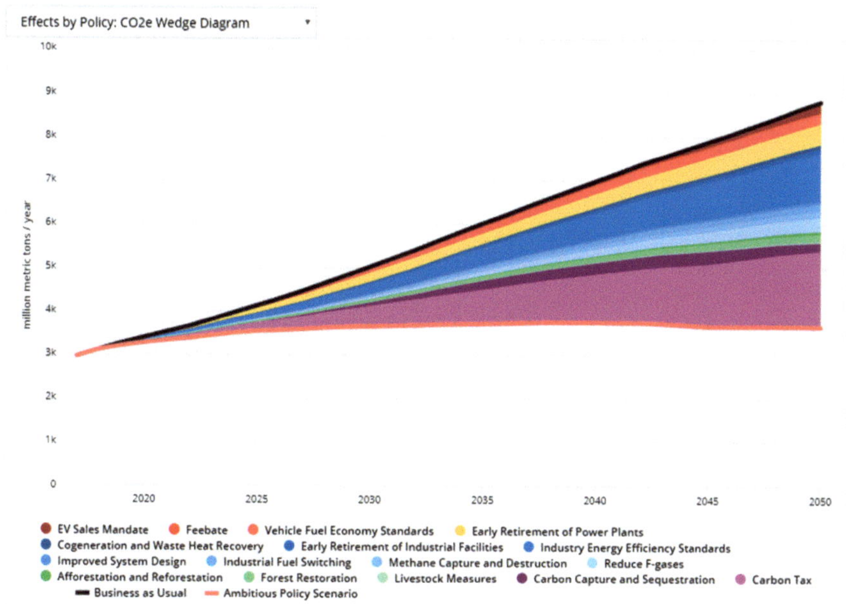


**Fig. 2** Reduction of GHG emissions in India compared with business-as-usual scenario: contributions of various additional policies and technologies (in million metric tons of $CO_2$-equivalent per year) over 2018–2050. *Source* Energy Innovation and WRI India (2018)

Transport

- Electric vehicle sales—100% of light duty vehicles (LDVs), buses, and motorbikes, and 50% of trucks
- Feebate on light-duty vehicles—100% of global best practice rate
- Increased fuel economy standards—Increases of 100% for LDVs, 66% for HDVs, 74% for motorbikes.

Electricity supply

- Early retirement of coal power plants by 6000 MW per year.

Industry

- Cogeneration and waste heat recovery—90% of potential
- Convert hard coal to natural gas equipment—25% of on-site coal use in Industry
- Early retirement of outdated facilities—90% of potential
- Fuel efficiency standards for industrial equipment—33% reduction in fuel use per unit product
- Improved system design—90% of potential
- Methane capture and use—90% of potential
- Methane destruction—90% of potential

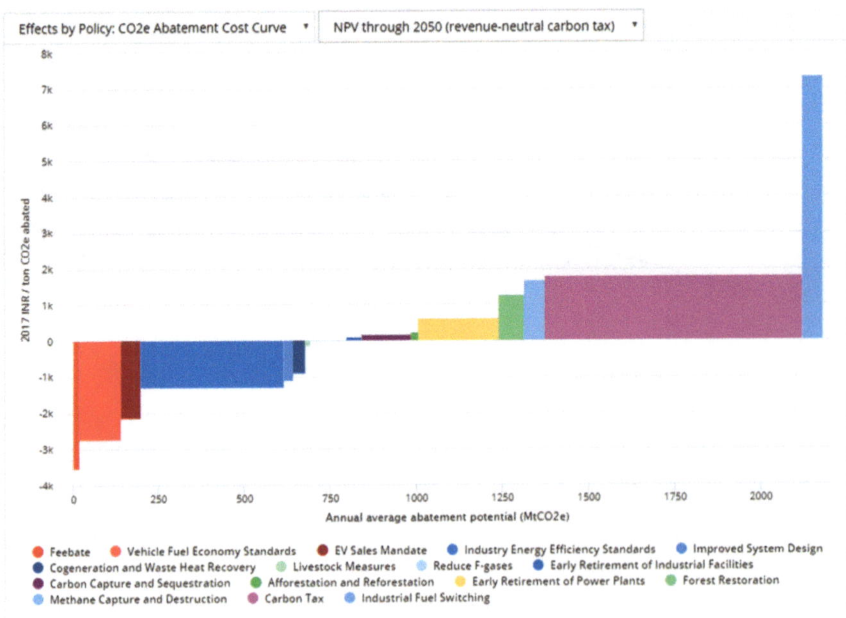


**Fig. 3** Abatement cost curve for selected GHG emission reduction technologies and policies in India over 2018–2050 (in 2017 Rs per ton of $CO_2$ reduced) *Source* Energy Innovation and WRI India (2018). *Note* Carbon pricing is assumed to be revenue-neutral

- Substitute other chemicals for F-gases—90% of potential.

Land use and agriculture

- Afforestation and reforestation of 1.4 million acres per year
- Livestock abatement measures—90% of potential
- Forest restoration—1 M hectare per year by 2020 and 0.5 M hectare per year between 2021 and 2050.

Cross-sector

- Carbon capture and sequestration—50% of potential
- Carbon price—Rs. 2500 per ton.

Figure 3 presents the same illustrative policy scenario in terms of the costs of mitigation relative to the mitigation potential of each technology or policy by 2050.

# 3 Transformative Low Carbon Technologies: Case Studies in Three Major Sectors

## *3.1 GHG Reduction Potential of Electric Vehicles*

Road transport is an important source of greenhouse gas (GHG) emissions in India, contributing 221 million tonnes of carbon dioxide equivalent in 2014, which is 8.5% of the country's total emissions (MoEFCC 2018). With rapid urbanization, India's transport sector emissions could quadruple by 2030 (Vieweg et al. 2018). Increasing the share of electric vehicles (EVs) presents an opportunity to reduce GHG emissions from road transport, as these have higher operational efficiencies than internal combustion engines. Increasing the deployment of EVs, as part of an integrated strategy of promoting public transport, shared mobility, and increased adoption of renewable energy can reduce carbon dioxide emissions from this sector by an estimated 37% by 2030 relative to business-as-usual (NITI Aayog and RMI 2017).

The net impact of EV deployment, however, depends on the source of the electricity used to manufacture and operate these vehicles.

Though EVs replace fossil fuels like petrol and diesel, EV charging draws electricity from the grid. Today 80% of India's electricity is generated from fossil fuels and only 17.5% from clean sources like solar, wind, and hydropower (CEA 2018a). Even if India achieves its current targets for installing renewables, only 22% of its electricity will be generated from renewable sources by 2032 (Thambi et al. 2018).

There could be also be variations across space and across time in the extent to which fossil fuel-based electricity is used. The southern region for instance has 51% share of thermal (coal, lignite, gas, diesel) in installed capacity, while the eastern region has 81% share of thermal in installed capacity (CEA 2018b). Charging a growing fleet of EVs at peak hours would tend to add natural gas-based electricity to the grid

since gas-based power plants can be ramped up and down relatively quickly to meet peak electricity demand.
Another aspect to consider is the GHGs emitted during the manufacturing of EVs. According to one estimate, for instance, in a country like Germany, where coal accounts currently for 40% of grid electricity, manufacturing a 500 kg electric car battery could emit up to 74% more $CO_2$ than manufacturing a conventional car (Berylls Strategy Advisors 2018).

Considering GHG emissions over the entire life cycle of EVs, the GHG impact is projected to reduce over time with greater penetration of renewables in the grid in the coming decades. Worldwide, $CO_2$ emissions per km of EVs are projected to keep falling by 3–10% annually (Bloomberg NEF 2019).

## 3.2 Moderating the Demand for Space Cooling

India developed a draft cooling action plan in 2018 for phasing out hydrofluorocarbons (HFCs) used in air-conditioners (ACs) and refrigerators. All countries, including India, have pledged to reduce HFCs by 80% by 2047. However, simply changing these chemicals will not reduce global warming caused by ACs, if we keep manufacturing and running more and more ACs using electricity from coal, oil and gas. 80% of India's electricity is generated from such fossil fuels and only 17.5% from solar, wind, and hydropower.

Over the next two decades, India's cooling demand is projected to grow eight-fold. Some of it will be used to refrigerate vaccines in rural health centers. Some to preserve perishable farm produce (fruits, vegetables, and milk) so that it boosts farmers' incomes. But these cold chains will account for a mere half per cent of the cooling demand, while a staggering 90% is expected to come from ACs in buildings and cars. Moreover, this growing demand for air conditioning is unevenly distributed—in 2011, only 5% of Indian households owned cars or ACs, but well-off urban families are expected to buy their second or third AC while the masses continue to be exposed to the elements on two-wheelers.

Even if new and efficient technologies are introduced, if people consume at a higher rate, there is bound to be an overall increase in consumption and GHG emissions—as the Jevons Paradox states. This is what will happen if we only rely on technological improvements and do not introduce strong policies to moderate the demand for air conditioning from high income population segments.

There is a need to distinguish between basic cooling need and excessive air conditioning demand. More and more buildings are expected to get air conditioned, but there is a difference between essential services like hospitals and luxury consumption like hotels and malls. That lifestyle can be encouraged to become more sustainable through policy incentives. For example, in specific seasons, green roofs that use plants to bring down temperature may be sufficient: homes with such roofs could be offered rebates on taxes or loans.

India's cooling action plan estimates that energy consumption from space cooling in buildings will double in the next decade and quadruple in the next two decades. But even a decade after the Energy Conservation Building Code (ECBC) has been introduced, its adoption by states is far from widespread. We need a detailed action plan for enforcement of this Code by builders and municipal bodies in all new construction.

## *3.3 Reducing the Carbon Footprint of Digital Technologies*

Data centres that process and store email, social media posts, shared work files, and streamed videos, generate vast amounts of heat and have to be cooled with air conditioning or running water. Running and cooling these data centres and data networks takes 2% of all the world's electricity and emits as much carbon as the entire airline industry (IEA 2017; Jones 2018). Internet companies are taking several measures to reduce the carbon footprint of their data centres. Many companies are locating their data centres in Scandinavian countries so that they can use the icy Arctic air and water for cooling. Microsoft has put a small data centre into the sea near Scotland which will release its excess heat into the surrounding sea water. But if this becomes a common practice, the heat from large server farms could adversely affect marine life. The waste heat from data centres is used to heat homes in Finland, a swimming pool in Switzerland, and a greenhouse in Paris. But so far, waste heat can only be piped over short distances and used nearby. IT companies buy renewable energy to compensate for their use of fossil fuel electricity from the grids where they operate. But this does not mean that they have stopped using electricity produced from coal, oil, and gas. Worldwide, only 24% of electricity is generated by solar, wind, and hydropower. IT companies are using artificial intelligence to detect inefficiencies in their systems and to match as closely as possible the varying availability of solar and wind power as weather conditions change during the day and over the seasons.

But the total energy used by data centres might continue to increase to meet our growing digital needs. As with any form of consumption, making supply more efficient does not reduce total consumption if demand is also not moderated. There is a need for policies that can help moderate the overall growth of fossil fuel energy use and greenhouse gas emissions from data centres in India. First, measuring and publicly reporting carbon dioxide emissions from energy use should be made mandatory for all data centres located in India. Second, state governments can make site clearance for a new data centre contingent on the company meeting part of its electricity use by generating solar power through rooftop panels or by purchasing renewable energy. The site clearance can also be made conditional on the company offsetting its use of thermal power by planting native species of trees that can absorb the equivalent of the data centre's greenhouse gas emissions. Siting within SEZs can be encouraged so that the waste heat from data centres can potentially be used by other industrial units nearby. Third, the Perform-Achieve-Trade scheme of the central government, which aims to make large industries energy efficient, can be extended to the IT industry. This would allow more efficient data centres to sell energy saving certificates to less efficient energy users. And finally, over the long term, consider putting a tax on carbon so that renewable energy becomes relatively more attractive than thermal power for industry.

# 4 Social and Ecological Tradeoffs of Low Carbon Technologies

## *4.1 Low Carbon Technologies and Jobs*

It is feared that the introduction of low carbon technologies and policies could lead to job losses in fossil fuel-based industries like coal mining, petroleum refining, thermal power generation, or manufacturing or internal combustion engine vehicles. The International Labour Organization (ILO) estimates the loss of 6 million jobs by 2030 as a result of such shifts (ILO 2018). But there are also growing economic opportunities with the emergence of low carbon industries like renewable energy, electric vehicles, green buildings, and recycling. In 2017, more people were employed in renewable energy than in coal—more than 10 million worldwide (IRENA 2018). The ILO estimates that 24 million new "green" jobs will be created by 2030, including 2.5 million jobs in renewable energy (ILO 2018). For India, a 2017 study estimated that the installation of solar and wind power capacity can directly create 330,000 new jobs in India by 2022 (Fig. 4) with an additional 45,000 jobs in manufacturing solar modules (CEEW and NRDC 2017). While the number of new green jobs may eventually offset the old polluting jobs, there is a need to ensure that the transition to a low carbon economy does not create hardship in the interim.

The new jobs that are emerging in the renewable energy sector need new skills and training. In India, for example, the Skills Council for Green Jobs offers vocational training courses for a range of new job opportunities such as rooftop solar PV installer, wind power site surveyor, solar water pumping station engineer, solar lighting technician, portable improved cookstove assembler, and biomass depot operator. The Suryamitra skill development programme of the Ministry of New and Renewable Energy also provides free training programmes across the country for solar jobs. There is a strong need to keep scaling up and increasing the reach of such training opportunities to poor people who lack the information, educational qualifications, and resources to acquire such skills. The timing and location of such programmes need to be made more conducive to the participation of women. Placement guidance and recruitment platforms need to be provided so that people, especially in rural areas, can access job openings in a timely manner.

Improving access to finance, new business models, and prudent investment are all needed to fully realise the employment generation potential of the low carbon economy. Banks should make it easier for small entrepreneurs, especially in rural areas, to access finance to set up solar charging stations, battery swapping stations, rooftop

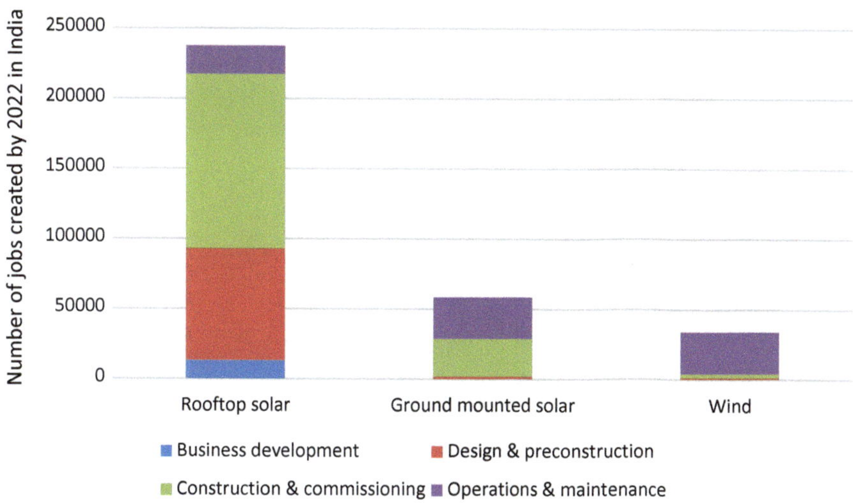


**Fig. 4** Estimated number of renewable energy jobs created in India by 2022. *Source* CEEW and NRDC (2017)

PV installation businesses, green building construction, and other such clean energy enterprises. Timely information and simpler requirements will make it possible for small entrepreneurs to be nimble and adapt to changing market demands.

A 2017 study by WRI India found that the jobs created so far in the solar PV sector in India tend to be contractual in nature and do not provide job security or benefits (WRI 2017). Social protection and safety nets are needed to ensure that this sector continues to grow and attract talent. Social protection and safety nets are crucial for occupations that are directly at risk from low carbon policies, such as coal mining, petroleum refining, and thermal power generation. Government, industry, and citizens can also work together to provide a space for social dialogue with trade unions, civil society groups, and consumer forums.

### *4.2 Low Carbon Technologies and Natural Resources*

Thermal power plants and nuclear power plants require freshwater to a considerable extent for cooling. Figure 5 maps the location of India's thermal power plants against water stressed areas. Only a few plants in Gujarat and Tamil Nadu use sea water for cooling. As India's electricity generation increased by about 40% over 2011–16, water consumption by power plants also increased at the same rate. Of the top 20 electricity utilities in India, 14 experienced at least one shutdown due to water shortages and had revenue losses of a billion dollars. Instead, if India were to meet its renewable energy targets and meet notified regulations for thermal power plants,

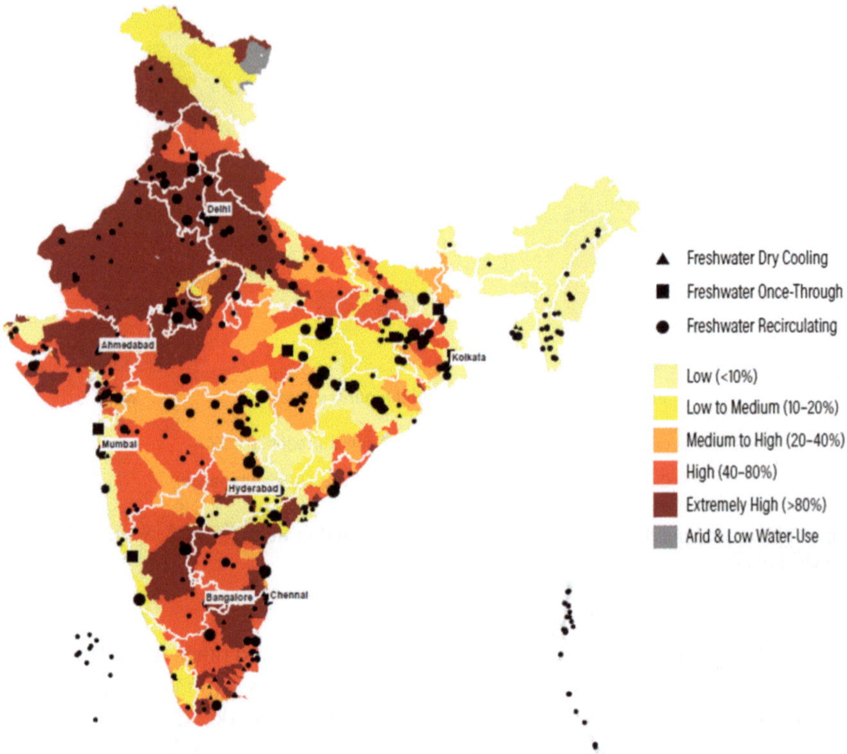


**Fig. 5** India's freshwater-cooled thermal utilities mapped against baseline water stress. *Source* Luo et al. (2018)

freshwater consumption by thermal power plants can be capped at below 2016 levels even in 2027 (Luo et al. 2018).

Another tradeoff is with regard to bioenergy with carbon capture and storage (BECCS), which the IPCC (2018) report presents as an important technology for staying within 1.5 °C warming. Widespread use of this technology may increase the demand for land for biomass, but a more sustainable method is using agriculture residue or municipal solid waste.

## 4.3 *Economic Opportunities of Low Carbon Technologies*

Recent research from the Global Commission on the Economy and Climate uses the E3ME global macroeconomic model to show that ambitious climate policies (like carbon pricing, withdrawal of fossil fuel subsidies, and circular economy) can create economic benefits of US$ 26 trillion and 65 million new jobs globally by 2030 compared with business-as-usual (NCE 2018).

The G20 has committed to phase out fossil fuel subsidies over the medium term. Fossil fuel subsidies and tax concessions amounted to around US$373 billion per year worldwide in 2015 (NCE 2018). The G20 can be bolder and make the price of coal- and oil-based energy signal its scarcity and its true social cost. This will provide policy signals that can encourage renewable energy, energy efficiency, public transport, etc. It can spur technological innovation in green building techniques, passive cooling design, and efficiency in the lifecycle use of energy—for manufacturing, raw materials, transport, service, and disposal. The High-Level Commission on Carbon Pricing has estimated that a carbon price of US$40–US$80 per tonne of carbon dioxide equivalent by 2020 is needed, rising to US$50–US$100 by 2030. It is estimated that subsidy reform and carbon pricing could generate an estimated US$2.8 trillion in government revenues per year in 2030 that could be used to invest in sustainable development actions (NCE 2018).

Another key element is financial disclosure. Large companies should take responsibility for reducing fossil fuel use in their supply chains, in the process helping small enterprises that are their suppliers or distributors to make this transition. Financial institutions, including public banks, mutual funds, insurance companies, and pension funds, should disclose their investments in fossil fuel assets that might become unprofitable over the coming years as climate regulations become more stringent. If fossil fuel investments continue, and 2 deg C policies are implemented, low cost producers will sell out their assets. Stranded fossil fuel assets of US$12 trillion by 2035 could vanish from their balance sheets (NCE 2018). The Task Force on Climate-related Financial Disclosures (TCFD) provides an approach for companies and banks to voluntary assess the climate-related risks of investments and report this as part of mainstream financial filings. Such disclosure is mandatory in France and being discussed in the EU, Canada, and China. As of September 2018, 500 major companies and banks responsible for assets of US$100 trillion have committed to such financial disclosure.

Finally, climate finance is required to support the technological transition to a low-carbon climate-resilient world. In the UNFCCC process, countries pledged in 2009 to provide US$ 100 billion of "new and additional" climate finance each year by 2020. In 2017, the annual climate finance provided amounted to US$ 87 billion. At the 24th session of the Conference of Parties (COP-24) to the UNFCCC, held in Katowice, Poland in December 2018, countries agreed to start negotiations in 2020 to set a new climate finance goal for the period after 2025. They also agreed to assess the climate finance needs of developing countries every four years. Industrialized countries have to communicate their projected future finance provision every two years. They are also required to report more details on their climate finance transfers. For instance, the different types of funding categories allowed were—grants, loans, equity, and "other". Now, guarantees and insurance have to be reported separately. Also, earlier funding for both renewable and non-renewable energy projects was reported under the "energy" sector, but now funding must be reported separately for each sub-sector.

But in addition to negotiations about mobilizing "new and additional" climate finance flows from developed countries to developing countries, there is a need to "mainstream" the entire global stock of financial capital of US$ 386 trillion so that it is consistent with low-carbon and climate-resilient development. There is a need to ensure that other finance flows are not counterproductive e.g. fossil fuel subsidies of US$ 373 billion in 2015 exceed the amount of climate finance flows mentioned earlier and are incompatible with climate goals. Multilateral development banks (MDB) have a key role to play in financing infrastructure but climate finance is less than a quarter of all MDB finance. WRI (2018) found that 40% of MDB country strategies make no reference to the country's NDC goals and only 27% of MDB country strategies specify how they will support the country's NDC goals. MDBs have committed to aligning all their investments with the goals of the Paris Agreement and this commitment needs to be operationalized.

## 5 Conclusion

We have the scientific understanding, the technical capacity, and the financial means to tackle climate change. But we need to change a host of policies that are protecting the old, inefficient, polluting economy. Emerging economies like India can enhance their NDC actions to contribute more to the transition required for 1.5 °C warming. Where tradeoffs are involved, we must strive to discuss them with those who are most affected. And policies like financial disclosure, fossil fuel subsidy report, and carbon pricing must be employed to send clear economic signals in India and globally.

## References

Berylls Strategy Advisors. (2018). *The dirt on clean electric cars*. https://www.bloomberg.com/news/articles/2018-10-16/the-dirt-on-clean-electric-cars.

Bloomberg NEF. (2019). *New energy outlook 2018*. https://www.bloomberg.com/news/articles/2019-01-15/electric-cars-seen-getting-cleaner-even-where-grids-rely-on-coal.

CEA (2018a). Growth of electricity sector in India from 1947 to 2018. Central Electricity Authority, Ministry of Power, Government of India. http://www.cea.nic.in/reports/others/planning/pdm/growth_2018.pdf.

CEA (2018b). Executive summary on power sector: Dec-18. Central Electricity Authority, Ministry of Power, Government of India. http://www.cea.nic.in/reports/monthly/executivesummary/2018/exe_summary-12.pdf.

CEEW and NRDC. (2017). *Greening India's workforce: Gearing up for expansion of solar and wind power in India*. Issue Paper. Natural Resources Defense Council and Council on Energy, Environment and Water. https://www.nrdc.org/sites/default/files/greening-india-workforce.pdf.

Energy Innovation and WRI India. (2018). *India Energy Policy Simulator*. https://india.energypolicy.solutions.

Gillingham, K., & Stock, J. H. (2018). "The cost of reducing greenhouse gas emissions". *Journal of Economic Perspectives*, 32 (4): 53–72. https://www.aeaweb.org/articles?id=10.1257/jep.32.4.53.

IEA. (2017). *Digitalization and energy*. Paris: International Energy Agency. https://www.iea.org/publications/freepublications/publication/DigitalizationandEnergy3.pdf.

ILO. (2018). *World employment and social outlook 2018: Greening with jobs*. Geneva: International Labour Organization. https://www.ilo.org/weso-greening/documents/WESO_Greening_EN_web2.pdf.

IPCC. (2018). Summary for policymakers. In V. Masson-Delmotte, P. Zhai, H.-O. Pörtner, D. Roberts, J. Skea, P. R. Shukla, A. Pirani, Moufouma-Okia, C. Péan, R. Pidcock, S. Connors, J. B. R. Matthews, Y. Chen, X. Zhou, M. I. Gomis, E. Lonnoy, Maycock, M. Tignor & T. Waterfield (Eds.), Global Warming of 1.5 °C. An IPCC Special Report on the impacts of global warming of 1.5 °C above pre-industrial levels and related global greenhouse gas emission pathways, in the context of strengthening the global response to the threat of climate change, sustainable development, and efforts to eradicate poverty(p. 32). Geneva, Switzerland: World Meteorological Organization. https://www.ipcc.ch/sr15/.

IRENA. (2018). Renewable energy and jobs: Annual Review 2018. Abu Dhabi: International Renewable Energy Agency. https://irena.org/publications/2018/May/Renewable-Energy-and-Jobs-Annual-Review-2018.

Jones, N. (2018). How to stop data centres from gobbling up the world's electricity. *Nature* 561: 163–166. https://www.nature.com/articles/d41586-018-06610-y.

Luo, T., Krishnan, D., Sen, S. (2018). *Parched power: Water demands, risks, and opportunities for India's power sector*. http://www.wri.org/publication/parched-power.

MoEFCC. (2018). India: Second Biennial Update Report to the United Nations Framework Convention on Climate Change. Ministry of Environment, Forest and Climate Change, Government of India. https://unfccc.int/sites/default/files/resource/INDIA%20SECOND%20BUR%20High%20Res.pdf.

Mangan, E., Mitra, A., & Rissman, J. (2018). *A tool for designing policies to achieve India's climate targets: Summary of methods and data used in the India energy policy simulator*. Technical Note. Washington, DC: World Resources Institute. www.wri.org/publication/achieve-india-climate-targets.

NCE. (2018). *Unlocking the inclusive growth story of the 21st century: accelerating climate action in urgent times*. New Climate Economy, The Global Commission on the Economy and Climate. https://newclimateeconomy.report/2018/.

NITI Aayog and Rocky Mountain Institute. (2017). *India leaps ahead: Transformative mobility solutions for all*. https://www.rmi.org/insights/reports/transformative_mobility_solutions_india.

Thambi, S., Bhatacharya, A., & Fricko, O. (2018). *India's energy and emissions outlook: Results from India energy model*. Working Paper. Energy, Climate Change and Overseas Engagement Division, NITI Aayog, Government of India. http://niti.gov.in/writereaddata/files/document_publication/India's-Energy-and-Emissions-Outlook_0.pdf.

Vieweg, M., Bongardt, D., Hochfeld, C., Jung, A., Scherer, E., Adib, R., Guerra, F. (2018). *Towards decarbonising transport – A 2018 Stocktake on sectoral ambition in the G20*. Report on behalf of Agora Verkehrswende and Deutsche Gesellschaft für Internationale Zusammenarbeit (GIZ). https://www.agora-verkehrswende.de/fileadmin/Projekte/2017/Verkehr_und_Klima_in_den_G20_Laendern/15_G20_WEB.pdf.

WRI. (2017). *Can renewable energy jobs help reduce poverty in India*? World Resources Institute. https://wri-india.org/resources/publications/can-renewable-energy-jobs-help-reduce-poverty-india.

WRI & UNDP. (2018). Long-term low greenhouse gas emission development strategies: Approaches and methodologies for their design. Input Document for the G20 Climate Sustainability Working Group. A paper prepared by World Resources Institute and the United Nations Development Programme for the G20 Climate Sustainability Working Group under the Argentine G20 Presidency. https://www.wri.org/publication/designing-G20-long-term-strategies.

# Chapter 9
# Climate Ambition Needs Targeted Technology Collaboration

**Arunabha Ghosh, Vaibhav Chaturvedi and Shikha Bhasin**

**Abstract** It is widely accepted that technology development and diffusion is critical to meet climate targets, yet specific stakeholder and institutional roles, as well as integration costs, remain largely undefined at a macro level. This chapter sheds light on the elements that hold key to actualising technologies through frameworks that allow for cooperative and collaborative arrangements of burden-sharing, rather than maintaining strategic competitive advantages. It highlights, first, the kinds of technologies that will be crucial for meeting climate goals and the uncertainties associated with them. Uncertainties pertain to development pathways, economic growth, technological development and costs, socio-political factors, and secondary and tertiary impacts. Next, the chapter examines existing multilateral frameworks for technology development and diffusion to identify the gaps therein. Finally, it outlines the principles for more effective technology partnerships to meet stringent climate stabilisation targets and submits templates for three alternative modalities for technological development, ranging from those that are ready to scale but need commercial pilots, to horizon technologies that have significant risks.

## 1 Introduction

In September 2015, at the United Nations General Assembly, Indian Prime Minister Narendra Modi called for a "global public partnership to harness technology, innovation and finance to put affordable clean and renewable energy within the reach

The original version of this book was revised: Missing abstracts of chapters 3, 6, 8, 9 and 11 have now been included. The correction to this book can be found at https://doi.org/10.1007/978-981-13-8106-5_12

A. Ghosh (✉) · V. Chaturvedi · S. Bhasin
Council on Energy, Environment and Water (CEEW), New Delhi, India
e-mail: arunabha.ghosh@ceew.in

V. Chaturvedi
e-mail: vaibhav.chaturvedi@ceew.in

S. Bhasin
e-mail: shikha.bhasin@ceew.in

 
R. Kathuria and P. Kukreja (eds.), *20 Years of G20*,
https://doi.org/10.1007/978-981-13-8106-5_9

of all." (Modi 2015). A few days later, on 2 October, when India submitted its Intended Nationally Determined Contribution (INDC) to the UN Framework Convention on Climate Change (UNFCCC), it proposed "global collaborative research [on] clean coal..., energy management and storage systems for renewable energy." India intended to "build capacities, create [the] domestic framework and international architecture for quick diffusion of cutting edge climate technology...and for joint collaborative R&D..." (GoI 2015).

India was right to argue that low-carbon growth would need much greater focus on shifting technologies "from lab to field". This was not just a need for India but for all major economies, which have the potential to collaborate on the technologies that could avert a climate catastrophe. The Paris Agreement on climate change aims to limit temperature rise to 'well below 2 °C' above pre-industrial levels. A shift towards a 1.5 °C target requires a step change in technological collaboration, development, testing, deployment, and manufacturing and commercialization at scale. Action, thus far, has not been in line with ambition.

It is widely accepted that technology development and diffusion is critical to meet climate targets, yet specific technological roles and their integration costs remain largely undefined at a macro level. This chapter sheds light on the elements that hold key to actualising technologies through frameworks that allow for cooperative and collaborative arrangements of burden-sharing, rather than maintaining strategic competitive advantages. It highlights, first, the kinds of technologies that will be crucial for meeting climate goals, but more significantly the uncertainties associated with them. Uncertainties pertain to development pathways, economic growth, technological development and costs, socio-political factors, and secondary and tertiary impacts. Next, the chapter examines existing multilateral frameworks for technology development and diffusion to identify the gaps therein. Finally, it outlines the principles for more effective technology partnerships to meet stringent climate stabilisation targets. It submits the templates of three alternative modalities for technological development, ranging from those that are ready to scale but need commercial pilots, to horizon technologies that have significant risks.

## 2 Technological Uncertainties in a World of Rising Ambition

The IPCC Special Report on 1.5 °C states that 'in comparison to a 2 °C limit, the transformations required to limit warming to 1.5 °C are qualitatively similar but more pronounced and rapid over the next decades (high confidence) (IPCC 2018)'. In essence, this implies that the set of technologies that are required for mitigation would in all probability be the same, just the application of these has to come in force rapidly—and at scale. In this context, it becomes critical to assess uncertainties related to technologies in a world of rising ambition.

## *2.1 Dimensions of Technology-Related Uncertainties*

Uncertainties are complex to understand, and there could be various dimensions of uncertainties in different contexts. Here we highlight the important dimensions of mitigation technology related uncertainties that are relevant for the discussion on cooperation between the G20 economies (Fig. 1).

### 2.1.1 Development Pathways-Related Uncertainties

The world could move towards alternative futures that are very different from each other. In the past 40 years or so, countries across the world have accepted the idea of globalisation and trade liberalisation as the desired future towards which the world should move. Of late, in the last few years, the idea of globalisation has been questioned by leaders across many countries, and the world appears to be heading in a different direction. The development pathway that the world charts and the future that we end up in will have important implications for technology cooperation and mitigation in a high ambition world. The Shared Socio-Economic Pathways (SSPs) provide a framework for assessment of alternative futures for the world (see, for example, Dellink et al. 2017; KC & Lutz 2017; Riahi et al. 2017; Kriegler et al. 2017; and IPCC SAR WG3 1996). The five SSPs paint alternative futures, where-in the world can move in the direction of sustainability, regional rivalry, inequality, fossil-fueled development, or somewhere that can be classified as middle-of-the-

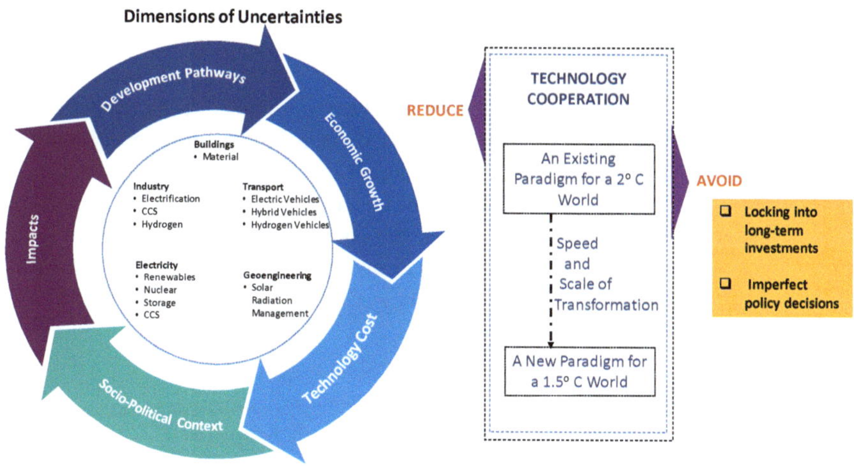


**Fig. 1** Technology cooperation can reduce uncertainties and avoid lock-ins and imperfect policy decisions to ensure speed and scale of low carbon technology penetration for a 1.5 °C world

road scenario reflecting current trends.[1] Depending on which path the world takes, the dynamics of technology cooperation would be very different, that need to be explored and understood.

### 2.1.2 Economic Growth-Related Uncertainties

It is logical to assume that in scenarios with deep inequality or rivalries across countries, the economic growth would be hit for most countries of the world. But for any given development pathway, economic growth could be high or low on average. Economic growth is important not only from the perspective of purchasing power of mitigation technologies, but is also bound to impact technology innovation across countries and the scale at which a mitigation technology penetrates in countries across the world. A high level of GDP implies that countries can invest more in the research and development of mitigation technologies, as well as incentivise their deployment and scale up through financial support. Even if countries want to cooperate for mitigating climate change, the dynamics of technology cooperation could be different in a world that is beset by lower GDP and economic growth as compared to a world with high GDP and growth.

### 2.1.3 Technology Cost-Related Uncertainties

Experience has shown that a drop in cost has a significant impact on the penetration of mitigation technologies.[2] The pace of penetration of solar technology has accelerated only after the sharp drop in its cost. Nuclear penetration in India, and in many countries across the world which are not philosophically against nuclear energy, has not picked pace largely because the comparative cost of nuclear-based electricity has been too high.[3,4] Economic modelling of future technology scenarios has shown that how the relative cost of fossil and non-fossil electricity generation technologies evolves will determine the extent to which the electricity system will move towards non-fossil energy.[5] The pace of decline in the cost of electric vehicles will determine their penetration in the market.[6] However, the pace of decline of the cost of either renewable technologies or electric vehicles is anybody's guess. Better understanding of this issue is important for devising a strategy.

---

[1]Dellink et al. (2017), KC and Lutz (2017), Riahi et al. (2017), Kriegler et al. (2017) and IPCC SAR WG3 (1996).

[2]Chaturvedi et al. (2018).

[3]Chaturvedi et al. (2017).

[4]Hultman et al. (2007).

[5]Chaturvedi et al. (2018).

[6]Chaturvedi et al. (2018).

### 2.1.4 Socio-political Uncertainties Related to Technologies

How society reacts to a technology has proven to be either an impediment, or a facilitator to the penetration of mitigation technologies. Germany, for example, has chosen not to include nuclear energy in its response to climate change. In some Nordic countries, wind farms have led to decline in the value of real estate due to the visual impact of wind farms. On the other hand, solar power has found many backers in developing economies due to its potential for distributed application which can have a positive impact on electricity access as well as livelihood opportunities. How societies—and the political class as the representative of societies—respond to various trade-offs associated with a given technology in the medium and long run will have a bearing on the evolution of these mitigation technologies.[7] Institutions will respond to the position taken by key stakeholders and decision makers in the society.

### 2.1.5 Uncertainties Related to the Short and Long-Term Impact of Technologies

Technologies have potential impacts. For example, opponents to nuclear power plants highlight the nuclear disasters experienced with these as a proof of the danger in going ahead with this technology. Experts have raised questions on the disposal and impact of solar panels as well as chemical batteries once their technical life is over. Horizon technologies like solar radiation management (SRM) could have drastic impacts on monsoon cycles, which could negatively impact the livelihoods of many in the developing world.[8,9] A high bio-energy world, as required for deep decarbonisation, could impact cropping pattern and food prices across countries. Each mitigation technology is bound to have its own set of impacts that are uncertain at best, and which would have implications for technology cooperation. SRM would necessitate global cooperation on technology governance,[10] while other mitigation technologies will have their own nuanced impacts related to cooperation.

## 2.2 *Why Uncertainties Matter for Technology Cooperation*

The choice of mitigation technology portfolio could change significantly depending on how various dimensions of uncertainties evolve and interact with each other. Valuation of robustness and timeliness of information could provide interesting insights

[7] See, for example: Riahi et al. (2017), Chaturvedi et al. (2018), Dellink et al. (2017), KC and Lutz (2017), Kriegler et al. (2017) and IPCC SAR WG3 (1996).

[8] Pasztor et al. (2019).

[9] Ghosh (2018a).

[10] Ghosh (2018a).

into how much longer decision-makers could wait for better information related to a technology. However, it is imperative that for achieving the 1.5 °C scenario, investments need to happen as early as possible. A wait-and-watch approach is increasingly not within the portfolio of choices. In such a scenario, a better characterisation of uncertainties and attempting to reduce these through technology cooperation could help in:

Informing government policies: For devising policy packages for incentivising mitigation technologies, it is important to have a good understanding of uncertainties related to mitigation technologies. There are different objectives of policy, for which different kinds of instruments are required. Policies could be for promoting research and innovation, for addressing imperfect or asymmetric information, or for inducing stakeholders to act on the basis of available information. All these objectives deal with different levels of uncertainties. Technology cooperation could also be at either of these levels, and would impact how uncertainties shape the development of a given technology. Ideally, technology cooperation should be able to reduce uncertainties rather than enhance them. Technology cooperation, hence, should not just be driven by government policies, but should also aim to inform government policies by reducing uncertainties for specific mitigation technologies of interest.

Avoiding lock-ins: As argued above, technology cooperation could inform how investors view uncertainties related to mitigation technologies of interest. Ultimately, a higher degree of certainty related to the long-term technical and financial viability of mitigation technologies should help to avoid locking into fossil fuel-based technologies. Thereby, the chances of stranded assets in energy infrastructure would also be reduced. In moving from 2 to 1.5 °C, investments need to happen at a faster pace, with less time for better understanding and responding to uncertainties. In other words, the higher the climate ambition, greater would be the probabilistic bets that policymakers would have to place on a set of mitigation technologies. Protocols for cooperation would have to reduce the range of the probabilities while increasing the willingness to place joint technology bets.

## 2.3 *Key Technologies Across Sectors, and Uncertainties Around These, for Achieving 1.5 °C*

Fast and deep transformations need to happen across sectors. Here we discuss the key technology-related uncertainties across various mitigation sectors.

### 2.3.1 Transport

The transport sector energy consumption, across the world, is dominated by oil. In the alternative low-carbon vehicle debate, electric vehicles (EVs), hybrid vehicles (HBVs), and hydrogen vehicles (HVs) are being discussed. Many European countries appear to be moving the EV way, while few other countries like Japan have seen a higher penetration of HBVs as compared to electric or hydrogen. Many countries and companies are also experimenting with hydrogen vehicles, particularly for buses. On the technology front, it could be argued that the technologies are well understood and mature, but the economics associated with them are impeding their adoption with speed and at scale. Of these, the cost of EVs has fallen most rapidly with a fast decline in battery costs. Cost declines in the other two have not been able to match up with the decline in the cost of EVs. It is fairly certain, at least in the public debate, that EV costs will continue to fall rapidly and it is just a matter of time for EVs to dominate global vehicle sales. Progress in the other two technologies is probably more uncertain. For a hydrogen economy, it is also imperative to create a hydrogen supply infrastructure, which is a significant investment and further impedes its penetration in the market. However, if hydrogen were chosen by governments as a low-carbon fuel for industrial applications, it could provide fillip to its usage in the transport sector as well.

### 2.3.2 Industry

Research has highlighted two main options for the decarbonisation of the industrial sector. The first is electrification. In India, for example, fossil fuels account for more than 80% of industrial energy use. It is imperative to electrify end-use processes to reduce direct emissions from the industrial sector. However, there are many different kinds of industrial processes, and technology substitution possibilities might vary across these. We need to better understand the technological as well as economic barriers towards electrification of industrial energy use. As of now, knowledge on this issue is fairly limited leading to uncertainty for decision-makers.

The second option is carbon capture and storage (CCS). In scenarios with continued dependence on fossil fuels for industrial energy use, CCS becomes an imperative. Progress on this technology, however, has been far from satisfactory. Experiments are ongoing, but there has been no long-term experience with the technical and commercial viability of all components across the CCS value chain. CCS has remained expensive, and is expected to be pushed only if carbon is explicitly valued. Under scenarios with explicit cap or tax on carbon dioxide emissions, there is a possibility of CCS becoming viable. In scenarios wherein technologies are incentivised through direct fiscal support, CCS technology might be a loser as mature technologies are favoured by policymakers for near-term policy and fiscal support. Overall, uncertainties related to CCS are far higher than those related to electrification of industrial energy use.

Along with these two options, a third option—hydrogen—is now emerging in the debate. Research on hydrogen-based applications for industrial energy use is fairly limited, but shows promise. Industrial investments have long gestation periods, and if transition towards alternative fuels does not happen in the near term, the world might be locked into fossil investments for a long time. Any technology cooperation paradigm has to account for all the low-carbon options.

### 2.3.3 Electricity

Mitigation technologies in the electricity generation sector are generally mature in terms of their technical progress. Be it solar photovoltaic or solar thermal, wind energy, or nuclear energy, the technologies have proven themselves. Nuclear power generation technologies have witnessed significant progress in terms of their safety features, although accompanied by increased costs. Still, this technology faces socio-political uncertainties. Germany, for example, has decided not to have this technology in its mitigation portfolio, and other nations could choose the same in the future.

For higher penetration of renewable energy, storage technologies become critical. Although in the last few years there have been significant advances in storage technologies, research with alternative materials for batteries is still ongoing. The batteries of the future could be very different from the batteries of today. Due to this uncertainty, large-scale investments in specific types of battery manufacturing plants may become risky. Only investors with deep pockets can take this risk. The future impact of batteries is uncertain, and their disposal could become an important issue in the future.

Another big uncertainty in this sector is related to CCS. It does appear that the world is moving in the direction of renewable energy, and the role of both nuclear energy and CCS is fairly muted at this time. Unless significant reduction happens in the cost of these technologies, expecting rapid penetration of these is arguably optimistic at best.

### 2.3.4 Buildings

The buildings sector is viewed in the mitigation discourse mainly through the perspective of energy efficiency. Appliances and lighting devices have become more and more efficient in the last few years on the back of policy support across the world. The biggest uncertainty, however, has been in terms of the kind of buildings that the world will see and needs to see in the long-term future. Building stock is a very long-term investment. Within India, it is expected that the building stock will grow three times in the next two decades. Will these buildings still be made with carbon-intensive cement, or will there be modified or alternative low-carbon materials is a big uncertainty? Changing the existing manufacturing set up to give way for new industries is a big challenge, and also a big uncertainty.

Irrespective of the building material, how efficiently buildings are designed would be important to reduce the cooling/heating loads and the requirement for lighting. Use of appropriate insulation material and natural lighting has implications for electricity demand. However, world over, we are not witnessing a surge in energy-efficient buildings though the knowledge has been there for some time. The biggest uncertainties in this space are institutional and regulatory, given that regulating the real estate sector has been a challenge in many countries, especially developing economies.

#### 2.3.5 Climate Geoengineering

Climate geoengineering is gaining increasing attention, as the world seems to be on a path that is well on track for more than 3 °C of warming on average. Climate geoengineering interventions are being conceptualised as a way to break the link between increasing carbon emissions and rising temperatures, either by removing carbon from the atmosphere (carbon dioxide removal) or by reducing the amount of solar insolation reaching the Earth's surface (solar radiation management (SRM)).[11,12]

There are a number of uncertainties surrounding the technical feasibility, economic viability and political motivation behind various SRM technologies.[13] For instance, injecting sulphate particles into the stratosphere could reflect sunlight back into space but could also affect regional rainfall patterns and crop production. The second and third order effects of SRM (such as the termination effect whereby stopping an SRM experiment could result in a rapid increase in surface temperatures) add to the technological—and political—uncertainties.

## 3 How Have Existing Tech-Focused Initiatives Fared?

For technological cooperation on mitigation technologies to enable low-carbon transformations, a strong normative imperative push within the climate regime, and a multitude of platforms for climate action at the national, bilateral and multilateral level are needed to tackle uncertainties highlighted above. Mission-oriented programmes and policies, as well as targeted technology platforms and partnerships have emerged in response to such needs. However, while most multilateral platforms recognise the need for multi-level and multi-institutional systemic changes to bring about technological transformations at scale and with speed, on-ground reality does not reflect such thinking adequately.

### *3.1 Multilateral Initiatives*

UNFCCC's Technology Mechanism: Technology transfers have been a key demand within the UNFCCC climate negotiations for several years.[14] In response, the UNFCCC's Technology Mechanism was designed to include a "policy arm" (the Technology Executive Committee or TEC) and an "implementation arm" (the Climate Technology Centre and Network or CTCN).[15]

---

[11]Ghosh (2018a).

[12]Pasztor et al. (2019).

[13]Ghosh (2018a).

[14]See, for example, UNFCCC (1992) and UNFCCC (2006).

[15]UNFCCC (2010).

The TEC was created to provide "an overview of needs" to enable development and transfer of climate technologies and suggest interventions and policies for 'technology cooperation' (UNFCCC 2010). Since its inception in 2011, the TEC has produced a significant number of policy briefs that are relevant for encouraging technology cooperation.[16] However, its primary composition, and audience, continues to be climate negotiators and officials from countries' environment ministries that reflect a lot of the same deadlocks as are seen in the negotiating rooms; and it has not grown into an influential authority for encouraging technology cooperation, as it was envisaged to be. Its expertise does not even reflect in the work of the CTCN, which is meant to be its implementation counterpart. For example, while the TEC has developed and published excellent knowledge pieces on how countries can undertake technology cooperation, the number of requests posed to the CTCN on R&D and market creation are less than 5% of the total since its inception.[17]

The CTCN was expected to "facilitate national, regional, sectoral and international technology networks, organizations and initiatives to mobilize and enhance global clean technology capabilities, provide direct assistance to developing countries, and facilitate prompt action on the deployment of existing technologies"[18] (UNFCCC 2010). It is noteworthy that the CTCN, although established as the implementation arm for technology cooperation "does not provide funding directly to countries, but instead supports the provision of technical assistance provided by experts on specific climate technology sectors".[19] It does so through its network that includes public and private, civil society and research entities. In essence what was meant to be a multilateral platform to enhance capabilities and undertake technology cooperation has become a project-specific request-stop for countries. Since its inception in 2014, 69 requests to the CTCN have been completed.[20] However, looking at the entire portfolio of requests put to the CTCNs from especially constituted Nationally Designated Entities in countries, usually based at the environment ministries in developing economies, over 80% of these requests are focussed on technology identification, feasibility and sectoral roadmaps, and policy and legal recommendations; and less than 20% of requests are on undertaking pilots, facilitating financing, conducting R&D, setting up markets, and engaging with the private sector.[21] While these requests are country-led, the notion of CTCN being an enabler for technology identification and provider of initial support to identify relevant technologies and initiate readiness projects is also commonplace now. R&D requests, for example, constitute less than 3% of all requests made to the CTCN. As a platform for technology cooperation, it must actively seek to shed itself of this image, and attract countries to apply for projects that alleviate technology risks and uncertainties and

---

[16]See, for example, publications listed here: http://unfccc.int/ttclear/tec/documents.html.

[17]https://www.ctc-n.org/technical-assistance/request-visualizations.

[18]UNFCCC (2010).

[19]Climate Technology Centre and Network (2019a).

[20]Climate Technology Centre and Network (2019b).

[21]Climate Technology Centre and Network (2019b).

encourage innovations. However, to do so, structural financing to meet its goals must also be mandated.[22]

The Technology Mechanism that emerged within the UNFCCC is explicitly aimed at enhancing climate technology development and transfers, and building innovation systems; but has so far fallen quite short even in enabling technology cooperation that is transformational or distinctly different from other multilateral technology focussed projects.

Mission Innovation: Mission Innovation (MI) was established to ‘make clean energy widely affordable’ by doubling investments into R&D and innovations by member countries. It aims to tackle the financial burden of disseminating technologies through increased public investments, public-private partnerships, and targeted innovation programmes.

Globally it’s been challenging to gather information on technology collaborations (and the funding supporting it) outside of specific programmes. MI has signed agreements with IEA and IRENA to improve data collection and management of public and private sector R&D spending on clean energy.[23] Such data sharing initiatives could help ascertain the gaps in funding for technologies and support the development of partnerships across national borders and may also encourage other countries to increase their spending towards low-carbon technologies’ innovations.

Over 40 ‘collaboration’ initiatives, many of them public-private partnerships, have been announced among member-countries since Mission Innovation’s inception in 2015.[24] These range from setting up open data platforms to understand building efficiencies for HVAC solutions, to creating MRV capacities in high-carbon sectors such as oil and gas, establishing innovation prizes for energy storage and climate-friendly cooling, and undertaking resource and site assessments for geothermal energy development. In addition, MI has set out eight ‘innovation challenges’ on technology areas that include smart grids, off-grid electricity access, CCS and storage and others, the most recent challenge area being on hydrogen. The mid-term results of these innovation challenges, presented in summer 2018, largely include research and gap analysis for these technologies, workshops, as well as the establishment of innovation-focussed prizes and funding calls.[25] It is not clear yet how far these innovation challenges will facilitate the curtailment of uncertainties associated with large-scale technology deployment.

Several other cases of multilateralism which have technology transfer and cooperation as a key goal remain limited in offerings for technological transformations towards low-carbon pathways, and have largely catered to softer capacity and capability efforts through knowledge sharing. Some key climate partnerships reflecting this reality have been captured in the Table 1.

---

[22]The CTCN does not benefit from any structural funding—this is a key barrier to fulfilling its mandate. Its request-realisations are contingent on raised funds, several of which are tied to financing terms and preferences.

[23]Mission Innovation (2018a).

[24]Mission Innovation (2018b).

[25]Mission Innovation (2019).

**Table 1** Climate partnerships: motivations and intentions

| Partnership | Knowledge sharing and coordination | Research, development and demonstration | Technology transfer | Deployment mandates, standards and incentives |
|---|---|---|---|---|
| *Forums for research and policies* | | | | |
| Asia-Pacific Partnership on Clean Development and Climate | ✓ | X | ✓ (Project implementation) | X |
| Climate Technology Initiative under the International Energy Agency | ✓ | ✓ | ✓ (Soft transfer) | X |
| Economic Community of West African States Centre for Renewable Energy and Energy Efficiency | ✓ | X | ✓ (Soft transfer) | ✓ |
| Global Green Growth Institute | ✓ | X | X | X |
| International Renewable Energy Agency | ✓ | X | ✓ (Soft transfer) | X |
| Renewable Energy Policy Network for the 21st Century | ✓ | X | ✓ (Soft transfer) | X |
| *Forums with a regional focus* | | | | |
| Asia-Pacific Economic Cooperation Energy Ministerial | ✓ | X | X | X |
| Baltic Sea Region Energy Cooperation | ✓ | X | ✓ | X |
| European Green Cities Network | ✓ | X | ✓ (Demonstration) | X |
| Latin American Energy Organisation | ✓ | X | X | ✓ |

(continued)

**Table 1** (continued)

| Partnership | Knowledge sharing and coordination | Research, development and demonstration | Technology transfer | Deployment mandates, standards and incentives |
|---|---|---|---|---|
| Regional Centre for Renewable Energy and Energy Efficiency | ✓ | ✓ | X | ✓ |
| Renewable Energy Support Program for ASEAN | ✓ | X | X | X |
| US-Asia Pacific Comprehensive Energy Partnership | ✓ | ✓ | ✓ (Soft transfer) | X |
| *Forums for city-level action* | | | | |
| C40 | ✓ | X | ✓ (Soft transfer) | X |
| Cities Development Initiative for Asia | ✓ | X | X | X |
| Local Governments for Sustainability | ✓ | X | X | X |
| *Forums with specific focus* | | | | |
| Carbon Sequestration Leadership Forum | ✓ | X | ✓ (Soft transfer) | X |
| Clean Technology Fund of the World Bank | X | X | ✓ | X |
| Climate and Clean Air Coalition | ✓ | X | ✓ (Soft transfer) | |
| Climate Technology Centres and Networks | ✓ | ✓ | ✓ (Soft transfer) | X |
| EC-ASEAN COGEN Programme | X | X | ✓ (Demonstration) | |

(continued)

**Table 1** (continued)

| Partnership | Knowledge sharing and coordination | Research, development and demonstration | Technology transfer | Deployment mandates, standards and incentives |
|---|---|---|---|---|
| Global Bio-energy Partnership | ✓ | X | ✓ (Soft transfer) | X |
| International Framework on Nuclear Energy Partnership | ✓ | ✓ | X | X |
| International Low Carbon Energy Technology Platform | X | ✓ | X | X |
| International Partnership for Energy Efficiency Cooperation | ✓ | X | X | ✓ |
| Renewable Energy and Energy Efficiency Partnership | ✓ | X | X | ✓ |

*Source* Ghosh et al. (2015)

## 3.2 *Bilateral Initiatives*

Examples also abound of bilateral technology cooperation among G20 countries. But they have fallen short of objectives.

The India-US Joint Clean Energy R&D Centres were launched in 2012 to jointly develop technologies. Initial enthusiasm was such that rather than match the 50 per cent contribution (of the $100 million budget) from the two governments, the research consortia pooled in $75 million.[26] Initiatives included research on solar, energy efficiency, advanced biofuels, and energy storage. The first R&D phase was for five years but the commercialisation phase has stalled.

The Indo-German solar energy partnership focuses on solar rooftops, solar parks connected to renewable energy corridors, and off-grid installations. The Indo-German Energy Forum has discussed energy security, energy efficiency in homes and indus-

[26]Ghosh (2017a).

tries, efficient cooling, and investments in renewable energy. Yet, there is no major initiative to jointly develop the next generation of energy technologies.[27]

France and India together launched the International Solar Alliance (ISA) in late 2015, with solar-related R&D as one of its main pillars.[28] Again, no work programme has been launched on this front, whereas work has begun on affordable finance and scaling existing technologies.[29]

US and China's Clean Energy Research Centre (CERC) was set up in 2009 to encourage joint research, development and deployment of clean energy technologies, and to understand commercial viability and cross-border market access for climate-friendly technologies. The CERC has birthed several invention disclosures and patents (39), research outcomes (44) and product launches (15), in part thanks to a strong and unique IP strategy that builds trust across actors in sharing information, and retaining rights for new technologies.[30] However, despite attempting to fill a trust deficit as well as actually undertaking R&D and creating patented technologies, the CERC has been critiqued for not quite 'jointly' undertaking research and collaborations, in that only a small part of the IP has been generated as a result of 'cross-national collaborative activities'.[31]

## 4 Taking Stock: What's not Happening, Why, and What Is Needed?

The experience of multilateral and bilateral initiatives for nearly two decades reveal several reasons why technology partnerships have not met their potential or promise.

The first challenge is the absence of targeted research. Open-ended research is harder to engender between countries, whose research capacities and market conditions might differ significantly. Instead, technological collaboration can be more targeted if participating countries defined technical and/or commercial parameters and then gave the freedom to research consortia to develop technologies that met those criteria.

Innovators respond to market signals, especially when public policy can nudge R&D in specific directions. For instance, a carbon price, directed R&D investment or advance market commitments to guarantee a market for low-carbon technologies could foster collaboration among research institutions and industry in markets where investors might be hesitant to enter. The US Department of Energy's SunShot Initiative offered incentives for innovators to reduce the cost of solar, leading to sharp decrease in solar technology prices. In India, the Domestic Efficient Lighting Programme used large-scale public procurement and subsequent resale to consumers

---

[27] Ghosh (2017a).

[28] Ghosh and Chawla (2018).

[29] Ghosh (2017a).

[30] US-China Clean Energy Research Centre (2019).

[31] Lewis (2014).

as a strategy to slash costs of LED bulbs by 60 per cent within three years. Similar strategies could spur multi-country collaborations as well.[32]

Secondly, technology collaborations require technical and financial capacity.[33] But perceived lack of capacity is also a reason why partnerships do not come to fruition. Participating countries and institutions can contribute to joint efforts even without injecting hard currency. Member countries and institutions can pool resources via research staff, offering scientific facilities, or land for demonstration projects. In order to be inclusive and effective, technology partnerships also need to develop capacity in weaker partner countries.[34]

Thirdly, intellectual property (IP) restrictions often impede deep collaboration. One approach is to design partnerships with participating institutions (firms or research labs) retaining their original IP but jointly holding IP rights over new technologies that the consortium develops.[35] This approach has been followed in other global technology partnerships, such as the Consultative Group on International Agricultural Research, the Human Genome Project, the CERN particle accelerator, and the International Thermonuclear Experimental Reactor.

Fourthly, the absence of an ecosystem for venture capital investment in many countries makes it harder to sustain technology partnerships. Partnerships cannot rely solely on public financing. Private investment and credit have to be crowded in. Many innovators struggle to prove technical concepts at scale that could eventually attract private equity and commercial debt. This gap could be potentially bridged via targeted public investment.[36]

Beyond the technical development stages, commercial pilots need strategic investment to test technologies in the market. Entrepreneurs need upfront financing to cover capital costs of clean energy technologies, working capital to hold inventories, and funds to pay IP license fees. Without private investment, many innovations remain restricted to the laboratories, thereby creating further scepticism about the value of multi-country collaborations.

## *4.1 Guiding Principles*

In order to overcome these barriers, new tech partnerships have to adhere to six guiding principles.

### 4.1.1 Objectives Matter

Technology cooperation is likely to fail if the participating countries/firms/research institutions are not agreed on the specific objectives of the initiative. For some,

---

[32]Ghosh (2015).

[33]Ghosh et al. (2015).

[34]Ghosh and Ray (2015).

[35]Ghosh et al. (2015).

[36]Ghosh (2015).

controlling temperature rise might seem obvious. But for others, delivering access to clean energy technologies might take priority. This would be the case for many developing countries.

In the case of developed countries, where energy access might not be of concern, the security and resilience of the energy system remains a driver for investments in new energy infrastructure. These could include investments in distributed renewables and distributed storage in order to insure against vulnerability for a centralised grid. For emerging economies dependent on energy imports, energy security is also a matter of concern, since it depends on the availability of critical resources, at predictable prices, with minimum supply disruptions, while ensuring environmental sustainability for future generations.

Still others might find mercantilist commercial motive in developing and controlling access to new low-carbon technologies. A range of trade disputes at the World Trade Organization over clean energy technologies indicate that protecting domestic markets or grabbing overseas market share are often more dominant priorities than climate mitigation.[37]

These priorities could yield co-benefits for the climate but the starting points for collaboration could vary. Clarity on the objectives would help to reduce uncertainties related to development pathways or socio-political impacts.

### 4.1.2 Prices Matter

Investments in clean energy R&D still account for a very small share in research investments because of high costs of technology development and alternative economic priorities. Energy technologies are changing rapidly and disrupting national and global markets. Many energy investments have long gestation periods (nuclear, for instance) and assets remain in operation for a long time (say, gas-based infrastructure). Technology cooperation needs a degree of price certainty to avoid frequent renegotiation of terms. Moreover, citizens would oppose cooperation on developing new technologies if they believe that their governments have locked them into price trajectories that are not in consonance with technological evolution.[38]

Economy-wide costs and benefits would also come into consideration. Low-carbon technologies have a greater chance of success if they generate wider economic benefits, such as in adding to industrial value addition or in having high employment coefficients. For instance, micro and nanoelectronics could support digitalisation of energy systems and promote the use of efficient and interactive appliances, thereby expanding the scope of application and making many low-carbon technologies more feasible to deploy.[39] Similarly, rooftop solar systems create seven times more jobs

[37]Ghosh (2016).

[38]Ghosh (2017b).

[39]Gupta et al. (2016).

in India compared to ground-mounted utility-scale solar plants, which in turn create more jobs per unit of electricity than thermal power.[40]

### 4.1.3 Pooling Resources

Technology collaborations have a greater likelihood of success if participating countries are able to pool resources, in cash or in kind. This approach also helps to partially overcome concerns about IP infringement or about sharing the royalties in future.

The challenge lies in identifying the right institutions and firms, which could be members of a technological alliance, while aligning their incentives. For instance, public funding would have to rely on reporting regularly to and getting annual approvals from parliaments and/or the executive branch. But for participating private sector institutions, investments of resources have to be approved by their Boards (easier for unlisted firms) or many disparate shareholders (in the case of listed companies).

Pooling resources is better done in a calibrated manner, with each stage of the technological development, testing and commercialisation securing new tranches of funding or in-kind contributions. Open-ended technology platforms with promises of multi-year funding seem promising at the outset but often fail to deliver resources in due course.

### 4.1.4 Innovative Finance

Related to pooling resources is the matter of hard finance. Renewable energy and energy efficiency need higher upfront capital investment, which bear risks of a different kind from risks pertaining to fossil-fuel prices. Such infrastructure requires large doses of de-risked institutional capital. It also requires patient capital to invest in energy R&D. The energy transition in many emerging economies would be incomplete without international cooperation on innovative finance and new modalities for technology co-development. Some joint R&D initiatives have begun, and small bilateral lines of credit are available. The real game-changers —such as energy storage technologies; hedging multiple financial risks simultaneously; deepened bond markets —are still largely absent.

### 4.1.5 Risk and Responsibility

Many horizon technologies for climate mitigation, such as SRM or CCS, entail significant known and unknown risks.[41] In such cases, technology partnerships serve two purposes: They could draw in a broader set of actors to independently conduct

[40] Kuldeep et al. (2017).

[41] Ghosh (2017c).

regular risk assessments as the technologies evolve; and, secondly, they could serve as a countervailing bulwark against any risky, unilateral behaviour by rogue scientists or technologists.

With risk assessments also come the assignment of responsibility and clear rules for liability. Technological innovation within single countries can be governed by the domestic laws. But multi-country partnerships need clarification on who bears what kind of responsibility should anything go wrong. Liability provisions are have informed nuclear energy collaborations, for instance. Similarly, if a coalition of countries decided to implement a large CCS facility and there were some leakage, the liability of the actual deployment (not just the tech development) has to be clearly established in advance.

#### 4.1.6 Voice in Governance

The final principle relates to the voice of various stakeholders. Of course, countries participating in a tech initiative might be keen to have a voice in the governance of the initiative. The rules governing voting rights, decision-making procedures, transparency and prior information for affected parties/communities would have to be determined in advance and revised or updated as the technology evolves or more countries get involved in the field pilots and commercial testing.

### *4.2 Alternative Modalities*

The uncertainties associated with various mitigation technologies, the failures of past tech initiatives and the guiding principles for effective partnerships help to design a few templates for collaboration. The three proposals outlined below focus on: technologies needing commercial pilots to scale; those that still need significant early stage investments to prove technically viable; and horizon technologies with high mitigation potential but also significant risks. The objective functions are different, as are cost-related uncertainties, the need for different kinds of finance, and appropriately designed governance structures.

#### 4.2.1 Enterprise-Driven R&D for Tech Applications

A $1 billion (replenishable) venture investment fund to promote innovative clean energy solutions would offer early-stage grant funding, so that innovators can test their products and business models and achieve sufficient scale to attract commercial investment. The bulk of the risk here would be assumed by the enterprises since the technologies are close to commercialisation. These could include, among others, electric public transport (using different battery charging models), deployment of superefficient appliances in residential and commercial buildings, energy efficiency interventions in micro, small and medium enterprises (which have little freed up working capital and small profit margins), and alternative business models for deploying rooftop and distributed renewable energy at scale.

Participating governments would co-finance the Fund while philanthropic foundations could supplement the resources. The Fund would aid: (a) technology demonstration; (b) project preparation for commercial investors; and/or (c) underwrite risks to lower cost of finance for innovators. Any company registered in a participating country with pre-established credentials of operating in these markets would be eligible.[42] Once commercial scale is reached in such low-risk investments, the enterprises would return the initial capital investment, which would replenish the fund for another round of financing in other technologies or geographies.

### 4.2.2 Innovation Fund for Low-Carbon Technologies

A $10 billion five-year programme for R&D in energy and other low-carbon technologies, with time-bound goals and parameters, could focus on: (a) increasing efficiency of solar cells; (b) low-cost manufacturing of solar modules; (c) distributed and utility-scale energy storage; (d) low-carbon cement; (e) innovations for thermal comfort; and (f) reduced demand for critical minerals in manufacturing climate-friendly products.[43]

In addition to universities and research laboratories, participating entities would have to necessarily include commercial enterprises. The programme would be co-financed by partner governments up to 49 per cent. Private enterprises would contribute the remainder, including contributions in kind (laboratory facilities and research personnel). Consortia members would co-own the resulting intellectual property. Advanced market commitments from governments to procure new products that meet specified parameters would give an added incentive for private investment. Pooled resources and aggregated demand could give the necessary push to drive the next stage of innovation.

### 4.2.3 G20 Platform for Horizon Tech

A $500 million pooled fund to promote joint investments in horizon technologies. By horizon technology we mean those that are likely to have significant mitigation potential (against a 1.5 °C target) but also carry many inherent risks. The risks could be about technological failure but also second-order risks, such as adverse impacts for the hydrological cycle or biodiversity, or tertiary risks in terms of trade disputes over industrial policy or geopolitical tensions. In this category would be, but not limited to: (a) renewables-based hydrogen for industry; (b) modular nuclear reactors; (c)

[42]Ghosh (2017a).

[43]Ghosh (2018b).

carbon capture storage and utilisation; (d) other carbon dioxide removal methods; and (e) solar radiation management.[44]

Risk and responsibility and voice in governance would be the key principles for designing this innovation platform in order to avoid unilateral technology development and deployment that might have many unintended transboundary consequences. The objectives here would be to not only consider high mitigation potential for prospective technologies but also assess their risks against inaction or insufficient action on climate mitigation. A risk-risk comparison would help to improve transparency about ongoing and planned activities, give voice to all G20 members (even those not directly involved in a research programme) and optimally pool resources amongst the world's leading technological and economic powers.

Why should these proposals work? One, emerging economies (in partnership with advanced economies) could serve as the test-beds for technologies applicable in other developing countries. Moreover, joint development mitigates concerns around intellectual property theft. And, the budgetary outlay would reduce for governments the more other countries and firms joined. Since 2009, the U.S. Advanced Research Projects Agency-Energy has funded more than 580 projects with just $1.5 billion; 74 projects have attracted more than $1.8 billion in private funding. Small investments can crowd in significant resources.[45] If a critical mass of G20 members created multi-country and multi-institutional low-carbon technology R&D platforms, they too could trigger a wave of research and transformative technologies.

## 5 Conclusions

Over a hundred developing countries have set out technology cooperation, development and/or transfers as a conditionality within their NDCs. The NDCs, even if achieved in full, are a far cry from 1.5 °C target. This chapter establishes the need for technological transformations as a key element for curtailing climate change to 1.5 °C, and suggests ways to enable these through effective partnerships.

Technological transformations will play a critical role in meeting global ambitions of curbing climate change. To be effective to this end, these transformations must occur with speed, and at scale. Given the range of uncertainties that exist in deploying and diffusing low-carbon technologies, from costs to governance to impacts, technology partnerships will have to strategically surge ahead as platforms to tackle these uncertainties through targeted research, development and deployment. So far, only a few such partnerships have been realised for low-carbon technologies - ambition is not yet reflected in actions sufficiently. To check this, guiding principles for new technology partnerships have been put forward, as have alternative modalities that include: enterprise-driven R&D for technology options; innovation fund for low-carbon technologies; and a G20 platform for horizon technologies. These encompass

[44]Ghosh (2017a).

[45]Ghosh (2017a).

three urgent spheres of technology development that need simultaneous focus and support: addressing technology diffusion challenges in the short term, anticipating upcoming challenges and minimizing these for the medium term, and ensuring that technological opportunities of the future are not lost to impact and governance uncertainties.

## References


Chaturvedi, V., Shukla, P. R., & Ganesan, K. (2017). A perspective on the cost of nuclear energy. In J. Nanda Kumar, G. Pant, & R. B. Grover (Eds.), *Resurgence of nuclear power: Challenges and opportunities for Asia*. Springer Nature Singapore Pvt Ltd.

Chaturvedi, V. Nagar Koti, P., & Chordia, A. R. (2018, April). *Sustainable Development, Uncertainties, and India's Climate Policy: Pathways towards Nationally Determined Contribution and Mid-Century Strategy*. Council on Energy, Environment and Water.

Climate Technology Centre and Network. (2019a). *Technical assistance*. Retrieved March 2, 2019, from https://www.ctc-n.org/technical-assistance.

Climate Technology Centre and Network. (2019b). *Request visualizations*. Retrieved March 2, 2019, from https://www.ctc-n.org/technical-assistance/request-visualizations.

Dellink, R., Chateau, J., Lanzi, E., & Magne, B. (2017). Long-term economic growth projections in the Shared Socioeconomic Pathways. *Global Environmental Change, 42,* 200–214.

Ghosh, A. (2015, October 16). Effective climate tech partnerships. *Business Standard*. http://www.business-standard.com/article/opinion/arunabha-ghosh-effective-climate-tech-partnerships-115101501416_1.html.

Ghosh, A. (2016). Clean energy trade conflicts: The political economy of a future energy system. In T. Van de Graaf, B. Sovacool, A. Ghosh, F. Kern, & M. T. Klare (Eds.), *The Palgrave handbook of the international political economy of energy*. London: Palgrave.

Ghosh, A. (2017a, October 24). The world's lab for energy tech. *Business Standard*. http://www.business-standard.com/article/opinion/the-world-s-lab-for-energy-tech-117102301285_1.html.

Ghosh, A. (2017b, May 23). Energy cooperation: First principles. *Business Standard*. http://www.business-standard.com/article/opinion/energy-cooperation-first-principles-117052201673_1.html.

Ghosh, A. (2017c, April 25). Time for geoengineering governance? *Business Standard*. http://www.business-standard.com/article/opinion/time-for-geoengineering-governance-117042401371_1.html.

Ghosh, A. (2018a). Environmental institutions, international research programmes, and lessons for geoengineering research. In J. J. Blackstock & S. Low (Eds.), *Geoengineering our climate? Ethics, politics, and governance*. Earthscan-Routledge.

Ghosh, A. (2018b, March 27). A Wild West for minerals? *Business Standard*. http://www.business-standard.com/article/opinion/a-wild-west-for-minerals-firms-are-rushing-to-buy-mines-overseas-118032601192_1.html.

Ghosh, A., & Chawla, K. (2018, March 16). The Global Solar Alliance must catalyse innovation. *Hindustan Times*.

Ghosh, A., & Ray, S. (2015, November). *Fixing climate governance through effective technology partnerships*. CIGI Fixing Climate Governance Series—Paper No. 3. Waterloo, ON: Centre for International Governance Innovation. https://www.cigionline.org/publications/fixing-climate-governance-through-effective-technology-partnerships.

Ghosh, A., Vijayakumar, A., & Ray, S. (2015, October). *Climate technology partnerships: Form, function and impact*. CIGI Fixing Climate Governance Series—Paper No. 2. Waterloo, ON: Centre for International Governance Innovation. https://www.cigionline.org/publications/climate-technology-partnerships-form-function-and-impact.

Government of India (GoI). (2015, October 2). *India's nationally determined contribution: Working towards climate justice*. http://www.moef.nic.in/sites/default/files/press-releases/INDIA%20INDC%20TO%20UNFCCC.pdf.

Gupta, V., Ganesan, K., & Ghosh, A. (2016, February). *Make in India: How could we be strategic?* CEEW Report.

Hultman, N. E., Koomey, J. G., & Kammen, D. M. (2007). What history can teach us about the future costs of U.S. nuclear power. *Environmental Science & Technology, 41*(7), 2087–2094.

IPCC. (2018). In V. Masson-Delmotte, P. Zhai, H. O. Pörtner, D. Roberts, J. Skea, P. R. Shukla, A. Pirani, W. Moufouma-Okia, C. Péan, R. Pidcock, S. Connors, J. B. R. Matthews, Y. Chen, X. Zhou, M. I. Gomis, E. Lonnoy, T. Maycock, M. Tignor, & T. Waterfield (Eds.), *Global Warming of 1.5 °C. An IPCC Special Report on the impacts of global warming of 1.5 °C above pre-industrial levels and related global greenhouse gas emission pathways, in the context of strengthening the global response to the threat of climate change, sustainable development, and efforts to eradicate poverty*.

IPCC SAR WG3. (1996) In J. P. Bruce, H. Lee, & E. F. Haites (Eds.), *Climate change 1995: Economic and social dimensions of climate change*. Contribution of Working Group III to the Second Assessment Report of the Intergovernmental Panel on Climate Change. Cambridge University Press. ISBN 0-521-56051-9 (pb: 0-521-56854-4).

KC, S., & Lutz, W. (2017). The human core of the shared socioeconomic pathways: Population scenarios by age, sex and level of education for all countries to 2100. *Global Environmental Change, 42,* 181–192.

Kriegler, E., O'Neill, B. C., Hallegatte, S., Kram, T., Lempert, R. J., Moss, R. H., et al. (2017). The need for and use of socio-economic scenarios for climate change analysis: A new approach based on shared socio-economic pathways. *Global Environmental Change, 42,* 807–822.

Kuldeep, N., Chawla, K., Ghosh, A., Jaiswal, A., Kaur, N., Kwatra, S., et al. (2017, June). *Greening India's workforce: Gearing up for expansion of solar and wind power in India*. CEEW-NRDC Report.

Lewis, J. (2014). Managing intellectual property rights in cross-border clean energy collaboration: The case of the U.S.–China Clean Energy Research Center. *Energy Policy, 69,* 546–554.

Mission Innovation. (2018a, May 23). *Letter of Intent on Collaboration between the International Renewable Energy Agency and Mission Innovation*, Sweden.

Mission Innovation. (2018b, June). *Country highlights*. 3rd Mission Innovation Ministerial.

Mission Innovation. (2019). *Innovation challenge*. Retrieved March 7, 2019, from http://mission-innovation.net/our-work/innovation-challenges/.

Modi, N. (2015, September 25). *Statement on adoption of the Post-2015 Development Agenda*. United Nations Summit, United Nations, New York.

Pasztor, J., Harrison, N., Chen, Y., Ghosh, A., Jumeau, R., Nobres, C., et al. (2019, February). *Geoengineering: the need for governance*. Carnegie Climate Geoengineering Governance Initiative (C2G2), New York. https://www.c2g2.net/wp-content/uploads/Geoengineering-Need-for-Governance.pdf.

Riahi, K., Vuuren, D. P., Kriegler, E., Edmonds, J., O'Neill, B. C., et al. (2017). The Shared Socioeconomic Pathways and their energy, land use, and greenhouse gas emissions implications: An overview. *Global Environmental Change 42*, 153–168.

UNFCCC. (1992). *United Nations Framework Convention on Climate Change*, Bonn.

UNFCCC. (2006). *Synthesis report on technology needs identified by Parties not included in Annex I to the Convention*, Bonn.

UNFCCC. (2010). *Report of the Conference of the Parties on its sixteenth session*, held in Cancun from 29 November to 10 December 2010, Bonn.

US-China Clean Energy Research Centre. (2019). *Intellectual property*. Retrieved March 7, 2019, from http://www.us-china-cerc.org/intellectual-property/.

# Part V
# Financing Infrastructure for Sustainable Development

# Chapter 10
# Infrastructure Financing in India—Trends, Challenges and Way Forward

**Kumar V. Pratap and Mira Sethi**

**Abstract** This paper highlights the infrastructure financing history of India, how this has changed over the years, and the factors responsible for it. The actual infrastructure financing experience has been compared with the financing requirements, to lead to a discussion on the need for deepening and diversifying sources of infrastructure financing and the challenges and issues that need to be addressed. Since the actual infrastructure investments in India are way below the required investments, the paper draws lessons from other countries, to identify the instruments and mechanisms which can be adopted to mobilize increased infrastructure finance. The paper also highlights the lessons that India holds for other countries on infrastructure financing.

## 1 Introduction

The need for infrastructure development for integration and economic prosperity of the world cannot be overemphasized. Infrastructure spending has a positive spin-off on the growth and overall development of the economy. Lack of infrastructure not only results in reduced economic output, it also translates into additional costs in terms of time, effort and money to access essential services. Rapid economic growth in recent years has put enormous pressure on existing infrastructure in India, particularly in transport, energy and communications, impacting her competitiveness. Though the ranking has improved in recent years, as per the World Economic Forum's Global Competitiveness Report 2018, India still ranks 63rd out of 140 countries on infrastructure. Since the overall ranking of India is 58 as per the same Report,

Views are personal and may not correspond with the views of the organization where the authors are employed.

K. V. Pratap (✉) · M. Sethi
Infrastructure Policy & Finance Division, Department of Economic Affairs, Ministry of Finance, Government of India, New Delhi, India
e-mail: kv.pratap@gov.in

M. Sethi
e-mail: mira.sethi@gov.in

 
R. Kathuria and P. Kukreja (eds.), *20 Years of G20*,
https://doi.org/10.1007/978-981-13-8106-5_10

infrastructure, which is one of the 12 pillars on which this ranking is based, is acting as a drag on the overall Indian competitiveness.

Experience suggests that the fast growing countries of East Asia have spent 7–8% of GDP on infrastructure. The Growth Report of the World Bank (2008) states that this is the right number for infrastructure investments for countries desiring to join the ranks of these fast growing countries. Given that India's GDP is $2.6 trillion in 2018, India needs to spend about $200 billion annually on infrastructure in the near term. Over 75% of this requirement is from the power, transport and urban sectors (CRISIL Infrastructure Yearbook 2017). The country, on the other hand, has spent about $1.2 trillion on infrastructure in the past decade (2007–17), thus leading to an average shortfall of about $80 billion on a per annum basis. This is manifested in India's over-crowded roads and airports, slow average speeds of trains, both passenger and freight, high turnaround time of ships, etc. which is impacting the overall Indian competitiveness.

India is currently the fastest growing large economy in the world, with a growth rate of 6.7% in 2017–18 which is expected to go up to 7.3% in 2018–19 (World Bank 2019). But for the infrastructure constraint to India's growth, it is likely that the growth rate would have been still higher, putting India on course for becoming a $10 trillion economy by 2030. High infrastructure investments would also make this rapid economic growth inclusive, thus bridging the distance between economic growth and economic development.

As already stated, India has invested about $1.2 trillion on infrastructure in the last decade (2007–17), out of which little over a third has come from the private sector. The world over, public sector has been providing the bulk of infrastructure investment, given the inherent public goods nature of infrastructure, large investment requirements, and long payback periods. Boston Consulting Group[1] estimates that two-thirds of the investment of $2.7 trillion that is being made on infrastructure the world over (as against a demand of $4 trillion annually), comes from the public sector. In that sense, India's split between public and private sector shares of investment, is in sync with rest of the world.

Given the unmet need for infrastructure (as per McKinsey, India has the second highest infrastructure deficit in the world), and fiscal constraints that leave little room for expanding public investment at the scale required, there is an urgent need to accelerate the flow of private capital into infrastructure.

The existing financing sources lack the capacity to meet such requirement. Apart from budgetary sources, banks have been the main financiers for infrastructure sector in India. However, in the recent past, high stress in the infrastructure sector has affected the balance sheets of both banks and investors (the twin balance sheet problem), thus affecting fresh investments. Banks are refraining from infrastructure financing due to project, sponsor and sectoral exposure constraints, capital constraints, rising Non-Performing Assets (NPAs)/stressed asset levels and asset-liability mismatch. Other sources like Non-Banking Financial Companies (NBFCs), pension

[1] Boston Consulting Group. 2013. Bridging the Gap—Meeting the Infrastructure Challenge with Public-Private Partnerships.

and insurance funds also face restrictions due to regulatory exposure norms, credit rating norms, etc. and may not be able to meet the funding requirement. Hence, there is a need for alternate sources to meet the funding requirement of the sector. It is imperative that innovative financing instruments are deployed which match the risk, return and time horizon requirements of various sources of capital to the profiles of underlying infrastructure assets.

## 2 Infrastructure Financing Trends

There are three main sources of financing infrastructure: Gross Budgetary Support (GBS), Internal and External Budgetary Resources (IEBR) of the Public Sector Enterprises, and Private Investment. The later half of the last decade (2007–12) saw a steady rise in infrastructure investment in India (as a percentage of GDP) which peaked at around 8.4% of GDP in 2011–12.[2] This period (2007–12) saw average infrastructure investment rise to 7.5% of GDP from about 5% in the previous five years (2002–07).[3] The share of private sector went up from 1.1% of GDP (2002–07) to 2.7% of GDP in the period 2007–12. In recent years, on an average, the public sector (GBS and IEBR) has been spending just over 4% of GDP on infrastructure. So, the entire upsurge in infrastructure investment to GDP ratio seen in the period 2007–12 can be explained in terms of the upsurge in private investment.

However post-2012, there was a relative slowdown in infrastructure investment due to sharp decline in private investment. In recent years, public spending on infrastructure has risen leading to a marginal rise in overall infrastructure investment which was estimated to be 6.1% of GDP in 2017.[4] On an average, in the period 2012–17, the proportion of infrastructure investment to GDP was about 5.8%, substantially lower than in the period 2007–12.

Based on projections of the erstwhile Planning Commission, during the period 2012–17, in order to attain a 9% real GDP growth rate, infrastructure investment of about 10% of GDP was needed on an average.[5] However, India spent only an average 5.8% of its GDP on infrastructure in the period 2012–17, implying infrastructure investment shortfall of about 4 percentage points of GDP. The reasons behind the shortfall in investment included issues with the Public Private Partnership (PPP) projects especially in power and telecom sectors, stressed balance sheet of private companies and banks, delays in land acquisition, environmental and forest clearances, and utility shifting, poor performance of contractors and delays in resolution

[2]Mid-Term Appraisal of Eleventh Five Year Plan (2007–12), Planning Commission, Government of India.

[3]Investment in Infrastructure during the Eleventh Five Year Plan, Planning Commission, Government of India, January 2011.

[4]NITI Aayog Appraisal Document of Twelfth Five Year Plan (2012–17), Government of India.

[5]Report of the Working Sub-Group on Infrastructure: Infrastructure funding requirements and its sources over the implementation period of the Twelfth Five Year Plan (2012–17), Government of India.

of disputes and claims etc. leading to time and cost overruns, and absence of commensurate long-term financing avenues.

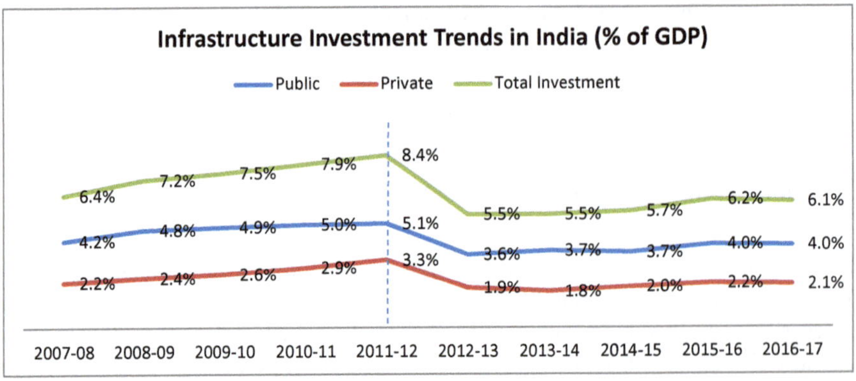


*Source* NITI Aayog Appraisal Document of Twelfth Five Year Plan (2012–17) and Planning Commission Mid-Term Appraisal of Eleventh Five Year Plan (2007–12), Government of India

Recognizing that infrastructure is key to enable economic growth and trying to make up for the loss in momentum of private infrastructure investment, the government has effected a massive thrust on infrastructure spending in recent years. Government's estimated budgetary (GBS) and extra budgetary expenditure (IEBR) on infrastructure for 2018–19 increased to $85 billion (or Rs. 5,970 billion) against estimated expenditure of $70 billion (or Rs. 4,940 billion) in 2017–18, an increase by almost 21% over the previous year.[6] Schemes such as Bharatmala Pariyojana, Sagarmala, Smart Cities Mission, Regional Connectivity Scheme or Ude Desh Ka Aam Nagrik (UDAN) Scheme, Ujjwal Discom Assurance Yojana (UDAY) as well as several initiatives by Government to mobilize infrastructure investment through the private sector like mainstreaming Public Private Partnerships (PPP), debut of the Toll-Operate-Transfer (ToT) model, launching of innovative financial vehicles such as Infrastructure Investment Trusts (InvITs), Real Estate Investment Trusts (REITs), Infrastructure Debt Funds (IDFs), Municipal Bonds, National Investment and Infrastructure Fund (NIIF) etc. are all expected to lead to massive investments in infrastructure over the next 5 years.

Until the mid-2000s, there was no major demand from the financial system to fund infrastructure investment as it was fairly low (around 3–5% of GDP) and financed largely by budgetary allocations, internal resources of public sector enterprises engaged in infrastructure, and tax free bonds. In the period 2007 to 2012, however, infrastructure spending picked up substantially with an important role played by the private sector implying greater recourse to the financial system. Most of the debt financing came from Banks, Non-Banking Financial Companies (NBFCs), and

[6]Union Budget Speech 2018–19, Ministry of Finance, Government of India.

External Commercial Borrowings (ECBs), followed by insurance companies.[7] Apart from budgetary sources, which was estimated to constitute around 45% of the infrastructure spending in the period 2012–17, the estimated share of debt and equity sources of funding infrastructure in the same period may be seen in the figure below.

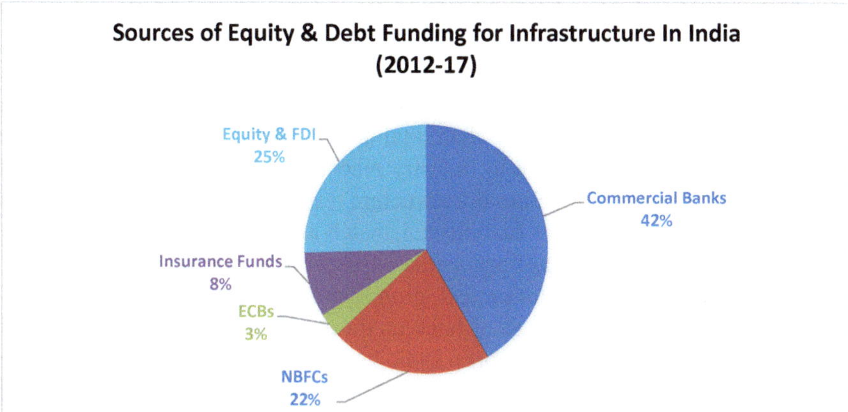


NBFC: Non-Banking Financial Companies; ECB: External Commercial Borrowing; FDI: Foreign Direct Investment. *Source* Report of the Working Sub-Group on Infrastructure-Infrastructure funding requirements and its sources over the implementation period of the Twelfth Five Year Plan (2012–17)

It is evident that infrastructure financing in India has largely been driven by the domestic sources, mostly commercial banks. The share of foreign sources (ECBs and FDI) in financing infrastructure has been low, as compared to countries in the East Asia and Latin American region. However, this may not necessarily be a drawback since foreign funding for domestic infrastructure projects suffer from the additional risk of currency mismatch as revenue streams in most infrastructure (except parts of the port and airport sectors) are denominated in domestic currency, and use of foreign capital may result in higher cost of capital (including hedging costs) and more risks.

The risk associated with use of foreign capital in infrastructure is borne out by countries that have experienced macroeconomic crises—Mexican peso crisis of 1994, East Asian crisis of 1997, Argentinean peso crisis of 2002, and Global Financial Crisis of 2008. These episodes of macroeconomic crises led to wholesale failure of infrastructure projects as foreign capital servicing became very expensive with local currency depreciation, and governments and public authorities being in no position to raise user charges to match the depreciation (Harris and Pratap 2009).

Infrastructure projects are often characterized by large financial outlays, long gestation periods, and long-term steady returns. In view of this, institutional investors

[7]Report of the Working Sub-Group on Infrastructure: Infrastructure Funding requirements and its sources over the implementation period of the Twelfth Five Year Plan (2012–17), Government of India.

with long-term horizon should ideally be the main source of financing infrastructure projects. However, in India, like elsewhere, infrastructure projects are mainly financed by debt from commercial banks with limited participation of long-term institutional investors (pension, insurance and sovereign wealth funds). Large exposure of bank funds to infrastructure sectors is accompanied with problems like asset-liability mismatch as bank liabilities (or deposits) are short-term and infrastructure assets are long-term. This implies refinancing risk, with associated costs and added risks.

The financial system was able to respond to the rapidly rising demand for credit by infrastructure companies largely because banks stepped up lending. Credit to infrastructure grew at a faster pace than total credit and the share of infrastructure in outstanding gross bank credit to industry reached around 33% in March 2013. This rapid growth in bank credit to infrastructure resulted in a greater concentration of risks in banks, due to Asset-Liability mismatch and project, group and sectoral exposure limits. The banks have prudential exposure caps for infrastructure sector lending as a whole as well as for project, groups and individual sectors.

After a period of rapid growth of bank credit to infrastructure, in recent years, bank lending to infrastructure sector in India has slowed down. Outstanding Gross Bank Credit to infrastructure sector witnessed a decline of 1.7% from $129 billion (or Rs.9,064 billion) as on 31st March 2017 to $127 billion (or Rs.8,909 billion) as on 31st March 2018.[8] Compound Annual Growth Rate (CAGR) of outstanding gross bank credit to infrastructure has declined from about 32% over Financial Year (FY) 2008–12 to about 4% over FY 2013–18 (Handbook of Statistics on Indian Economy 2011 and 2018). Gross Non-Performing Assets (NPAs) as a ratio of Gross Loans and Advances to infrastructure sector has increased from about 3% in FY 2015 to about 9% in FY 2017. Stressed advances ratio as a percent of total advances for infrastructure sector reached 22.6% as on March 2018 (Financial Stability Report 2018).

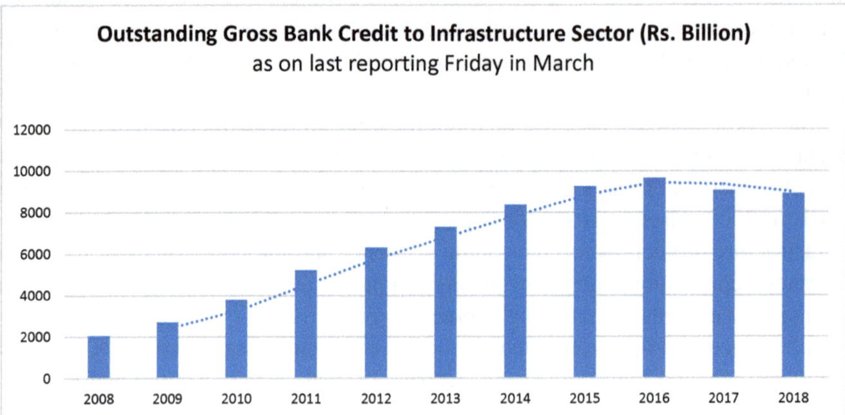


*Source* Reserve Bank of India (RBI) Handbook of Statistics on Indian Economy

[8]Data on Sectoral deployment of Bank Credit, March 2018, Reserve Bank of India.

Since budgetary spending is limited by fiscal constraints and bank financing to infrastructure (which suffers from asset-liability mismatch) has reached its exposure limits and declined in recent years, it becomes imperative that innovative mechanisms are developed to attract investments from the private sector and institutional investors into infrastructure to sustain the growth of the economy.

## 3 Challenges and Opportunities

The long-term nature of infrastructure assets matches the liability profile of institutional investors such as pension funds and insurance companies, whose liabilities often stretch across multiple decades. Infrastructure assets have the potential to yield steady, long-term returns that are often uncorrelated with business cycles and hence provide portfolio diversification opportunities to these investors, compared to traditional assets such as fixed-income debt securities or listed-equity investments.

Thus, institutional investors are increasingly being regarded as a potential source of financing for infrastructure projects. The International Monetary Fund estimates that globally more than $100 trillion is held by pension funds, sovereign-wealth funds, mutual funds, and other institutional investors. However, the participation rate of institutional investors in infrastructure remains considerably low, not just in developing economies, but also in developed countries. Institutional investors in OECD countries invest less than one percent of their assets in infrastructure (mostly brownfield), and very little in Emerging Market Economies (EMEs). A World Bank Report finds that the current level of institutional investor activity in new infrastructure deals is abysmally low and constitutes a mere 0.7% of total infrastructure investment in emerging markets and developing economies (EMDEs) in the period 2011–17 (Contribution of institutional investors to private investment in infrastructure, 2017).

There are several risks and barriers to institutional investment in infrastructure. Although, on the demand side there is a need for more resources to finance infrastructure and on the supply side institutional investors are looking for steady, long-term returns, matching the two has been a challenge, resulting in extremely low share of institutional-investor contributions to infrastructure investment. The reasons for the mismatch include lack of a significant pipeline of well-prepared and well-structured infrastructure projects in EMDEs, differing mandates and lower risk appetite of institutional investors, lower yields compared to risks associated with infrastructure projects, foreign-exchange risk and limited resources to set up the specialized infrastructure teams that are essential to assess and track investments in EMDEs. The high risk perception for infrastructure projects stems from the experience of implementation delays, cost overruns, poor cost recovery, and issues faced in stabilization of these projects. Institutional investors are credit-risk averse and restricted by regulations and/or internal investment policies from investing in securities rated below the AA category. They are also taken aback by political sensitivity and corruption often associated with these projects. User charges in many infrastructure sectors are way below cost recovery levels (e.g., water, power, metro trains, railways, etc.). For the long-run sustainability of these assets and for institutional investors to show investment interest, there would be a need for raising user charges to cost-recovery levels, which would subject any such move to political sensitivity, and possible failure. Similarly, since infrastructure projects involve large investments (e.g., a 4 GW thermal power project may cost about $4 billion, the cost estimate of the Mumbai-Ahmedabad High Speed Rail Project is about $16 billion), they suffer from allcgations of corruption in their procurement, which is an interest dampener for institutional investors.

However, the Canadian Pension Plan Investment Board (CPPIB) is a major investor having investments in India totaling $4.8 billion (as on 31st December 2017) (CPPIB 2018). While Canadian pension funds have invested in Indian infrastructure, the same has not been the case with the US, which has a much larger pool of pension fund resources to be deployed in projects that provide steady returns over the long term. The challenge is to attract other such institutional investors to Indian infrastructure.

The corporate bond market in India has grown in recent years accounting for as much as 30% of outstanding system credit in fiscal 2018, compared with 21% in fiscal 2013. Yet the level of penetration of corporate bond market remains considerably low in India, accounting for just 16% of GDP compared with countries such as Malaysia (46% of GDP), South Korea (73% of GDP) and the USA (120% of GDP) (CRISIL yearbook on the Indian debt market 2018). Bond financing of infrastructure is also severely constrained in India. This is mainly because, typically, infrastructure projects have low credit rating (generally BBB level), while the Bond market in India has appetite for higher rated bonds (AA and above). The credit ratings for infrastructure projects tend to be constrained on account mainly of their non-recourse (and limited-recourse) financing nature, high exposure to implementation risks, concentration on single asset cash flows, shorter debt tenure compared to the overall economic life of the project, and risks pertaining to counterparties, markets and operations. These risks make these projects to be rated low on conventional rating scale, based on the Probability of Default (PD) approach. In India, the regulatory threshold for funding by insurance and pension funds is AA which limits their participation in infrastructure projects. However, there is scope and opportunity to develop the corporate bond market to meet the future financing needs of infrastructure.

## 4 Initiatives and Way Forward

The challenge, therefore, is to mainstream bond financing of infrastructure and channelize long term institutional funding to infrastructure projects. The Roadmap to Infrastructure as an Asset Class endorsed by the G20 countries outlines work streams for the G20 nations to collaborate under the principal objectives of improving project development; improving the investment environment for infrastructure; and promoting greater standardization. This is to be taken up under five workstreams—improving project preparation, financial engineering, risk allocation and mitigation;

contractual and financial standardization; and bridging the infrastructure data gap to reduce information asymmetry and increase capital availability. At the project level, improving project preparation by carrying out robust feasibility studies and structuring projects with appropriate risk allocation is the key to increasing institutional-investors' interest. Also, standardization of infrastructure contracts with private parties and streamlining the project procurement process is essential to help scale up investment in such assets.

In recent years, India has taken several initiatives to mobilize infrastructure funding from various sources including the private sector and long-term institutional investors through mainstreaming Public Private Partnerships (PPP), monetization of brownfield infrastructure assets (asset recycling strategy), developing a new credit rating scale for infrastructure projects and a proposed dedicated Credit Enhancement Non-Banking Financial Company (NBFC) to raise credit rating of bonds floated by infrastructure companies. Some of these initiatives, as elaborated in the following sections, may find traction globally with countries which are trying to diversify sources of infrastructure investment.

## 4.1 Mainstreaming Public Private Partnerships

Infrastructure investment is perceived to be risky due to large upfront capital investment, high sunk costs that could lead to opportunistic behavior, long concession period and presence of multiple stakeholders with different objectives. However, infrastructure assets also provide steady, long-term revenue streams, which may be attractive to the private sector. Hence, private participation in infrastructure has been fairly successful in India. The main form of private participation in infrastructure is through Public Private Partnerships (PPPs), which are commercial arrangements between public and private sectors for providing a service traditionally provided by the public sector for an extended period of time. Appropriate risk allocation lies at the heart of a successful PPP. Risks should be assigned to the agency that has more control over the risk factor. Under this guideline, construction and commercial risks should be allocated to the private sector, political risk should be with the Government, while regulatory risks should be managed by autonomous regulatory institutions. Improper risk allocation may lead to project failure. In return for its obligations, the private sector gets a return either from user fees or government payments, or a combination of both. Widely used in sectors such as Highways and Electricity Generation, PPPs are seen as one of the solutions for government to meet the unmet infrastructure demand.

India is second in the developing world both by the number of PPP projects as well as associated investments as per the Private Participation in Infrastructure database of the World Bank (see Table 1).

Much of the Indian success in private participation in infrastructure is based on standardized procurement process and standardized contracts. Standardized bidding and contractual documents like Model Concession Agreements (MCA), Request

**Table 1** Private participation in infrastructure in India (1990–2018)

| Sector | Number of projects | Investment ($ billion) |
|---|---|---|
| Energy | 438 | 149 |
| ICT | 25 | 3 |
| Transport | 497 | 104 |
| Water and sewerage | 20 | 1 |
| Total | 980 | 257 |

*Source* Private participation in infrastructure database of the World Bank (ppi.worldbank.org)

for Qualification (RfQ) and Request for Proposal (RfP) have been introduced to streamline PPPs in infrastructure. Model documents aim at lending transparency, consistency and predictability to the procurement process, allowing decisions to be made objectively and expeditiously. India has more than 400 road sector projects based on standardized documents that can be replicated across infrastructure sectors.

However, PPPs are not popular in the social sectors like health, education, and water and wastewater in India. The quality of these services could do with some improvement in India. However, PPPs in these sectors are also more difficult because of small size of capital investments (say, a school or a primary health center) and the direct consumer interface, which increases the risk perception. Government is coming out with a new policy for mainstreaming PPPs is social infrastructure.

## 4.2 Developing Brownfield Assets as a Separate Asset Class for Infrastructure Investment

The Roadmap to Infrastructure as an Asset Class endorsed by the G20 countries acknowledges that financial vehicles need to be developed to tap into the changing risk profile of infrastructure projects over their lifecycle. Brownfield assets are considerably de-risked as compared to greenfield assets since they are past the stages of land acquisition, regulatory clearances (e.g., forest and environment clearances) and construction.

Two factors make it attractive to develop brownfield assets as a separate asset class. First, it has been observed that private financing structures are reasonably well-placed to manage the operational risks and private operators are capable of delivering good quality services through better operational management of infrastructure assets. Secondly, more than 50% of the debt financing in PPP Projects has come from banks, which suffers from Asset-Liability mismatch as the liabilities of banks are generally short-term while infrastructure assets are long-term. Institutional investment from pension, insurance and sovereign wealth funds in brownfield infrastructure assets does not suffer from this asset-liability mismatch. These twin objectives can be met through recycling of operational assets that are presently in control of the government and its agencies. This can be done through the strategy of Brownfield Asset Monetization for Infrastructure Investment (BAMII).

India is trying to develop brownfield projects into separate asset class to tap into the changing risk profile of projects over their lifecycle. To improve user services, augment infrastructure investment and create opportunities for the private sector, an asset recycling strategy for mature operational assets is proposed to be introduced in India across infrastructure sectors covering highways, railways, petroleum, telecommunications etc. through BAMII which involves transferring operational public sector infrastructure assets to institutional investors and private operators to unlock efficiencies and reinvest proceeds in new infrastructure projects.

BAMII can help accelerate infrastructure roll-out (in greenfield projects) by recycling brownfield assets that are considerably de-risked and can generate extra resources for infrastructure development, without incurring higher debt and levying additional taxes, as a fiscally sustainable option. Besides, this strategy can help attract long-term capital from patient investors like insurance and pension funds thereby enabling infrastructure investment without asset-liability mismatch typically associated with bank financing of infrastructure. Moreover, it can facilitate efficient Operations & Maintenance (O&M) through involvement of private sector.

Operating assets generating stable cash flows which are predictable, monitorable and transparent are considerably de-risked and suitable for BAMII, such as electronic tolled roads, metered electricity flows through power transmission lines, and metered flow of oil and gas through pipelines. Besides, a reliable regulatory structure for determining tariffs (which may be through a contract or independent sectoral regulator) is essential for BAMII. Moreover, the size of package needs to be large enough as packages below $200 million may not be attractive to foreign financial investors. But, this issue may be addressed through bundling of contiguous infrastructure assets.

Based on the above mentioned criteria, potential assets for BAMII may include assets across infrastructure sectors such as power transmission, railway lines, national and state highways, oil and gas pipelines, port connectivity projects and telecommunication towers. As per preliminary analysis conducted for India, cumulative monetization potential of existing assets of certain identified Central Public Sector Enterprises (based on Net Present Value of cash flows) amounts to over $80 billion which may be staggered over a period of four years. This will bump-up the infrastructure investments by $20 billion on a per annum basis, i.e., an increase of about 15–20% in current annual infrastructure investment.

Steps to mainstream BAMII across infrastructure sectors would involve setting up an institutional arrangement for identification of assets in consultation with concerned stakeholders and enabling standardized procurement processes which may include a two-stage bidding process consisting of Request for Qualification (RfQ) and Request for Proposal (RfP) and standardized documents such as Model Concession Agreement across sectors with clearly specified service level requirements (key performance indicators) and safeguards for protecting the public interest.

Asset recycling is common in several countries including US, UK and Australia. For example, New South Wales, Australia leased 3 electricity transmission and distribution assets for 99 years for $26.3 billion and buyers included pension funds

(CDPQ) and sovereign wealth funds (ADIA). Long-term lease of the Indiana Toll Road, USA for $3.8 billion is another example where net proceeds were used for 10-year program of state highway capital investment. Besides, Business Trust model for real estate (Real Estate Investment Trust-REIT) is fairly well developed in countries such as UK and Singapore. Globally, as of 2016, there have been over 500 REITs across 36 countries, with total market capitalization of approximately $1.7 trillion (Global perspectives: Real Estate Investment Trust (REIT), 2016).

India is trying to monetize brownfield assets through innovative models and mechanisms like ***Toll Operate Transfer (TOT)*** and Infrastructure investment Trusts (InvITs) which hold immense potential.

In the TOT model, Operation & Maintenance (O&M) obligations and right to collect user fees for operational infrastructure assets are transferred to the highest bidder for the concession period. The project operations are transferred from a public operator to a private operator for an upfront fee and the operator retains residual revenues. The additional revenue generated for increased infrastructure investments is the difference between bid price and reserve price (i.e. Net Present Value of future cash flows). The Ministry of Road Transport and Highways in India is monetizing its road assets constructed with public funds through the TOT scheme. This scheme envisages transfer of operational (post-construction) projects for a concession period of 30 years. The TOT model has seen interest from large private equity funds, pension funds and sovereign wealth funds. First TOT bundle of 9 highway projects (of total 680 km) was recently awarded for about $1.5 billion (Rs. 96.81 billion). The winning bidder included a foreign infrastructure investor (Mcquarie). The winning bid generated additional revenue (premium) of about $0.5 billion (Rs. 34.23 billion) above the reserve price, amounting to a premium of about $0.7 million (or Rs. 50 million) per kilometer of road.

***Infrastructure Investment Trusts (InvITs) and Real Estate Investment Trusts (REITs)*** are trust based structures which act as pooling vehicles to source funds from long-term institutional investors to invest in infrastructure and real estate projects respectively. A InvIT/REIT is an investment vehicle that owns infrastructure assets/real estate-related assets, which have stable cash flows, and allows investors to earn income produced through ownership of infrastructure assets/commercial real estate without actually having to operate these assets. Business Trust structures were launched with an aim to refinance/takeout existing high cost debt and equity with long-term lower cost capital, attract institutional finance to Indian infrastructure projects, and free up current developer capital for reinvestment in new projects. InvITs/REITs can raise funds by listing on the exchanges and issuing units to investors. The sponsor of the assets retain operational control of the assets and divest part of the holding over a period of time to realize the market value and raise significant capital from a wider investor base. These are hybrid instruments regulated by the Securities and Exchange Board of India (SEBI) and are mandated to pay at least 90% distributable cash flows to investors at least on a half-yearly basis [Securities & Exchange Board of India (SEBI) Infrastructure Investment Trust (InvIT) Regulations 2014]. Owing to their pass-through status, InvIT units offer tax-efficient returns and are ideally suited for long-term investors. India's first InvIT in the road sector whose asset base aggregated seven toll road assets raised over $700 million and had foreign Investors. So far, three companies have raised funds (close to USD 1.5 billion in aggregate) through the InvIT route in India in the roads and power transmission sectors. Robust management, strong governance and continuous addition of good quality assets will determine the yields generated, and eventually determine investor interest in this instrument.

## 4.3 New Credit Rating System for Infrastructure Projects

Infrastructure projects, post-completion and stabilization, tend to generate a steady stream of long-term cash flows. They often have a near monopoly market position and low technological obsolescence risk. Further, infrastructure projects implemented through PPPs have additional features like availability of termination payments, contractual protection through some form of non-compete clause, etc. Moreover, structural features such as ring-fencing of cash flows, well-defined cash flow waterfall mechanism, low incremental capex risk, and better governance, also act as risk mitigation factors. Given the focus on timely servicing of financial obligations, the conventional credit rating scale (based on the Probability of Default (PD) approach) has limitations in providing adequate weight to the above mentioned characteristics, thereby resulting in relatively lower ratings of infrastructure projects.

In order to overcome these limitations and provide broader information on associated risks to the prospective investors, a new credit rating system for infrastructure projects has been developed in India that would retain the valuable aspects of the PD approach adopted by the conventional rating scale and integrate the same with recovery prospects, thereby taking into account the unique features of infrastructure projects.

The new credit rating system for infrastructure projects is based on the 'Expected Loss' (EL) methodology [i.e. product of probability of default (PD) and loss given default (LGD)], which captures the recovery prospects of the asset under evaluation during the lifetime of the debt instrument and enables investors to take a long-term view on infrastructure projects by laying emphasis on the embedded factors, such as termination payments, contractually guaranteed payments etc., which are not captured by the existing PD based conventional rating scale. The EL based scale thus emphasizes the in-built credit enhancement features of infrastructure projects, instead of relying upon a standard perception of risk which often results in mispriced loans. The new credit rating scale based on the Expected Loss, will be assigned along with the existing conventional credit rating and will be on a seven-point scale from 'INFRA EL1' to 'INFRA EL7' where the instrument rated 'EL1' would be considered to have lowest expected loss and 'EL7' the highest expected loss.

While in the project's initial stage, there may not be much difference in the conventional PD and the EL-based Ratings, the latter will be less volatile and not susceptible to sharp downgrades as is the case in conventional rating system. This will be useful in case of infrastructure projects facing temporary cash flow mismatches as the ratings on EL basis will also factor in the project fundamentals and other protective factors. As the project progresses to the operational stage, with the stabilization of its cash flows, both PD and LGD are expected to reduce in an ideal situation, thus benefiting the EL-based rating of the project.

Regulatory recognition to the new rating scale for investment in infrastructure projects by pension and insurance funds can provide fillip and help channelize long term funding to the infrastructure projects. Based on empirical evidence, rating agencies in India have proposed that the prudential norms governing investment in infrastructure by insurance and pension funds could provide the option of either a minimum AA rating requirement as already stipulated in their guidelines or a minimum of INFRA EL2 subject to PD rating being investment grade (BBB- and above under the existing rating scale). INFRA EL2 rated exposure has been found to have annualized EL levels comparable to what is being priced by investors for AA rated papers under the PD scale. Besides globally, BBB rating is investment grade under PD scale and therefore presents a reasonable degree of comfort for investors.

The new credit rating system based on Expected Loss scale for infrastructure projects has been launched in India in 2017, at a time when banks are under stress and there is a need to diversify the source of funding and attract long term monies into infrastructure projects. The new EL based rating scale for infrastructure projects will provide a valuable input, in addition to the existing rating scale based on the PD approach, to investors for effective pricing of debt instruments, and consequently, investment decisions.

## 4.4 Dedicated Credit Enhancement Non-banking Financial Company (NBFC)

A dedicated NBFC to provide Credit Enhancement (CE) to bonds floated by infrastructure companies is going to be launched in India soon. The typical credit rating of bonds floated by infrastructure companies is BBB, while regulatory thresholds of pension and insurance companies do not allow them to invest in bonds rated lower than AA. The CE company would raise the credit rating of lower rated bonds and make them amenable to investment by institutional investors.

The CE Company would be set up as a joint venture among public sector entities (such as public sector banks, insurance companies, and financial institutions) initially having a share capital of about $70 million (Rs. 5 billion) which may be adequately increased going forward based on requirements. Initially, the CE Company may offer established first loss CE products such as Partial Credit Guarantee (PCG) and subordinated loans that have gained market acceptance. Going forward, after gaining experience, it may introduce an array of innovative CE products. Further, for the PCG facility, the CE Company may, in the initial years, focus only on brownfield projects that have been completed and therefore relatively less risky assets. In the later years, based on the risk appetite and absorption capacity of the CE Company, and the demand in the market, the PCG may gradually and carefully be extended to cover Greenfield projects.

The CE Company would assist in development of non-banking markets in infrastructure finance by linking institutional and capital markets with infrastructure projects. Through this, it will contribute to deepening of financial markets for infrastructure in India and development of more appropriate risk sharing mechanisms for sustainably supporting the sector. The company will play a vital role in the development of an array of non-funded and funded credit enhancement products and activities which would lead to stimulation of the infrastructure sector and corporate bond market. It would lead to replacement of bank financing to infrastructure sector with broader non-bank markets including debt capital markets and institutional investors. This would release exposure limits of the banks for supporting new pipeline generation and scaling infrastructure investments. This will not only diversify the resource mobilization avenues for the infrastructure projects into the bond market, but also de-risk the banking sector and strengthen its fundamentals. Improved fundamentals would in turn lower the capital requirement of the banking sector. Moreover, it would assist the infrastructure projects raise cost-effective fixed-rate long-term funds and also better structuring their liabilities with the receivables leading to a significant reduction in their financing cost.

Considering that infrastructure projects are capital intensive and highly leveraged, financing costs are a major expense. Support from the CE company would lead to improved viability of projects, lower user charges for the end-users and also de-risking of the banks' balance sheets. Hence, this is an innovative institutional initiative for infrastructure sector that will improve infrastructure financing thereby having multiplier effects for the entire economy.

Besides, several other measures are being taken to deepen the corporate bond market in India. The Securities & Exchange Board of India (SEBI) is considering mandating large corporates to meet about 25% of their financing needs from bond market.[9] Insurance and Pension Regulators are also moving towards lowering the minimum threshold for insurance and pension fund investments from "AA" rated bonds to "A" rated bonds. Operationalization of these measures will facilitate even lower rated borrowers in infrastructure sector (borrowers rated between AA and A) to raise funds from the bond market and institutional investors.

## 5 Conclusion

Historically, the Government and banks have been the most important sources of funding infrastructure projects in India. Both these traditional sources of funding infrastructure are constrained at present. Government has to bring down its fiscal deficit to the levels defined under the Fiscal Responsibility and Budget Management

[9]Consultation paper for Designing a Framework for Enhanced Market Borrowings by Large Corporates, Securities & Exchange Board of India (SEBI), July 2018.

Act. The banking system is weakened with several issues at present, including the Non-Performing Assets (NPAs) problem. On the other hand, the need for infrastructure investment is massive, given the infrastructure deficit in the country and the imperative of providing infrastructure to a fast growing economy. Given these factors, there is a strong recognition of the need for diversification of infrastructure funding sources, including introduction of new and innovative instruments of financing and enabling regulatory and institutional reforms. In this context, the untapped potential of long-term institutional investors such as insurance and pension funds and debt capital market offer both a challenge and an opportunity to meet the future financing needs of the sector.

In recent years, India has launched several new and innovative initiatives to channelize long-term funding to infrastructure sector such as Infrastructure Debt Funds, monetization of brownfield infrastructure assets (asset recycling strategy) through models such as Toll-Operate-Transfer and Infrastructure Investment Trusts, mainstreaming of Public Private Partnerships, developing a new credit rating scale for infrastructure projects and a proposed dedicated Credit Enhancement NBFC to raise credit rating of bonds floated by infrastructure companies. These new alternative financing instruments and avenues hold immense potential to provide fillip to infrastructure investment in India and may find traction with countries across the world who are looking to diversify their infrastructure financing options.

## References


Capital market instruments to mobilize institutional investors to infrastructure and SME financing in Emerging Market Economies: World Bank Group/IMF/OECD Report for the G20, September 2015.

Contribution of institutional investors to private investment in infrastructure: World Bank Group Report, 2017.

CPPIB Press release dated April 3, 2018.

CRISIL infrastructure yearbook 2017.

CRISIL yearbook on the Indian debt market 2018.

Financial Stability Report 2018, Reserve Bank of India.

Global perspectives: Real Estate Investment Trust (REIT): Ernst and Young (EY) Report, 2016.

Handbook of statistics on Indian economy 2011 and 2018, Reserve Bank of India.

Harris, C., & Pratap, K. V. (2009). What drives private sector exit from infrastructure. Gridlines, Note No. 46. Washington DC: World Bank.

Securities & Exchange Board of India (SEBI) Infrastructure Investment Trust (InvIT) Regulations, 2014.

World Bank. (2008). Commission on growth and development. 2008. The growth report: Strategies for sustained growth and inclusive development. Washington, DC: World Bank.

World Bank. (2019). Global economic prospects, January 2019: Darkening skies. Washington, DC: World Bank.

# Chapter 11
# The Problem of Financing Private Infrastructure in India Today

**Sebastian Morris**

**Abstract** Optimal approaches that recognize the specific kind of market failure/s, in the policy and design of infrastructure, greatly reduce the financing costs and improves the ability of to attract finance in the private provisioning of infrastructure. When state systems are weak organizationally it is first best to strengthen the state capacity so that it can minimally perform the roles of design, regulation, development of frameworks, and of monitoring, for the private provisioning of infrastructure. This is particularly so in the case where there are dual market failures arising out of both the natural monopoly and the appropriability failure aspect. The challenges in design and policy are large and with many false starts it is only now barely beginning to be considered in India. Thus infrastructure design rather than debilities in financial markets remain the key problem. The potential to use of foreign capital to finance infrastructure is often overstated. The forces leading to the current mess-up of the Indian banks and FIs in lending to infrastructure are brought in perspective. The key issues in developing state capacity, and the changes required for getting the design of infrastructure right, as also to bring functionality to the role of financial institutions in the private development of infrastructure are highlighted. Governance reforms that make for better development of infrastructure are highlighted.

## 1 Introduction

The movement from the public sector as the leading element in investments to the private sector is more or less complete. Prior to the reforms of 1991–92 and 1992–93, of the Narashima Rao government, the public sector as whole invested as much as 52% of the total investments (gross capital formation—GCF) taking place in India.

---

The original version of this book was revised: Missing abstracts of chapters 3, 6, 8, 9 and 11 have now been included. The correction to this book can be found at https://doi.org/10.1007/978-981-13-8106-5_12

---

S. Morris (✉)
Indian Institute of Management Ahmedabad, Ahmedabad, India
e-mail: morris@iima.ac.in



R. Kathuria and P. Kukreja (eds.), *20 Years of G20*,
https://doi.org/10.1007/978-981-13-8106-5_11

The highly successful reforms brought that down to under 25% over the next four years (Barua 2004). Although cold privatization of public sector units was not a success, the slew of measures including delicensing, abolition of the Industrial Policy Resolution of 1956—that had reserved many sectors for state enterprise—openness on foreign investments, and a general movement towards a laissez faire economy were factors in this relative decline. Unlike what was believed by many commentators including those supportive of the reforms this relative decline in public investments was very important to the success of the reforms since public investments were known to be very inefficient in terms of both cost and time overruns (Morris 1990, 2003c).

## 2 Macroeconomic Performance and Infrastructure

### 2.1 The NHDP and Economic Revival

From 1997 to 1998 with the slowdown, there was little further fall in the share of public investments despite the many measures to increase private investment in infrastructure. While in areas requiring little regulation or recast of subsidies—oil refining and mining, airlines, courier services, telecom (where the regulatory and licensing approaches were essentially right), private investment continued, after having completely dominated the manufacturing sector over the period since then. Private investments in infrastructure require detailed second generation reforms (appropriate regulation, PPP formats, legal changes making possible private ownership and holding of public assets, non-distortionary ways of subsidization), given the market failure/s in these sectors. That kind of second generation reforms being deeper and requiring a more specific understanding of sectors have yet to take place in many sectors—urban and municipal infrastructure sectors, city transportation, electricity among others. The slowing down of private investments in the period after 1997–78 was one of the causes of the overall economic slowdown. Reforms in the right direction in infrastructure have been few and far between since then, but when they have taken place the impact has also been large.

Indeed the revival of the Indian economy from 2003 to 2004 onwards, can in a large measure be traced to the National Highway Development Programme—popularly called the Golden Quadrilateral (GQ), which because of the essential correctness of approach, resulted in very large private investments in the highways, which was instrumental in lifting the economy out of the recession from 2003 to 2004 onwards. The setting up of a road fund which was nearly ring fenced, instituting a new land acquisition act specific for highways, an improved EPC format, a BT format for PPPs, and most importantly a workable annuity model for PPPs, besides the strengthening of the organization to drive the programme—the National Highway Authority of India (NHAI), the focus on the Quadrilateral, and allocative efficiency being upheld, all together created the framework for large private and public investments to take place into the highway sector. Such strategic action that could effectively create public and social value on the scale of the GQ has not been witnessed by the country since the early 2000. Indeed, it was quickly followed by the programme of building village roads—the Prime Minister's Gram Sadak Yojyna (PMGSY) which also saw administrative and contracting innovations to liberate Indian villages from poor last mile connectivity. Indeed these two programmes have remained to date, the major conduits for state spending in a way that is not wasteful.

The period over which growth was maintained at a high level through fiscal action saw larger than before investments in the infrastructure structure. The growth of 8.5% achieved over 2003–04 to 2007–08 saw the capital formation rise to as high as 37%, before it declined somewhat with the monetary tightening that took place as the RBI acted against a supply side inflation from 2007 onwards by raising the cash reserve ratio, and the last two/three quarters before the GFC when it did not any more accommodate the pressure for inflows into the economy. However this period of growth was led by service exports, the rise of manufacturing and with "normal" demand from the infrastructure sectors although the high growth had been kick started by the spending on the GQ as mentioned before. Since the fiscal stimulus saw a large part of counter action take the form of investments in infrastructure, the share of infrastructure in gross capital formation rose in this period (Morris 2014).

## 2.2 *The 12th Plan*

The 12th Plan (2012–17) laid out a programme for infrastructure including in areas of dual (natural monopoly and appropriability) market failure (sewerage, city roads, municipal water, sanitation) that was to have a large part of the same provided through private investments. The role envisaged for PPPs was considerable, and had the Plan (with an assumed growth rate of 9%) materialized, the target for PPPs would have been larger than for any other country in the world.

However as growth slowed down, the fiscal stimulus was withdrawn, the targets did not seem achievable and the Plan itself was scaled down (Morris 2005, 2012). With growth fall from 2011 to 2012 onwards the infrastructure sectors especially those that had been privately financed went into deep trouble, and the problems hurt the banking sector as well—especially the PSU banks, with their non-performing assets (NPAs) rising very rapidly.

## 2.3 *The Fiscal Stimulus*

The large fiscal stimulus to counter the demand depressionary effect of the Global Financial Crisis (GFC) has generally been blamed for the banking crisis from which the country has still not overcome. However it is not the act of the counteraction of macroeconomic demand fall, through the fiscal mode including through enhanced infrastructure spending that was per se the cause of the problem, as much as the fact the lending to infrastructure projects was based on ritualized assessment by the banks, and there were crucial deficiencies in the format for PPPs and their structuring. Also in the specific case of electricity generation, there were large risks to the state arising out of the bidding formats (Pandey 2014). Of course some increase in the NPA levels is only to be expected when there is a slowdown, with the fiscal stimulus having been withdrawn. Inherent organizational and governance weaknesses of the public sector banks made them particularly vulnerable and as we will argue bids by developers in many sectors may have been made to exploit this vulnerability as well.

Since 2011–12, when growth fell off sharply to under 6%, the rate of capital formation also fell first generally hover around 30% or below the same. Infrastructural investments also suffered. But from 2016 to 2017 onwards as the government enhanced the investments on highways now calling it the "Bharatmala" Project, with a hybrid annuity model, since apparently in its reckoning the earlier annuity model was limiting. Indeed, the NHDP and the PMGSY have been the only programmes that have allowed the government to enhance spending without sacrificing public and social value, since the core aspects of the design, bidding and other arrangements under the NHDP that had been developed during 1999–2002 in the Vajpayee era remains essentially functional and value creating.

Other large investments that took place which cannot be said to be successes when the important aspects are considered are the investments related to the two metro airports at Delhi and Mumbai. Since our focus is on financing we will not go over the experience sectorally, but would bring out the experience of financing private infrastructure and the lessons from the same.

The Maharashtra State Road Transport Corporation's (MSRDC's) much commented success in the excellent design and construction of the Mumbai-Pune expressway is remarkable for its near uniqueness. The personal involvement and leadership of the CEO of the MSRDC was responsible. MSRDC still retains some of the capabilities that it then had. However that has been exception to the public sector generally where the woes arising out delays and cost overruns have been typical. Cost overruns of the order of 40–60% and delays of the same order continue in government projects. That means a significant loss of value in capital formation and hence of the growth rate that is possible for the same savings rate. The shift of investments from the public to the private sector, while it would generate rents when with lax design or regulation nevertheless in a large way avoids the social loss that happens when projects have large cost overruns due to extra spending to create the assets, and to the assets being delayed in being put to production (Morris 2003a).

## 3 Financing Government Infrastructure

Financing public infrastructure when built and owned by government does not pose large problems in financial design since the government as the sovereign, and as an entity that can operate beyond the tenure of the longest loan that can be raised in the market, is expected to have the lowest cost of finance, and could potentially take up projects with large gestation periods and long asset lives. However inefficiencies in implementation, pricing and management, and loss of social value, would only get partially reflected in the accounts of the government, that being usually on a cash flow (single entry) basis. The cost of delays for example would not get reflected, unless a notional interest during construction is incorporated. Similarly, the risks in returns to the project would not get reflected—at least not fully—if the project has recourse to government funds; so that the low financing costs for the project could underestimate the risks and the value created. Implicit "guarantees" or assurances which are always there even when without formal guarantees can keep the financing costs "low" (Morris 2003b).

### 3.1 *Implicit Assurances Can Be Exploited*

Through SPVs it is possible to remove the benefit of recourse to government's budget as a whole for projects carried out through public SPVs, but then markets have a way of leveraging the implicit assurance by bringing projects to a situation where much public interest is involved to tie the government down to its debt commitments, even when the risks manifest much after the project is in place, but which could have been anticipated by debt markets.

Consider a risky project by government which is financed by raising debt in the market—say of a tunnel or a special turnpike, and without government guarantees. If the project does not have cash flow to cover debt repayments, then the market instead of taking a loss could lead to concentration among debt holders who could force the government to honor the debt payments of a project that was not formally guaranteed in the first place. This means that the initial premium that such finance would have attracted may systematically undervalue the risks, given such a probability of forcing the hand of the government.

## 4 Financing Privately Owned/Built Infrastructure

The challenges in private financing of infrastructure, especially in the case of PPPs, would require understanding of the issues in government financing as well, since the involvement of Government is active here as one of the parties. Even in the case of regulated entities where the ownership is entirely private, to the extent that there is asset specificity, and the industry is regulated, there would be an interface with government/regulatory/appellate authority that goes beyond what is the case in the case of industries without market failure. When, additionally, the goods/services are seen as being merit goods or necessities, there is always the additional aspect of government acting on behalf of consumer interest, which of can course affect the private financing through markets or otherwise in these sectors.

## 4.1 Governments Are Always Involved in PPPs

PPPs do not take away the government. When annuities are involved, government is essentially creating contingent liabilities to cover these annuities while the private entity puts in the risk capital. Obviously governments need to constraint themselves on the amount of such contingent liabilities they can take. In the Indian case the RBI has put in place measures that limit the exposure of state governments in this manner (RBI 1999). As the fiscal squeeze was put on state governments to meet the expenditure reduction that was part of the reform of 1991–92, 92–93, state governments had responded with increases in expenditure made by their own state owned enterprise (SOEs) and by giving guarantees to other entities some of them in the private/municipal sectors. The RBIs measures which were put in place from around 1999 soon put a near stop to these approaches by the state governments, although they continue to use the losses of state owned enterprises to cover programmes whose budgets have not been technically assented to the legislative assemblies.[1]

## 4.2 Endogenous Risks and PPPs Versus EPC

Consider a PPP. For simplicity we would consider an annuity highway project. Let us imagine that the design, unit costs, methods and technologies are symmetric as between a government department constructing the highway and the same being done by a private entity that has to raise some part of the funds in the market or through institutions.

In bidding out projects the public comparator can easily be considered in terms of the annuity payable (or the annuity equivalent of tolls discounted at the cost of capital for the "prime" private party) vis-à-vis a reference annuity. Government can set up a reference or reserve annuity based on its unit costs, assuming a life of the asset that is realistic −30 years in this case, and a return that is say 3% above the yield of a 30 year bond that it could float. This is say $9\% + 3\% = 12\%$. The annuity so determined now becomes the highest annuity that any private developer could bid for. This would serve as a public comparator. Even when governments and developers see the same unit costs, the failure of the state in construction of an experience good

[1]One of the reasons for the governments' reluctance to divest out of electricity, despite all the state systems being ready for divestment is that then they would not be able to bad but populist policy unless they took the cost on to their own budgets. The ability to pile up the deficits, and then pressure the central government to debt forgiveness continues. It was hoped that the debt forgiveness instituted once in 2002, (GOI 2001, 2002) would not have to be done again. But then that has not been the case since now after nearly 15 years the state DISCOM's balance sheets have been muddied with another similar dispensation now being proposed, without real reform on the distribution and subsidization side, by the government. Clearly reform has to be real. Similarly, large investment heavy sectors like irrigation, sewerage, bus transport, which could be easily divested from to reform and enhance public value, continue to be used wastefully, even when reform could actually have been politically rewarding.

like roads would give enhanced value in case done by the private capital through PPPs. It is precisely because it is virtually impossible to have low maintenance costs by building a shoddy road, that gives value to a BOT/Annuity.

## *4.3 EPCs Can Be First Best Sometimes*

There is a large opportunity to correct the problems in EPC frameworks, which as yet is only partly addressed by the many authorities that procure roads in India. It is only the National Highways Authority of India (NHAI) which has a reasonable organization, and the requisite autonomy to support EPC. The improved EPC which was part of the NHDP was certainly helpful. Of course it could have been far more capable by developing skills and competencies in network design, and in integrating highways with regional and urban transport networks, which are almost entirely absent. The necessity of sound organization at the operational level is because roads (as much as many other assets) are actually experience goods. Their quality cannot be assessed after the top surface has been laid. Only a responsible and incorruptible supervision that checks for the correctness, and functionality of each layer can ensure that what the procurer signs off on is a good asset. This capability having been virtually destroyed in Indian PWDs, compounded by archaic procurement formats, make them procure roads that are "guaranteed" to fail with the next monsoon. It is this inadequacy in supervision, compounded by the poor EPC formats that is common to most PWDs, that gives well crafted PPPs a great value over what is otherwise possible.[2]

The lack of financial resources with government is hardly an argument for PPPs since governments can always raise money cheaply if the same is used in efficiently creating social and public value. That PPPs are more in sync with government accounts which are on cash flow basis is of course more correct, and gives some advantage to PPPs. However, if there are ex-ante limits to how much of contingent liabilities governments can create, with the same being linked in some way to current revenues/outlays, (as in should be), then the financial argument disappears and only the arguments of better design, better construction and more efficient operations and lower prices through the ability to access markets not possible for the public sector[3] would hold.

---

[2]Public procurement has its frailties and cannot be replaced by procurement that is akin to procurement by private parties. See Pandey (2003) to for a discussion on the issues of relating to the private sector in public procurement.

[3]As for instance to access cheaper labour markets, given the "schism" in labour markets that is widely observed in many late industrializing countries.

### 4.4 Duration of Financial Markets

Yet there may not be (or should not be) bids for the same by the private sector in case there are no sources of finance with a tenure of 30 years. If corporate bond markets do not go beyond[4] say 15 years, then private firms would face interest rate (change) risk, that would not permit them to bid effectively for the project. Managing with loans of tenure of 15 years (assuming that the loan on the same terms can be rolled over after 15 years) exposes them to this risk. When financial institutions (FIs) are not supported by the state, loans from FIs would also have the same problem. Indeed FIs like banks would only offer term loans of much lower tenure. In this case because the concession period is say 30 years (being the life of the asset) which is much higher than the tenure of the finance available, worthy developers responsible to their shareholders would not be able to participate. However, some developers with little reputation and not answerable to their diffuse shareholders, but only to promoters, could bid "taking on this risk", but with the intent to shift the same on to others in case the same materializes, thereby resulting in adverse selection. That would keep worthy developers out. This "risk taking" can result in a high probability of winner's curse with abandonment risk being faced by the government. There are of course several possible solutions to the same.

### 4.5 The Concession Period

One is to limit the concession period to 15 years which matches the tenure of markets in which the developer can raise funds to result in financial closure. Then there is the problem of intergenerational pricing as when the tolls have to be higher than "cost" to reflect this shorter concession period over which all costs are recovered. But this may not be very large as between a concession period of 15 years and 30 years. However it opens the door to what is to be done after 15 years. Of course there must then be a transfer clause necessarily, and in order to avoid the risk that the developer does not maintain the road well over the last few years, it is imperative to either withhold payments for the last two years, to the year after the transfer (which is expensive); or to build in a clause where the current developer gets a handicap to bid for the same asset as an maintain operate and transfer (MOT) project after the concession period of 15 years. The "handicap" can easily be worked out knowing variances in costs across the private sector and acceptable "loss" to cover this risk. In most cases a 5% preference over the lowest annuity bid for the MOT after 15 years would be adequate since most of the costs after 15 years would be operational costs, which can easily be assessed and anticipated.

---

[4]Markets that go beyond this tenure are very thin, and/or are very heavily discounted in India.

### 4.6 *Covering Interest Rate (Change) Risk*

Another way out is that the FIs who do the lending, then assess this interest rate risk and insist on equity well beyond those suggested as a norm by the government, to cover this risk. Then the bidder would have to bid beyond the reserve annuity, or above those who are not constrained by such assessment. This again would bring in adverse selection if there are players of the latter type in the market. However if development finance institutions (DFIs) can cover this risk (through instruments such as take-out financing), then there should not be a problem even if the concession period is well beyond the tenure of the market.[5] Indeed this was acutely realized by the Infrastructure Development Finance Company (IDFC) and the instrument was created early enough to support private capital in infrastructure. However there being no compulsion to use the same, developers taking recourse to covering their interest rate (change) risk would be at a disadvantage, creating therefore an adverse selection problem despite a mechanism existing. There is therefore a need in the PPPs (in India most notably) to internalize the cost of covering the interest rate risk; i.e. the RFPs must lay down that the bidders must necessarily cover themselves if their bids are to be considered. That would of course raise the cost somewhat but would lead to large gains in terms of risk reduction, making for fewer failures of PPPs and hence of enhanced scope for private sector development. It would also allow for a somewhat lower level of due diligence required on the part of the banks, without exposing them to too large a mismatch between their assets and liabilities.

### 4.7 *Annuities and Tolls Linked to Cost of Capital*

Alternatively governments can cover this risk by linking a portion of the annuity to the interest rate on the debt instrument with the thickest market—a 10 or 5 year bond in the Indian case. Although the portion of the annuity to so cover is not very accurately determined, that is not important. Such an approach could for example make an irrigation or dam project efficiently financed by the private sector with additional benefits that come from efficient design and management. Or equivalently the cost of covering the risk can be compulsorily borne by the buyer, which is effectively the same as the previous one.

## 5 Role of BSFIS

Of course this limitation of the capital market need not result in adverse selection if the FIs that lend to the developers without exception understand this rather simple

[5]For the role of DFIs in a liberalized market that leads to development of financial markets, see Varma (2004).

problem and insist on covering the same either with an option like take out financing or through a higher equity contribution.[6]

## 5.1 *Failure of Indian PSU Banks*

Unfortunately the Indian public sector banks, having created a ritualized assessment process, and being subject to government suggestion, cannot be relied upon to have gone through the assessment deligently. Even if some particularly independent CEO did so, he would have been ruled out by the need for "objective" assessment or following each other, since most of the public sector banks would have lend without consideration of the risks. Indeed, most of the developers were borrowing at tenures of 5–8 years with interest being reset every one or two years! Since the equity to debt ratio was also as per the standard in the RFP, and the PPPs could only look to fixed annuities or to tolls whose rates were not in their control, the problems that the PPPs ran into in the period of rising interest rates was only to be expected. We may even suggest that many of the private developers took this risk knowingly since they always could pressure the government on one side to renegotiate the contracts, and that they could dump the negatives on the public sector banks, the ever willing to be the losers that they are.[7]

# 6 The Hybrid Annuity Model

Subsequently at least, in the NHDP, the new "Hybrid-Annuity" Model (HAM) was put in place. This provided for a capital grant of 40% of the project construction cost (bid value of the project cost i.e. the NPV of the construction and operating costs since these are non-overlapping in time) to be paid out over the construction period. And the annuities subsequently (fixed) to cover the rest of the bid value over the concession period. Government may or may not toll. The annuities as well as the capital grant is adjusted upwards with inflation based on a weighted average of CPI and WPI. Thus in the HAM the traffic risk as in the annuity model is on the government. This is not a major deviation from good project structuring, since the alternative of lane availability based annuity would anyway have the same risk allocation. However since there is early recovery (given the 40% support that happen before revenues), there could be some addition to the project abandonment risk. Since there is also a deemed termination clause, which was not there in either the BOT or

[6]It is important to realize that in competitive industries where revenue streams can rise due to price changes, as in the cases where there are no market failures, lending can be over much shorter tenure, and equity proportions can adjust, or be made to adjust to reflect these risks.

[7]An insight due to Prof. Ajay Pandey, shared with me over several discussions. See also Pandey (2014) for risk shifting behavior more generally by the private sector.

the annuity model that it replaced, that route could be used by making arguments that "force majeure" like conditions exist to quit early, in case of major difference between costs as estimated and as actually happens. These probabilities are apparently not very large. The indexation of both annuities and construction cost with inflation does reduce considerable the interest rate (change) risk that we mentioned earlier, since inflation over the longer period does track the interest rate.

## *6.1 Partial Coverage of Interest Rate Risk*

However since the inflation has been lower than the interest rate by much over 2% (high real interest rate policy of the RBI), if the same approach to macroeconomic policy continues, the HAM is likely to result in higher costs.[8] The interest build up though during construction is on the bank rate + 3%. Since the bank rate is a dead rate in a regime where the repo is used it would have been better to use the repo rate. However since the repo window has often been not fully open, it is even better to have used the low end (1 year) bond yield rates with a premium over the same. They could also be based on triple A corporate bonds with a term of around 5 years or more where the market in thick enough.

Since in the annuity model, there is no tolling by the developer, even when the tolls may be viable, but tolls could be levied by the NHAI, the framework provides an ample opportunity to move from cost based tolling to allocative use efficiency based tolling, even as in BOT projects the private sector does essentially cost based regulated tolling.[9] Even for the private sector, a congestion charge that is negative or positive, and dynamically allocated, can be collected by government with a view to manage traffic over a network.

Since it is well known that selective tolling can be distortionary, unless driven from the congestion angle, as the network develops (multiple paths for the same OD), there can be major gains in both social use value, and in the cost by resorting to differential tolling that takes into account optimal traffic considerations as well. They could then move to being dynamic as well. Similarly on BOT projects, the private entity must have the option of tolling under the regulated toll to enhance traffic flow as the network develops.[10]

---

[8]Many of the UKs PPP were contracted for during the period of high interest rates. Since then rates have fallen, especially so after the quantitative easing that followed the GFC. That has made annuity out payments very large to the chagrin of those arguing for PPPs. Had the annuities been indexed to bond rates, this should not have happened.

[9]Unfortunately the NHAI has not recognized the opportunity that is there even now (despite low network densities and alternatives today). Thus on the Ahmedabad Baroda stretch, the very large 6+ lane national highway sees very little traffic because the tolls are higher than on the Expressway (4+ lane). Had the tolls been rationalized to give trucks a lower relative toll on the Highway, and cars a relatively lower toll on the Expressway, the separation of truck and car traffic, would have improved the value to both (including safety), and enhanced the revenue as well.

[10]Today though this would only be of academic interest, since the tolls are very high in India constituting a significant part of cost to operators and road users. Equally importantly when a

The operations period once the construction happens is 15 years. Since anyway much of the interest rate risk is covered through inflation linked payments, or can be covered through an explicit incorporation of the interest rates in the annuities, the concession period can be made long enough to match the actual asset life, and the same model with some modifications can be used in other sectors such as irrigation, bridges, logistics, to name a few.

# 7 Load Flow and Network Effects

## *7.1 Efficient Network Design*

Network effects can be very large when the network densities are very high as in the highway sector. In India where the central place densities are high, very high traffic on arterials (GQ and GCross for example) is less a reflection of the OD and more one of route availability. To planners going by demands over segments as they are visibly revealed and not by OD, the value of grids like networks, and networks with multiple paths gets obfuscated. In the long run though national grid networks, with spurs to major urban habitats would have to be the approach of the design rather than the current incrementalism of expanding capacity wherever the traffic visibly grows. Without such a change over the expected huge rise in intercity and long distance traffic would become completely unmanageable,[11] as these already have around the major metros.

From the point of view of finance the load-flow aspects of road networks makes for a lower traffic risk for a set of roads as compared to road segments being considered separately. The approach if BOT and tolling has to be maintained, is to either create a market for tolls,[12] and/or allow for SPVs over various segments to merge given their negative incremental traffic correlation. Listed companies that hold many segments in China exists in China where toll roads are many.[13] Making the same possible

highway is being expanded, or in part redone to provide for underpasses or service roads, tolling continues without the value to road users, which actually could be challenged in a court of law. It is important that tolling is not carried out when the road is broken, under construction, or under large scale traffic diversion.

[11] Already the limitation of the current approach of by-passes, ring roads, (which all get quickly ribbonised and to become part of urban system) with regard to urban transportation, and radial (star) arrangements on highways, which come close to or intersect urban/rural habitats to bring about conflict between local and regional/long distance traffic takes away much public value in contrast to system design in almost any other country. The sacrifice of safety that the current approach entails is the reason for the almost 10–15 times higher loss of life due to road accidents that is there in India over the advanced countries, when correctly measured in terms of fatalities per vehicle km.

[12] See for instance Tilotia and Pawar (2004).

[13] Though most are in the public sector, the listing of such companies allows for secondary market participation. Cf. Thomas White (2010).

only after construction would only allow for leveraging developers risk capital since the road once it completes construction and enters the annuity/toll phase can be offloaded on to markets, the latter if a market for tolls can be created. Of course if these possibilities are there even before construction (which would mean efficient accounting separation with strong audit of particular roads businesses from the point of view of the government), then financing costs could fall somewhat as well. In any case the value of mergers after construction would allow for capital markets—especially of long tenure investors like pension and mutual funds to participate.[14]

### 7.2 *Segments Not Commercialisable*

Similarly in the case of gas pipelines the market failure arising out of the natural monopoly aspect enhanced by load flow characteristics would imply that if segments of the network are privatized then the risks emanating from load flow would necessitate that lenders (and developers) are protected from vast demand variation through take or pay contracts, which while it makes funding and construction by the private sector possible increases the cost of the service of transportation. Ideally the entire network should be considered as a single on with open access and common carrier principles being built into, with incentive regulation covering the transportation costs, to allow markets in gas to emerge. Only this can keep the costs down, and pave the way for functional expansion of the overall gas business that included production as well with private capital (Barua and Madhavan 2010).

## 8 Foreign Capital in Infrastructure

One of the important themes in the literature and in popular discussions, with the re-emergence of private sector in infrastructure, is the hope and belief that there is a large role for foreign capital both direct and portfolio. The reality is that the scope is highly constrained because infrastructure services being non-tradable would not typically be able to generate the foreign exchange to service debt and equity that is designated in foreign currency. One could counter this by stating that significant infrastructure creation by the private and municipal sectors in the late 19th century—railways, tramways, canal systems, sewerage systems had been so financed. The differences between the situation then and today though need to be appreciated. Most of the infrastructure sectors which raised private capital (including foreign capital) were still in the competitive phase of their evolution as natural monopolies and were unregulated.[15]

---

[14] See also Varma (2002).

[15] "Regulation" in the form of Antitrust had just come into the railways in the US. This was by no means price regulation but actually kept the competing "natural monopolies" from merging into a

That means they were able to operate like competitive firms with the ability to raise prices to cover exchange rate changes as much as other costs variation. Equally importantly since the Gold Standard ruled, the currency values could not deviate much from their sustainable values (at which the balance of payments is in equilibrium), so that the adjustment process of the exchange rate was much quicker, and not of a situation of compounding disequilibrium that could last long in currency markets. In other words, borrowing in external markets would automatically would lower the currency if the current account proved unsustainable with those additional capital inflows.

## 8.1 Deviation from Uncovered Parity and Resulting Distortions

Today with fixed and dirty floats characterizing most exchange rate regimes, the implications of borrowing from abroad to take advantage of a seemingly lower overall cost of capital, may well mean that disequilibrium continues for long, with the pressure to get back increasing which then manifests with a large fall in the currency to render the original perceived lower cost of borrowing infructuous. In other words, the uncovered parity condition is off in a significant way by as much as 200–400 basis points,[16] even for countries that are open to portfolio flows, results in some seeming advantages to finance projects through international borrowings and capital flows, when we also expect the interest rate differentials to also mirror the inflation differentials over the long term. But this can be misleading[17] especially for long duration infrastructure projects, with fixed price services, and revenue being realized in dollars, since the positive deviation from uncovered parity can suddenly reverse to turn deeply negative when the much lagged adjustment of same takes place.

## 8.2 Pension and Sovereign Funds

Yet there is the limited opportunity that arises out of foreign funds from developed mature economies that face slower growth rates as compared to the emerging economy in question, are of very long tenure (pension and insurance funds for instance).

few dominant monopolies. For a discussion on the evolution of natural monopolies (industries with sub-additivity of costs) from competition to the textbook natural monopoly with pricing power see Morris (2002). See also Varma (2001).

[16]Aliber (1993) argues that multinationals (MNCs) could have an advantage in being able to take advantage of the uncovered parity being positive, even as portfolio capital is not able to close the gap. In other words the so-called "country risk" when used to denote this deviation from uncovered parity, could be penetrated in part by MNCs.

[17]However for MNCs in host countries from where exports take place (operating in areas with no market failure), the positive deviation from uncovered parity becomes an "advantage" allowing it to finance/take over local firms, using foreign sources of funds, even when these are otherwise on other real factors like technology, organization and management no inferior to the MNC.

To take advantage of the longer tenure of foreign funds, the local government would have to set in place adequate long term cover, and manage the exchange rate such as to adjust quickly to be as near as the uncovered parity condition. Even then as agents who manage pension funds have sought significantly higher returns that what is possible for them in their own markets, the scope for such funds is limited. Sovereign wealth funds too are increasingly managed with incentives for high returns. As a result the scope for foreign financing of infrastructure is limited as well.

## *8.3 ELG Economies*

Export led growth economies, undervalue their currencies from the very start of their strategy, and also have low real interest rate policies. This means that the deviation from uncovered parity is not as high as in other emerging economies, allowing for financing with low risks in infrastructure. However, since there is no ex-ante revealed difference in the cost of local and foreign funds then, the uncovered parity condition (also sometimes called the fisher open) being nearly met, little flows would actually take place, and a certain functionality in the pattern of the sources of financing would emerge. Competitive entities with dollar revenue streams having more foreign capital inflows, and non-competitive entities having no dollar revenue streams being almost exclusively funded from local sources, which is what should be. As in such economies much of the infrastructure would, as is should get funded locally.[18]

## *8.4 Government to Government Credit*

Government to government credit given on long tenure, and at low rates, may have a functionality though. Often such credit being linked to sourcing of equipment for the construction could raise the price of equipment above that of suppliers without such linked finance. This was certainly the case in the 2000s and earlier. As World Bank has created frameworks for bidding in such cases of international funding, which are fairer to the recipient countries than what they would otherwise have been, it has helped to create an opportunity for such credit to supplement the IDA window of the World Bank. Relative to the needs of a large economy like India in its current phase of transition, such credit would be very small but not negligible.

[18]An additional consideration is the so-called "real economy" advantage that MNCs have which arises out of imperfections in the technology and product markets, and in organizational structure and practice. Kindleberger (1969). When the advantage that MNCs have is of such kind and especially when technological, rather than arising due to the fischer open (positive deviation from the uncovered parity), then the spillovers would naturally be large to benefit the host economies. Infrastructure sectors do not show large technological differences, which are also not appropriable. Hence foreign direct investments too into infrastructure tend to be low if these are not be dysfunctional.

## 9 Indian PSBS and DFIS

Indian public sector banks pose a particular threat to enhancing private sector participation in infrastructure. Their inability to truly understand risks (or more correctly the organizational difficulties in using the correct approach) negates one element that could have been a watchdog for ensuring that developers don't take on unwarranted risks. And they could have also nudged procurement and PPP formats to what is functionally desirable and in the interest of society. However with a pure private banking sector, it is also unlikely that hidden rent opportunities in PPPs would get exposed either.

### *9.1 Reform of PSB Urgent*

Hence reform of the PSU banks is very much integral to the issue of private infrastructure development, especially in the enhanced use of PPPs for developing public infrastructure. As entities with their money in, and yet not having an objective of profit maximization at all costs (including partaking in rent generation), they could have played an important role in ensuring that rent opportunities are not there in PPPs, and could have prevented developers from taking risks that are beyond their control. Yet their managers do not speak out against the inadequacies in government policy or in regulation, the frameworks for PPPs all of which have a bearing on financing. Lacking autonomy, their senior managers not have courage to contend with bad or incomplete infrastructural policy.

### *9.2 Policy Advisory Roles*

It is interesting that when one FI viz the IDFC had set up "policy advisory" sensing the need for the same if "good" projects in which private sector could participate were to be forthcoming, things really moved. The role played by the IDFC (programme and organizational design which was then adopted by the MOST) was crucial in the success of the both the NHDP and the PMGSY. But soon enough a variety of pressures emerged which forced the IDFC to withdraw from any such role. It also retreated from the developmental role even in the financial market and today is no more than a vanilla universal bank.

Other organisations like the ILFS and the IIFCL reached nowhere near the expected role of a DFI in a liberal financial sector, and lend largely from its own pockets to private infrastructure (without the leveraging of flow of funds from the market that they could have). Indeed they may have been lax enough to have contributed in a major way to the banking crisis. Approval by ILFS was akin to a green signal for all PSU banks to jump in without their own real assessment.[19] The tendency of PSU managers to never contest the views of government officials even when they were mistaken, removes all hope that the public sector banks would be able to reform themselves on the crucial function of credit assessment.

## *9.3 Lack of Autonomy Results in Failure of Accountability*

For some of the better PSU banks the problem was that they were "not allowed" to do correct credit assessment, since many of their managers were experts. The bigger tragedy of PSU banking is not than managers did not know (they could have learnt), but that the expertise which is so obviously there in PSU banks is not effectively brought to bear. This is due to the lack of autonomy which makes the interface with government dysfunctional enough for banks to ignore prudence, and be led by targets and other agenda brought in administratively by the government. The lack of autonomy[20] has allowed banks to, over a period, completely displace accountability to the primary task, so that the only corrective that can happen is to viciously punish managers who unluckily become the "fall" guys, as the crisis has emerged and the accountability to NPAs is insisted upon. This has today taken the level of demoralization of the bank managers to an altogether new level where it is only rational for them dissociate themselves from any lending at all. The probability then that those willing to act are motivated increases. "Internal" adverse selection then runs rife!

The RBI's regulatory role is no better either. In itemizing regulation it forced banks to adhere, at best, to the letter of regulation, and not the spirit. Thus credit assessment which is holistic with a key role for private information, hardly therefore amenable to a set of requirements which are considered independent of each other. Similarly regulating/controlling input and process measures, which was the penchant

[19]One's own experience being on the board of a PSU bank during this period of lax lending was that it was almost impossible to argue against lending to infrastructure. If ILFS had cleared a particular infrastructure project, for the mangers of PSU banks, who behaved more like bureaucrats over long years of an abused interface between the government and the bank, there was no question of seriously re-examining the proposal. Even if glaring risks like in the case of a power project projecting revenues with no firm PPA but through sales in the market at assumed prices based on past prices for short term deals, were pointed out, they could be easily overruled because "another PSU bank" had already taken the decision. RBI representatives would not typically be critical enough to look closely at endogenous risks being much more concerned about any ticks as laid out in the assessment procedure not being met.

[20]Government for example, carpet bombs the banks with office memos and Government Orders (some compulsory others advisory) and there could be as many as a few score over quarter, swamping the boards of the weaker banks (with very little countervailing power), so that response to these, as well as credit assessment much of which should have taken place lower down, uses up all the top management time. Most of these are internal and pertain to operations rather than strategy or policy, which leads to PSU banks being not able to maintain their boundaries—a necessary aspect of any "living" firm or system. Indeed the bane of government in India, is that it is singularly unable to distinguish strategy, plan and policy from operations.

of both the RBI and the government is the best recipe for losing accountability to the primary task. In other words the RBI was interfering rather than regulating, despite many sound measures and advice that it has brought on to the issue.

## 9.4 Poor Organisations for the Primary Task

Resulting from the lack of autonomy, the PSU banks have not been able to create organisational structures and processes that are in keeping with the performance of their primary task. This of course keeps them from seizing the opportunity even when there are narrow windows of opportunity under the very rare benign and well meaning minister and secretary who are able to differentiate the strategic and policy from the operational and organizational. This is of a course a general problem that all PSUs in India face which has denied effectiveness to PSUs (Sarabhai 1969; Morris 1991) in leading the economic transformation of the country, a role that they have well played in the countries that starting later have been successful—most notably the east Asian tigers and china, besides Japan in an earlier period.

There are many other design and policy aspects that act against public sector banking. Loan 'melas' and such periodic loan forgiveness, and administratively direction banks to political and social goals (instead of stating them in policy terms) are well recognized as being perverse. However, the aspect of title to land being very weak and risky, reducing the effectiveness of collateral based lending is not recognized. This hurts especially MSMEs. Similarly the angularity between recovery laws and the lending portfolio of banks is only now beginning to be recognize.

## 9.5 Law and Recovery

Indian law modeled on the Anglo-Saxon banking practice where banks only lend short with the stock as security. But banks actually lend long term as well in India, like the continental banks. However in recovery the option to change the management is not considered, which in the Indian context would mean getting rid of the promoter, and bringing new management. This option is very much part of the banking law in the continent, Japan and Korea, where term lending by banks is common. When lending long the functionality of this option being available to lenders is very important in the efficient direction and use of deposit resources that would be available to the banking system in a large measure. This lacunae is particularly limiting when lending to private infrastructure owing to the long tenure of the debt and the limitations in price adjustment than come with regulation.

The large amounts of capital that gets locked up in SLR assets (today about 22% of deposits) creates the need for higher interest margins in lending, which has brought about a disintermediation. This of course hurts the MSMEs in manufacturing most since they have a comparative advantage in borrowing from banks. The smaller infrastructure players too would be "unfairly" affected by this disintermediation.

## 10 "Good" Projects

### *10.1 Correct Returns, Not Rents*

The problem of bringing more private capital into infrastructure is much more that of the infrastructure sector not having many good projects, and less that of limitations in financial markets. The markets of course recognize "good" projects to be those which are profitable, even when some of the "profits" take the form of rents. But from a social and public point of view, "good" projects are not those that allow private developers to make abnormally high returns arising out of them taking high risks (that governments can mitigate), or because of rent opportunities that arise due to ill-designed PPPs and/or regulation. Such perversities would unnecessarily raise the direct and indirect cost of the services provided by the developer to high levels. The demand to that extent would then be far less than otherwise. But perhaps more importantly the rents and super-normal profits inevitably attract the hostile attention of the public, opposition parties, and other civil society organisations, and media to take PPPs more than a step backward.

While financial markets and analysts may have incentives to not talk loudly of such instances, the government as the upholders of the larger social interest and especially of value to the public, cannot but put its best foot forward in the design of infrastructure. Since government action ultimately in action by civil servants, the importance of legal covenants, and indeed an overarching legal frameworks for private infrastructure and especially for PPPs becomes necessary. Hence "good" projects are necessarily those that allow known returns ex-ante, while avoiding rents.

### *10.2 Legislation and Legal Frameworks*

When PPPs are pushed through pure executive action, since a change of the executive is always possible in democracies, the framework for the award of contracts has to have justification in law and in value, if not through objective assessment, then at least through well laid out processes that lead to choice, including that of location, shortlisting and final award of the contract. In countries like India where programmes of political parties are both fickle and populist[21]—in part arising out of the need to oppose—the risks due to change in governments, are very high.

The risks can be reduced through laws that specifically provide for PPPs and private sector participation and the attendant requirements that go with it, which override other possible legal barriers. The hurry of politicians to get through with PPPs through executive action without waiting for the cumbersome legislative pro-

[21] Pure populism without either a developmental or inclusion aspect is also partly the result of the state not having the capacity to strategise and pursue developmental goals. The lack of ability then makes politicians turn to the quickies that populist measures are.

cesses is usually a recipe for failure. And that gets reflected in the very high premiums for financing such projects, or in risk shifting behavior. Here the role of the civil servants become important, since they are in a position to point to such risks and of the need to mitigate these.[22] Having laws and frameworks and independent institutions that have defined roles, in place mitigates this risk to an extent.

## 10.3 MCAs

There is general agreement that model concession agreements (MCAs) are important to take PPPs further. One argument is favour is the savings in time. Also that in following the MCA closely the government promoting the project would have gone through a well analysed and developed framework. After all there is no point in reinventing the wheel. There being many hidden risks the MCA provides a path where these have apparently been identified and addressed. An added benefit is that it provides a way to take forward PPPs to the civil servant who is otherwise harried to give the attention to the detail which is required for PPPs. Also in a situation of little or no organizational capability, and where the embedding of learning within government departments in low, which is very much the case with government departments in India, and where "mistakes" can invite punishment on the "fall guy" ex-post, civil servants are in a better position to push for PPPs within the ambit of the MCA. These are all valid and MCAs are very important for countries like India that seek to provide much of their public infrastructure through private capital.

[22]One of the major plus points of the NHDP was that it had its own legislative basis both in the NHDP Act and in the special provision for land acquisition that the NHAI could use. As the Congress came to power displacing the Vajpayee led NDA government under whose leadership the NHDP happened, the initial reaction of the Congress government was to critically examine the NHDP. But finding the same to be successful in creating public value and being well entrenched in law, the new government actually enhanced the investments! On the other hand poorly crafted private investment arrangement for generation in the electricity sector under the IPP policy c.1995 which allowed returns up to 32% (much of it in the form of rents), invited a severe backlash, from which a partial recovery could happen only after 10 years with much change, and new policy in the form of the "Ultra Mega Power Policy" (Pandey 2010). Similarly, the two metro airport privatisations which involved much rents that were hidden in the earlier format. This is because the bid criteria was the share of revenue when the revenue was ill defined. There were other issues as well (Pandey et al. 2010). These, inter alia led to a period of retreat from privatization of other airports. And it is only now that the matter is back on the burner with an attempt to overcome the vast rent seeking opportunity created because of the bid criteria being the share of revenue, when revenue itself was ill defined. However since public value was enhanced considerably by the professionalization of design and management that these privatisations brought about, there was no adverse public reaction as such, and the realization of the mistake is confined to official and academic circles. Also the intervention of the court to deny a part of the rents, much after the project was completed, took some part of the sting away. But the matter can still be brought on into the public domain if the same is seen to provide a political opportunity.

## 10.4 Beyond MCAs

However it is a mistake to believe that there are no significant or crucial differences between PPPs in the same sector, and with the same objectives. Not only those due to geographical differences, but those emanating from the nature of demand especially in the differences in willingness to pay, the current condition of the publicly owned network, differences in the nature of the organizational situation, all imply that with hardly any exception PPPs have special characteristics which need to be addressed, even if a good starting point is the MCA. In other words the task of ex-ante subjecting the PPP (in the detail of all its agreements) to analysis (of risks and incentive compatibility) by putting oneself in the shoes of all stakeholders (developers, lender, consumers, ordinary citizens, the relevant public, governments—local, state and national, other authorities with the power to approve infrastructure (defense establishment, town planning authorities, cantonments, safety authorities, etc.), land owners and user of land, besides the interests that are likely to adversely affected. has necessarily to be gone through. Highways may be the sector, where MCA would encompass more of the risks as compared to other sectors where the specificities tend to be high. In the case of sewerage systems, ports, multimodal facilities, water systems, airports, etc., even with a standard approach the specifics would almost always have to be deeply considered to anticipate the risks and potential dispute points ex-ante as much as possible, even though we know that no contract can be completely specified.

## 10.5 Expert PPP Organisation

A good answer especially in India is to have a neutral expert body of lawyers, economists, finance and market experts, besides those with sectoral knowledge, which could whet proposals sent to it on a voluntary basis. Such an organisation should have independence and no executive or recommendatory powers, and most must importantly avoid any developmental role.[23] Its reputation gets built on its expertise, although it is funded by government. Its purpose is really to point out lurking risks and anomalies to the party that approaches it. Over a period, whetting by the same organisation would become a way by which sincere civil servants, lenders and developers (who seek genuine profits but not rents) could get their agreements and proposals double checked. The cost of such an organisation would be infinitesimally small vis-à-vis the social value it could render through PPPs and such modes of infrastructure development. Key to the success of such an organisation is non-interference from the government, and no influence of the private sector either. Having a budget

[23]In the budget of 2014–15 government proposed an organization called 3PIndia with these roles but was unfortunately also saddled with a developmental role, which would negate the primary purpose of being an expert organization!

that is not voted, and having the right stakeholder structure is most important to the ability of such an organisation to contribute to "good" PPPs.

## 10.6 Administrative and Civil Service Reform

Given the specific constraints and debilities that civil servants face in India,[24] the Indian system of decision making, especially with regard to PPPs and infrastructure can be highly problematic, and could lead to situations of large risks and/or rent opportunities, or to inaction. Having recourse to an organisation of specialists of the kind described above should result in a flood of "good" projects. This is especially so, since governance and organizational reform, (which involves both civil service reform and administrative reform in the Indian parlance) in the right direction, is hardly round the corner.

Similarly, enabling senior civil servants to have recourse to "owner's consultants"—who are unattached experts—could go far to develop a critical evaluation of the approach and strategy laid out by main stream consultants, who are who keep out of processes consultation that would typically follow the "framework or design" consultation. In other words, there is conflict of interest between the framework consultation and process consultation—the latter being large in size—which has the potential to distort the framework consultation recommendations.

## 10.7 Modes of Intervention

Recognizing the nature of the core market failures in particular sectors is paramount if they have to be addressed correctly. Thus while electricity has only the failure of being a natural monopoly, the city road sector is both a natural monopoly and suffers from appropriability problems due to lack of excludability as well. However, the sewerage sector is a natural monopoly but its excludability may not be of much meaning in a poor economy. This is because the very large positive externalities of use (actually the very large negative externalities of non-use even by a few) would keep the door open for avoidable infectious diseases which would hurt all. Therefore it would be necessary to include everyone and this implies subsidization as well.

With modern developments in contracting, measurement, data acquisition and analysis, it becomes possible to unbundle the electricity sector into generation, supply, ancillary services, transmission, and the wires part of distribution of which

[24]Civil servants are not experts. The high value placed "generalists", the frequent transfers, the disdain with which knowledge is considered all make for non-learning organisations. Also by design there is very little embedment of knowledge other than of the procedural variety. The result is person dependence rather than system dependence. In most other LDCs though with poor governance the reasons more often like in a politics that misdirects resources, or in a undertrained civil service, not in the kind of organizational failure that become the hall mark of Indian administration.

only the latter two segments are natural monopolies since the show sub-additivity of costs. Today we need only regulate these two to set free the other sectors. This means designed markets, the efficacy of which lies in the correctness of the design. For the approach relevant to the country.[25] The financing options would therefore follow such desirable change in the industrial organization the leads to markets.

| | Inadequate appropriation | No problem of appropriation |
|---|---|---|
| Competitive | Education<br>Public health services<br>Tertiary health care<br>Inoculation services<br>Extension services for agri.<br>Solid waster collection<br>*Efficient State, subsidies, contracting* | Domain of markets<br>Generation in electricity<br>Supply in electricity<br>Mobile (growing NM)<br>Airlines (contestable NM)<br>*Markets, designed markets, oversight/ interconnect regulation, bids* |
| Natural Monopoly | Sewerage networks<br>Water supply<br>City roads<br>Multimodal switches<br>Highways (overappr. Possibilties)<br>*State, PPPs* | Telecom (wires)<br>Electricity(transmission, wires distribution), gas pipelines<br>Market yards<br>*Incentive regulation,* |

Similarly, sectors like city cleaning have only appropriability problems. Efficient regulation would mean taking advantage of market creation as well as use of contracting. The modes of intervention that are appropriate are indicated schematically in the figure alongside.

## *10.8 Electricity*

Approaches to financing would have to recognize this optimal market structure and mode of intervention, and be in tune with the same. Thus in a regulated industry, market like electricity generation market borrowings to finance investment to cover a large part of the capacity when generation is unregulated would imply that the generation company pre-sells a large part of its capacity in long term contracts, which could of course become financial contracts in a world where the delivery of power is based on day ahead markets etc. Where the design of the markets necessarily involves the pre-selling of capacities prior to participation in the energy markets the financing risks are clearer since demand imbalances manifest quicker and capacity

[25] For example, Pandey and Morris (2009) lays out the framework for the design of electricity markets most appropriate to the needs of the country.

creation is quickly signaled without large gaps. When the market bundles capacity and energy cost recovery into a single price bid, capacity addition may get bunched together to create periods of low and high prices, with the risks that these can put on an individual firm.

## *10.9 Municipal Water and Sewerage*

Similarly, in recognizing the vast social and public benefits of total inclusion in sewerage and water systems, and the physical interaction of one with the other, bids would be for both sewerage and water together with strict penalties for non-coverage below nearly 100%, and with support if need be if some people are too poor to pay. The PPP structure and design would have to reflect this aspect and viability gaps to be covered by the state would be in order. Also being natural monopolies the tariff would have to be set, with increasing block to both allow for the judicious use of water, and to have access for all. Access subsidization rather than use subsidization would be functional. With the tariffs fixed and incentive regulation chosen it makes sense to have bids on the basis of the viability funds demanded. Since good i.e. to cost to serve tariffs may be higher than the initial willingness to pay (given the incredulity that people have with regard to the capability of the system to reform) a staged rise from tariffs that are no higher than the present to full cost recovery to all except the poor may be called for.

Volumetric metering and strict penalties against non-achievement of quality standards,[26] and coverage would be called for. One necessary standard among others is that water supply has to be 24*7 since there is no way to ensure potability of water, and control leakage with anything less than 24*7. Indeed given the massive wastage of water, most PPPs if correctly structured should see humungous rise in social value, and also make most projects be financially viable with the support being bid for turning negative if the RFP is in the direction suggested. This is only by way of example. The risk reduction that is thereby possible with upfront clarity would crowd in private finance.

Similar sector/service specific considerations are there in almost all areas of infrastructure. Major dysfunctionalities emerge if the tenets that follow from the schema in the figure are ignored. Thus, setting up of a regulated/unbundled industry like electricity which clearly has no appropriability problems as PPPs (as in the Case I and Case II or IIP models) are per se problematic and their financing would reflect these risks. Besides these, there are of course many other sector specific aspects which would need to be considered.

[26]The standards too have to be realistic. For sewage disposal a BOD of 10 ppm would be very expensive, while 30 which is very good would allow most cities have near 100% coverage via PPPs.

### 10.10 False Comfort of Cost Plus

Regulatory modes also influence the financing decisions. Thus in natural monopolies, when the regulation is cost plus, the "comfort of cost plus" reduces the cost of finance. However this comfort comes with all the attendant failures and distortions brought about by cost plus regulation that greatly subtracts from consumer and social values. The somewhat higher cost of financing investments when the regulation is of the incentive type is more than compensated by the vast gains in social efficiency and the lack of massive distortions that cost plus brings. This is well known in the literature, but neither associations of developers, nor the financial institutions would be inclined to highlight this aspect. If government officials are unaware of the nuances of regulatory modes on the financing costs then expensive errors are possible. The choice of cost plus which regulation which has slowly moved to "norms based" regulation instead of having used incentive regulation directly is one of the reasons for the problems in the sector.

### 10.11 Covering Vast Price Changes in Major Inputs

Similarly if prices of significant inputs are expected to fluctuate much and can only be anticipated very weakly, then the private sector cannot be expected to bear the risks from these large movements in prices, since they intrinsically lack the capacity. They would have to be pass thru, but be based on prices in the markets which are thick. The regulation ought to recognize the need for such defined pass thru ex-ante. This for example would be case of generation bids invited through competition for the market, where the fuel cost would have to be pass thru. It is only in the case where there are well developed market for energy (competition in the market) where the pass-thru arrangements need not be part of the ex-ante regulation, but result from the bid and market process that regulators can leave the cost of generation to the market.[27]

## 11 Brownfield Infrastructure

### 11.1 Completing Projects

The Ministry of Finance has been actively considering the potential of "brown-field" investments. Essentially there are two possible types of such projects. An asset that

[27]The core difficulties with both Cases I and II of the UMPP has been this. See Pandey (2014). Also being cast as PPPs with demand risk being completely taken off their backs, the policy has resulted in the ballooning of the capacity created to well above the realistic demands.

is probably not in adequate use, or in disuse which could be brought on stream with marginal capex and with opex to give high social value in such reworking. Examples would be highways not in good use because the surface is bad, or because in the interconnect was earlier ignored, city railway systems (Chennai's broad gauge old metro, Ring Railway in Delhi) which by marginal opex focused on access and interconnect could greatly create social value. Past incomplete irrigation projects (earlier done with much cost and time overruns by the department) but now could be completed by an appropriate PPP, canal systems (which is to be completed) of irrigation projects where the dams are in place would also fit this category. Herein the value to incremental expenditure is very high, provided there is a break from the past in terms of the framework. The scope for such investments is high given the poor performance of public investments, and of many mistakes made in the past that have prevented PPPs from being able to create social and economic value. Of course the challenge is to get the RFP right given the requirements and the true status of the asset keeping uppermost the social and public value that can be generated.

### *11.2 Operational Stage*

Another class of brownfield projects would be projects that have gone past their construction and start of commercial operations, and now face far lower level of risks. This would be the case in the operational phase of most road projects on annuities or tolls. They can be offloaded on to markets to free up entrepreneurial capital (Varma 2002, 2003). This would lead to enhancement of the space for private capital in infrastructure, and could push the development of long term bond markets. Indexation of annuities and tolls to the interest rates would help to speed up the process.

## 12 Conclusion

The approaches to financing infrastructure must arise out of the regulatory and design of the framework for private sector involvement, and these when they are derived from optimal approaches to overcoming the many market failures that are possible do result in better outcomes and lower overall cost of financing.

Having a commercially oriented banking sector is vital to the flow of funds to the infrastructure sector and to the exercise of due diligence in funding projects.

The role of DFIs in crafting instruments and approaches for overcoming the large interest rate (change) risks is very important.

The cost of covering interest rate risks over the entire concession period from the date of financial closure has to be internalized and PPP formats must incorporate this provision. It would help to reduce adverse selection.

Contracts and PPPs have to improve much before there are a larger number of "good" infrastructure projects into which private capital can flow. "Good" projects are not those through which rents can be sought, but those where profits are adequate and private capital does not bear risks that it is ill equipped to bear.

In networks like pipelines casting private projects out of individual segments of the network means that the risk of load flow would be enhanced inviting take or pay contracts and hence larger cost and lower social value. The better approach would be to have a few network players who are subject to incentive regulation who act as common carriers to competitive businesses in gas production, storage, and consumption. The financing requirements for the network would then fall.

The scope for use of foreign capital in infrastructure is limited. With limited technological and real advantages, there can only be the seeming "advantage" of a positive fischer open (deviation from uncovered parity being positive) only open the door to major exchange risks when debt inflows are contemplated.

The Indian public sector banks need to be reformed, and the mess has gone far enough that nothing short of disinvestment would now work. The government cannot be relied to keep from its dysfunctional interference, that necessarily results in the banks being able to displace their accountability.

Ultimately it is the weakness within the government (non-learning organisations, lack of a systems approach, little ability to coordinate across many government departments, mind space of decision makers being too busy with fire fighting, procedures, and the mundane, and person centricity) that results in enhancing risks and in failure. Correction of the same would require civil service and administrative reform on lines that are yet to emerge (Morris (2002) in Morris and Shekhar (2002)).

## References


Aliber, R. Z. (1993). The multinational paradigm (edn. 1, vol. 1, number 0262511517), January. MIT Press Books.

Barua, S. K. (2004). The disinvestment story, Chapter 4.1. In S. Morris (Ed.), *India infrastructure report 2004—ensuring value for money*. 3inetwork, Oxford University Press.

Barua, S. K., & Madhavan, T. (2010). At the crossroads: Pipeline infrastructure for oil products. In S. Morris (Eds.).

GOI. (2001). Report of the expert group on restructuring SEBs, Chaired by Dr. Montek Singh Ahluwalia, Government of India.

GOI. (2002). Report of expert committee on state-specific reforms—structuring of APDRP, reform framework and principles of financial restructuring of SEBs, Ministry of Power, Government. of India, September. Government of India.

Kindleberger, C. P. (1969). *American business abroad*. New Haven: Yale University Press.

Morris, S. (1990, November 24). Cost and time overruns in public sector projects. *Economic and Political Weekly*, *25*(47), M154–M168. https://www.jstor.org/stable/4397023.

Morris, S. (1991, November 30). Holding companies, performance contracts, and task orientation in public sector. *Economic and Political Weekly,* M137–M144.

Morris, S. (2002). The challenge to governance in India. In S. Morris & R. Shekhar (Eds.).

Morris, S. (2003a). Public investments in India: Delays and cost overruns, Chapter 5.1. In S. Morris (Ed.).

Morris, S. (2003b). Expenditure accountability in India—The interlinkages. In S. Morris (Ed.).
Morris, S. (Ed.). (2003c). *India infrastructure report 2003—Public expenditure allocation and accountability*. 3iNetwork, Oxford University Press.
Morris, S. (2005). Understanding export led growth and late industrialisation to explain the differences in the post reform performance of India and China, WP No 2005/03/02. March, Indian Institute of Management, Ahmedabad.
Morris, S. (2012). In I. Hirway, A. S. Shah, & G. Shah (Ed.), *Growth or development: Which way is Gujarat going?* New Delhi: Oxford University Press.
Morris, S. (2014). A comparative analysis of Gujarat's economic growth, Chapter 2. In I. Hirway, A. Shah, & G. Shah (Eds.), *Growth or development: Which way is Gujarat going*. Oxford University Press.
Morris, S., & Shekhar, R. (Eds.). (2002). *India infrastructure report 2002—Governance issues for commercialisation*. 3iNetwork, Oxford University Press.
Pandey, A. (2003). Public procurement and the private sector. In S. Morris.
Pandey, A. (2014). Adani Power Ltd (A, B and C): Renegotiating long term electricity contracts, IIMA/PSG0114 (A, B and C). Ahmedabad: Indian Institute of Management.
Pandey, A., & Morris, S. (2009). Electricity reforms and regulation—A critical review of the last 10 years experience, March 25, Indian Institute of Management. (http://forumofregulators.gov.in/Data/Reports/FOR_IIMA_STUDY%20ON%20ELECTRICITY%20REFORMS%20AND%20REGULATIONS%20-%20A%20CRITICAL%20REVIEW%20OF%20LAST%2010%20YEARS%20EXPERIENCE-%2017.06.2009.pdf).
Pandey, A., et al. (2010). Structuring PPPs in aviation sector: Case of Delhi and Mumbai airport privatization, W.P. No. 2010-11-03 November. Ahmedabad: Indian Institute of Management.
RBI. (1999). Report of the technical committee on state government guarantees. Reserve Bank of India.
Sarabhai, V. (1969). Control and management of public sector enterprises, mimeo Administrative Staff College of India, Hyderabad.
Thomas White. (2010). Bric spotlight report—Toll roads in China: Speeding up growth, August. https://www.thomaswhite.com/pdf/bric-spotlight-report-china-toll-roads-expressways-august-10.pdf. Accessed January 28, 2019.
Tilotia, A., & Pawar, S. (2004). Traffic-risk management—Derivatives in the transport sector, Chapter 11.6. In S. Morris (Ed.), *India infrastructure report 2004—Ensuring value for money*. 3iNetwork, Oxford University Press.
Varma, J. R. (2001). Regulatory dilemmas in infrastructure financing, Chapter 4. In S. Morris (Ed.), *India infrastructure report 2001—Issues in regulation and market structure*. 3iNetwork, Oxford University Press.
Varma, J. R. (2002). Private finance to private entrepreneurship, Chapter 6.1. In S. Morris, & R. Shekhar (Eds.), *India infrastructure report 2002—Governance issues for commercialisation*. 3iNetwork, Oxford University Press.
Varma, J. R. (2003). Putting 'Private' finance back into private finance initiative, Chapter 7.1. In S. Morris (Ed.), *India infrastructure report 2003—Public expenditure allocation and accountability*. 3iNetwork, Oxford University Press.
Varma, J. R. (2004). Development financial institutions and the development of financial markets, Chapter 6.1. In S. Morris (Ed.), *India infrastructure report 2004—Ensuring value for money*. 3iNetwork, Oxford University Press.

# Correction to: 20 Years of G20

**Rajat Kathuria and Prateek Kukreja**

## Correction to:
## R. Kathuria and P. Kukreja (eds.), *20 Years of G20*, https://doi.org/10.1007/978-981-13-8106-5

The original version of the book was inadvertently published without abstracts for the chapters 3, 6, 8, 9 and 11. The missing abstracts have now been included. The book has been updated with the changes.

---

The updated version of these chapters can be found at
https://doi.org/10.1007/978-981-13-8106-5_3
https://doi.org/10.1007/978-981-13-8106-5_6
https://doi.org/10.1007/978-981-13-8106-5_8
https://doi.org/10.1007/978-981-13-8106-5_9
https://doi.org/10.1007/978-981-13-8106-5_11
https://doi.org/10.1007/978-981-13-8106-5



R. Kathuria and P. Kukreja (eds.), *20 Years of G20*,
https://doi.org/10.1007/978-981-13-8106-5_12

MIX
Papier aus verantwortungsvollen Quellen
Paper from responsible sources
FSC® C105338

If you have any concerns about our products,
you can contact us on
**ProductSafety@springernature.com**

In case Publisher is established outside the EU,
the EU authorized representative is:
**Springer Nature Customer Service Center GmbH**
**Europaplatz 3, 69115 Heidelberg, Germany**

Printed by Libri Plureos GmbH
in Hamburg, Germany